FAMINE:
THE IRISH EXPERIENCE
900-1900

FAMINE:
THE IRISH
EXPERIENCE
900-1900

Subsistence Crises
and Famines in Ireland

Edited by
E. MARGARET CRAWFORD

JOHN DONALD PUBLISHERS LTD
EDINBURGH

ISBN 0 85976 219 X

Distribution in the United States of America and Canada by
Humanities Press Inc., Atlantic Highlands, NJ 07716, USA.

Phototypeset by Beecee Typesetting Services
Printed in Great Britain by Bell & Bain Ltd., Glasgow

PREFACE

'Famines and Subsistence Crises in Ireland' was the theme of a symposium held on 1 April 1987 at The Queen's University of Belfast under the auspices of the Economic and Social History Society of Ireland. Eight papers were presented spanning the ninth to the nineteenth centuries. These are now published, together with an abstract of Sir William Wilde's table of famines (1851), and a concluding essay.

In 1845-9 Ireland suffered the last major famine to be seen in the western world. Its intensity, duration and the timing have given to the Great Famine a notoriety unsurpassed in Irish history. Like other western societies, however, Ireland experienced famines in earlier times, one or two possibly even more serious than that of 1845-9. But their impact has been minimal in the pages of history. Despite Ireland's unenviable place in famine history there is a distinct paucity of scholarly work on the subject, except of course for the Great Famine.

The most widely read popular monograph is *The Great Hunger* by Cecil Woodham-Smith published in 1962. In 1956 Dudley Edwards and Desmond Williams edited a collection of scholarly essays on the Great Famine which remains a classic volume. However, recent research has superseded many of the contributions. Two new surveys, one by Mary Daly, *The Famine in Ireland* (1987), and the other by Cormac Ó Gráda, *Ireland Before and After Famine: Explorations in Economic History, 1800-1925* (1988), are the latest contributions to the subject. Both draw heavily on Joel Mokyr's *Why Ireland Starved: A Quantitative and Analytical History of the Irish Economy, 1800-1850* (1985), surely the most provocative book published on Irish economic history for decades. It is, though, less a history of the Great Famine than a profound analysis of the Irish economy in the half-century leading to the famine crisis.

The one notable exception to the concentration on the Great Famine is Michael Drake's essay on 'The Demographic Crisis of 1740-1' in *Historical Studies* VI (1968). More comprehensively there is William Wilde's table of famines compiled for the 1851 census, more correctly entitled 'Table of Cosmical, Phenomena, Epizootics, Famines, and Pestilences in Ireland'. As a tool for social historians this encyclopaedic document is essential though, until recently, much under-used.

There is an obvious need for further research on famines in Ireland. The purpose of this volume of essays is to remedy in part the neglect of food crises other than the Great Famine, and to explore new aspects and to re-examine old themes relating to the 1845-9 crisis.

Without the assistance of several organisations and many individuals the symposium would not have taken place nor the following essays have appeared in print. First, I thank Dr Raymond Gillespie and Ms Bernadette Cunningham for planting the idea of the symposium. The financial assistance of the Nuffield Foundation and the Economic and Social Research Council allowed the idea to grow into a reality, and the co-operation of the Institute of Continuing Education and the Department of Economic and Social History Departments at Queen's University greatly facilitated the practical arrangements. Mrs Valerie Fawcett provided valuable assistance in the preparation of the manuscript, and Ms Gillian M. Alexander skilfully prepared the graphs. Last but not least, a great debt is owed to the contributors, without whom this volume would not exist.

E. Margaret Crawford
Department of Economic & Social History
The Queen's University of Belfast

CONTRIBUTORS

Professor L.A. Clarkson	Department of Economic and Social History, The Queen's University of Belfast, Northern Ireland.
Dr E. Margaret Crawford	Department of Economic and Social History, The Queen's University of Belfast, Northern Ireland.
Dr David Dickson	Department of Modern History, Trinity College, Dublin.
Sir Peter Froggatt	The Queen's University of Belfast, Northern Ireland.
Dr Raymond Gillespie	Ministry of Finance, Eire Government, Dublin.
Dr Christine Kinealy	Ulster Historical Foundation, Public Record Office N. Ireland, Belfast, Northern Ireland.
Dr Mary C. Lyons	British Library, Great Russell Street, London WC1B 3DG.
Dr T.P. O'Neill	Department of History, University College, Belfield, Dublin.
Dr Peter Solar	Centrum voor Economische Studien, Katholieke Universiteit, Leuven, Belgium.

ABBREVIATIONS

Annales, E.S.C.	*ANNALES Economies Sociétés Civilisations.*
B.L.	British Library, London.
Bodl. Lib.	Bodleian Library, Oxford.
Brit. Parl. Papers	British Parliamentary Papers.
Cal. S. P. Ireland	*Calander of State Papers, Ireland.*
D.J.M.S.	*Dublin Journal of Medical Science.*
D.M.P.	*Dublin Medical Press.*
H.C.	House of Commons.
H.L.	House of Lords.
H.M.C.	*Historical Manuscripts Commission.*
Jnl. Eur. Econ. Hist.	*Journal of European Economic History.*
J.R.S.A.I.	*Journal of the Royal Society of Antiquaries of Ireland.*
N.L.I.	National Library of Ireland.
N.U.I.	National University of Ireland.
Proc. R.I.A.	*Proceedings of the Royal Irish Academy.*
P.R.O.	Public Record Office, London.
P.R.O.I.	Public Record Office, Ireland, Dublin.
P.R.O.N.I.	Public Record Office, Northern Ireland, Belfast.
Q.U.B.	The Queen's University of Belfast.
R.I.A.	Royal Irish Academy
S.P.O.	State Paper Office, Dublin.
T.C.D.	Trinity College, Dublin.
U.C.D.	University College, Dublin.

CONTENTS

1

WILLIAM WILDE'S TABLE OF IRISH FAMINES 900-1850

Edited by E. Margaret Crawford

Assuming that such a disaster as the Great Famine was unavoidable, it could scarcely have occurred at a more fortunate time for historians. The mid-nineteenth century was the golden age of the statistical inquiry, when political economists counted everything quantifiable,[1] and the Famine was located between two products of this statistical movement, the 1841 census and its successor, the census of 1851. Indeed, the historian is twice blessed, for in William Wilde, architect of a major section of the 1851 census, and an important contributor to the 1841, he is faced with a stastician and social inquirer of exceptional talent.

Ireland lagged behind the rest of the United Kingdom in enumerating its people. The first abortive attempt at a national census was in 1813. This was followed by censuses in 1821 and 1831. But it was the 1841 census which set new standards in the compilation of economic, social and demographic information. These standards were maintained in the 1851 census, which in size and variety of information even surpassed its predecessor. One of the innovations was to present not merely the number of deaths in Ireland but cut fresh ground and provide the number of deaths according to cause:[2] no civil registration of births, marriages or deaths existed for Ireland until 1864. The fact that the Great Famine occurred midway between these two detailed censuses makes possible serious attempts to reconstruct and quantify in economic, statistical and social terms the impact of this extensive and intense famine.

One of the architects of these achievements invited by the Commission to undertake the specialised task of collating and analysing the data on deaths statistics for the 1841 census was William R.W. Wilde. Wilde was an excellent choice. A young Irish surgeon freshly returned from a European study tour, his interest in Irish history, language and folk habits combined with his statistical and, more importantly, his medical knowledge made him a most fitting person for the job. By 1851 Wilde's plans for the census were even more ambitious than those for 1841. In addition to tables of disease and deaths he compiled a tabular presentation, chronologically arranged, of

1

Irish pestilences, cosmical phenomena, epizootics and famines from 'pagan or pre-Christian period' to 1850 as part of his master plan in political arithmatic. Wilde felt that

> in recording the fact, as well as analysing, the extent, causes, and concomitants of the recent 'plague, pestilence, and famine,' with which it has pleased Providence to afflict this country, we naturally looked back to native history for parallels; and having found that from the earliest period to which past chronicles refer down to the present time Ireland has suffered sometimes alone, and sometimes in common with Great Britain and the rest of Europe, from various epidemic pestilences, we collected and tabulated the circumstances attending them in the table . . . From an examination of this epitome of the most remarkable epidemic pestilences, as well as of the famines, epizootics, cosmical phenomena, and other circumstances, influencing, or supposed to influence mortality, we perceive that so far as the annals and records of the country afford information, Ireland has from the earliest period of its colonisation to the present time been subjected to a series of dire calamaties, affecting human life, arising either from causes originating within itself, or from its connexion with Great Britain and other parts of Europe.[3]

This section of the report, as Sir Peter Froggatt has pointed out, 'is a classic of great scholarship, erudition and industry, and is the standard reference work in the subject.'[4]

The preamble contains a survey of the methodology employed in the compilation of the material. First, Wilde explains the three temporal divisions he makes: the pre-Christian Period, extending 'from the earliest time to which tradition refers . . . to the reception of Christianity';[5] the Historic Period, 'dating from the arrival of St Patrick, A.D., 432, to about the middle of the seventeenth century';[6] and finally the Scientific Period, 'from about the year 1650 to the present time.'[7] Secondly, he provides a brief outline about the Annals utilised, and the annalists themselves. This is followed by information on the medical and other texts consulted. Wilde's knowledge of sources is impressive although, notwithstanding his extensive combing of Irish manuscripts and texts, he does not identify all periods of famine. For example, in the period focused upon here there is no reference in the table to the severe famine of 1629.[8]

The table presented below focuses specifically on famines and subsistence crises. It is an abridgement of the entries gathered by Wilde, though to avoid repetition it excludes entries presented in the tabular Appendix of Dr Lyons' paper.

Sir William Wilde's Table of Irish Famines, 900-1850

Date	Event and Circumstance	Authority
963*	'A great famine [*ascolt*], and cold and scarcity of corn.'	*Chronicon Scotorum.*
964	'A great miserable dearth in Ireland that the father sould his sonn and daughter for meat.'	*Annals of Ulster.*
997	'Many churches of Munster laid waste this year by famine and feuds.'	*Annals of Innisfallen.*
1011	'There was a great scarcity of corn and victuals this year in Ireland, insomuch that a hoope was sold for no less than five groats, which came . . . to a penny for every barron.'	*Annals of Clonmacnoise.*
1047*	'. . . A great famine [*gorta*] came upon the Ulidians, so that they left their country and went into Leighlin [Leinster] . . .'	*Chronicon Scotorum.*
1076*	'There was a great scarcity of provisions this year.'	*Annals of the Four Masters.*
	'A scarcity of food this year.'	*Chronicon Scotorum.*
1077	'The scarcity of victualls continued for this year.'	*Annals of Clonmacnoise.*
	'There was a great scarcity in this year also.'	*Annals of the Four Masters.*
1099	'Great dearth of provisions in all Ireland.'	*Annals of Ulster.*
	'Plunderings, and the evil deeds of war and famine . . .'	*Annals of Innisfallen.*
1116	'A great famine [*gorta*] in this spring, during which the man sold his son and daughter for food, and the people even ate each other . . . Almost the whole of Leinster was depopulated, and the people dispersed through Erinn by the hunger.'	*Chronicon Scotorum.*
	'A great plague, [*Plaigh mor*] and famine this year in Munster and Leinster; so that churches and fortresses, territories and tribes, were desolated; and they also spread throughout Ireland and beyond the seas afterwards.'	*Annals of the Four Masters*
	'Great pestilence and famine yet in Munster and Leinster both; that the churches, towns, and canthreds were dispeopled throughout Ireland, and beyond seas . . .'	*Annals of Ulster*
1137	'A great scarcity [*tacha*], in the province of Connaught, of which multitudes died.'	*Annals of Kilronan.*
1153	'A great famine raged in Munster, and it spread all over Ireland, being occasioned by the vehemence of the war.'	*Annals of Innisfallen.*

* See also Appendix of Dr M.C. Lyons' paper

Date	Event and Circumstance	Authority
1179	'The churches of Tyrone, from the mountains southwards, were left desolate, in consequence of war and intestine commotion, famine, and distress.	*Annals of the Four Masters.*
1188	'A great scarcity of food in the north of Ireland this year.'	*Annals of Kilronan.*
1200	'A cold, foodless year, the like of which no one of those times has seen.' There was a wasting intestine war this year, which was perhaps the cause of the famine.	*Annals of Kilronan.*
1202	'There was great scarcity of victuals throughout all Ireland this year, that infinite numbers of the meaner sort perished for want; and there was plenty of milk.'	*Annals of Clonmacnoise.*
1203	'A great famine [*gorta*] in Ireland this year, so that the priests used to eat flesh meat in the Lent.'	*Annals of Kilronan.*
1225	' . . . This hot, heavy, death sickness, not sudden as the *tamh*, was probably our Irish typhus, which succeeded to the war and famine which desolated large portions of Ireland at this period; . . . Women and children, the feeble, and the lowly poor, perished by cold and famine in this war!'	*Annals of the Four Masters.*
	. . . A great dearth prevailed in Connaught for several years afterwards in consequence of these wars. The same annals state that 'during this war women, children, young lords, and mighty men, as well as feeble men, perished of cold and famine.'	*Annals of Kilronan.*
1227	'A great famine [*gorta*] in this year throughout all Ireland, and an epidemic [*Teidhm*], and a great mortality [*ar*] upon men, and various distempers, that is, of cold, and hunger, and of all kinds of diseases.'	*Annals of Connaught.*
1228*	'An intolerable dearth prevailed in Connaught, in consequence of the war . . .' Many of the clergy and upper classes of the laity were banished 'into foreign and remote countries, and others of them perished of cold and famine.'	*Annals of the Four Masters.*
	'Great famine in Ireland;' and in the year following [*i.e.,* A.D.1229] 'great devastations in Connaught.'	*Annals of Boyle.*
1262	[See Appendix of Lyons' paper]	
1268	'An insupportable famine in Erinn this year.'	*Annals of Ulster.*
1270	'A great famine and pestilence, the natural consequences of war, spread over all Ireland, and sorely afflicted the whole kingdom.'	*Hibernia Anglicana.*
1271*	'Pestilence and famine in the whole of Ireland.'	*Dowling's Annals.*
	'A great and severe scarcity in Ireland; and a multitude of people died by famine.'	*Annals of Multifernan.*

* See also Appendix of Dr M.C. Lyons' paper.

Date	Event and Circumstance	Authority
	'Plague, famine, and sword, raged this year, particularly in Meth.'	*Camden's Annals.*
	'A great famine occurred in Ireland, and a heavy pestilence.'	*Clyn's Annals.*
1294*	'On the festival of the Blessed Virgin Mary there was lightning and meteors destroying the blades of corn, whence proceeded very great scarcity, by which many perished of famine.'	*Clyn's Annals.*
	'Great dearth and death reigned in Ireland this yeare and the two yeeres next insuing.'	*Flatisbury's Chronicle.*
	'This year and the two following there was a great dearth and pestilence throughout Ireland.'	*Camden's Annals.*
1315*	'The pestilential period of the 14th century was, both in duration and intensity the most remarkably calamatous . . . It dates from 1315, and lasted almost without interruption for 85 years. It commenced with the foreign invasion of the Scots, under Edward Bruce, at a time when the country was labouring under the double scourge of famine and partial civil war, and its effects were, to increase the one and render the other general.'	
	'Wonderful and numerous distempers [*Teidhmanna*] throughout Ireland that year; such as destruction [*dith*] of people in great multitudes in it, and famine and various fatal distempers [*galra*] and an intolerable and damaging inclemency of weather also.'	*Annals of Kilronan.*
	'There reigned many diseases generally throughout the whole kingdom, a great loss of the inhabitants, great scarcitie of victualls, great slaughter of people, and in summer ugly and foul weather.'	*Annals of Clonmacnoise.*
1316	'To all these misfortunes was added that of a prodigious dearth; wheat was sold for three-and-twenty shillings the crenoge, oats six shillings, and wine eighteen pence a quart, and other things proportionably; so that many died from want.'	*Hibernia Anglicana.*
1317*	'The Scots increased in strength and courage, who spoiling of the countrie, caused such horrible scarcitie in Ulster, that the soldiors . . . prolled and pilled insatiablie wheresoever they came, without need, and without regard of the poore people, whose only provision they devoured. These people now living in slaverie under The Bruce starved for hunger, having first experienced manie lamentable shifts, even to the eating of manie dead carcasses . . . A great dearth this yeare afflicted the Irish people; for a measure of	*Hooker's Chronicles.*

* See also Appendix of Dr M.C. Lyons' paper.

Date	Event and Circumstance	Authority

wheat, called a chronecke, was sold at foure and twentie shillings, and a chronecke of otes at sixteen shillings, and all other vittels likewise were sold according to the same rate, for all the whole countrie was sore wasted by the Scots, and them of Ulster, insomuch that no small number of people perished through famine.'

'This year corn and other provisions were exceedingly dear, wheat sold at 23s the cranock, and wine for 8d., and the whole country was in a manner laid waste by the Scotts and those of Ulster. Many housekeepers, and such as were formerly able to relieve others, went a begging, and great numbers dy'd of hunger. The pestilence and famine were so severe that many of the poor dy'd.' *Camden's Annals.*

1318 [See Appendix of Lyons' paper]

1330 ' . . . That year was dear and hurtful to all men; and many died from hunger; for a cranock of corn was sold in winter for a mark and more, but it was worth little more in summer on account of the [imported] corn of foreign parts.' *Clyn's Annals.*

' . . . about the feast of St. John Baptist, there began to be a great dearth of corn in Ireland, which lasted till Michaelmas. A crannoc of wheat was sold for twenty shillings, and a crannoc of oats, peas, beans, and barley, for eight shillings. This dearth was occasioned by the immoderate rains, so that a great deal of corn could not be cut before Michaelmas.' *Camden's Annals.*

1331 'In 1330 the seasons were wet and crops indifferent. In the next year Ireland was distressed by famine; . . .' *Webster's History.*

'A great famine afflicted all Ireland in this and the foregoing year; and the city of Dublin suffered miserably. But the people in their distress met with an unexpected and providential relief: for about the 24th June a prodigious number of large sea-fish, called Turlehydes, were brought into the bay of Dublin, and cast on shore . . .' *Harris's Dublin.*

'The 27th of June when there was a great famine in Ireland; through God's mercy there came ashoar such a vast number of sea fish, called Thurlhedis . . .' *Camden's Annals.*

'Ireland was grievously distressed by a famine; but Dublin was seasonably relieved by a shoal of fishes called Thurlheds come to land.' *Short's Chron. History.*

1339 [See Appendix of Lyons' paper].

1410* 'There was great scarcity of corn this year.' *Marleburgh.*

* See also Appendix of Dr M.C. Lyons' paper.

Date	Event and Circumstance	Authority
1433	'This is a greedy summer; and it is called the non-knowing summer' [samhradh na mearaithni].	*Annals of Kilronan.*
	'A starving summer came this year; the summer of non-recognition it was called, because no one knew friend or relative in it, from the greatness of the famine.'	*Annals of Ulster.*
	'There was a famine in the summer of this year; called for a long time afterwards, *samhra na mearaithne* [the summer of slight acquaintances], because no one used to recognise friend or relative, in consequence of the greatness of the famine.'	*Annals of the Four Masters.*
1447*	'Vast numbers died in Dublin of a plague and famine this year, which afflicted all parts of the kingdom.'	*Harris's Dublin.*
1465	[See Appendix of Lyons' paper]	
1491	'In 1491 appeared a comet; the season was very wet; . . . and a famine afflicted Ireland.'	*Webster's History.*
	'This year there was such a famine all over Ireland, that it was called The Dismal Year; numbers died of the same during the summer season, which was exceeding wet.'	*Smith's Cork from M.S. Annal*
	'This year was commonly called by the natives the Dismal Year, by reason of the continual fall of rain all the summer and autumn, which caused great scarcity of all sorts of grain throughout Ireland.'	*Ware's Annals.*
	'The summer and harvest were so wet in Ireland that the corn could not be saved, and therefore a great dearth ensued, which was accompanied with a disease — called The Sweating Sickness — which now came to be first felt and known in Ireland.'	*Hibernica Anglicana.*
1492	' . . . A great famine [*ascolt*] in Erinn this year.'	*Annals of Ulster.*
1496	' . . . A great dearth [*ascolt*] throughout nearly the whole of Erinn this year'.	*Annals of Ulster.*
1497*	'A great famine throughout Ireland this year.'	*Annals of Kilronan.*
	'There was a great dearth this year through most of Ireland, but especially in Ulster. At and about Dublin it was not so great; for a peck of wheat, being almost four English bushels, sold for 10s., and malt for 8s.'	*Harris's Dublin.*
	'So great a dearth of corn did this year afflict almost all Ireland that many perished by famine, especially in Ulster'.	*Ware's Annals.*
1504	'The pestilence raged this year in this province [Munster]; and the next season was followed by a great dearth, of which also great numbers perished.'	*Smith's Cork.*

* See also Appendix of Dr M.C. Lyons' paper.

Date	Event and Circumstance	Authority
1505	' . . . a great dearth of corn . . . by reason of the continual rains that fell in summer and harvest.'	*Ware's Annals.*
	'This plague was followed with a famine, by reason of the wetness both of summer and autumn . . .'	*Hibernia Anglicana*
1520	'There is so great a scarcity and dearth in Ireland that the soldier cannot live on four pence a day.'	*Hibernia Anglicana.*
1523	'Great famine in Ireland . . .'	*Dowling's Annals.*
	'There was great scarcity of corn this year in Ireland, by reason of the continual rains in summer.'	*Ware's Annals.*
1525	'The last year there was a great dearth by reason of a wet autumn . . .'	*Hibernia Anglicana.*
1545	'Great dearth [prevailed] in this year, so that six-pence of the old money were given for a cake of bread in Connaught, or six white pence in Meath.'	*Annals of the Four Masters.*
1552	'In this year there was such a scarcity of corn in Ireland, that a peck of wheat . . . was sold in Dublin for twenty-four shillings; and a peck of malt for eighteen shillings, a price, considering those times, extraordinary . . .'	*Ware's Annals.*
1586	Describing the wars of Desmond, and the miseries consequent thereon, the Chronicles of Ireland affirm, 'after this followed an extreme famine; and such as whom the sword did not destroie, the same did consume and eat out; verie few or none remaining alive, saving such as dwelled in cities and townes, and such as were fled over into England; and yet the store in the townes was verie far spent, and they in distresse, or albeit nothing like in comparison to them who lived at large.' The author, in enumerating the hardships which were then experienced, asserts that human flesh was eaten in the County Cork, and that around Limerick Bay 'the common people who had a long time lived on limpets, orewads, and all such shell-fish as they could find,' and which were soon spent, 'eate the bodies of drowned sailors', and not long after death and famine did eat and consume them. 'The land itself, which before those wars was populous, well-inhabited, and rich in all the good blessing of God, being plenteous of corne, full of cattel, well stored with fish and sundrie other good commodities, is now become waste and barren, yielding no fruits, the pastures no cattel, the fields no corne, the aire no birds, the seas, though full of fish, yet to them yielding nothing. And whosoever did travell from the one end unto the other of all Mounster, he should not meet anie man, woman, or	*Hooker's Chronicle.*

Date	Event and Circumstance	Authority

child, saving in townes and cities, nor yet see anie beast, but the verie wolves, the foxes, and other like ravening beasts; manie of them laie dead, being famished, and the residue gone elsewhere.'

1589 'Did not the said [Earl] Desmond bring his countrie to that miserie that one did eate another for hunger, and himselfe with all his posteritie and followers to utter ruinne.'   *Payne's Description of Ireland*

Edmund Spenser, describing, the miserable condition of the country after 'the late warres of Mounster,' writes, 'Out of every quarter of the woods and glynnes, they came creeping forth upon their hands, for their leggs could not beare them; they looked like anatomies of death; they spake like ghosts crying out of their graves; they did eate the dead carrions, happy where they could find them; yea, and one another soone after, insomuch as the very carcasses they spared not to scrape out of the graves; and if they found a plot of water-cresses or shamrocks [wood-sorrel] there they flocked as to a feast for the time, yet, not able long to continue therewithall; that in short space there were none left, and a most populous and plentiful country suddenly left voyde of man and beast. Yet sure, in all that warre, there perished not many by the sword, but all by the extremitie of famine, which they themselves had wrought.'   *Spenser's View of the State of Ireland.*

1600 . . . The seventeenth century was marked, at its commencement, by a severe frost, followed by very tempestuous weather; then a great scarcity of food, amounting in some places to absolute famine, and plague followed after.

1601 ' . . . Already a very great dearth is began, and a famine must ensue, the rates of all things being incredible.' Oats 7s. 6d. the barrel, in time of plenty the ordinary rate of oats in Ireland was then but twelve pence the barrel. 'All things here are already grown so dear and scarce; and the decaiss by sicknesse are already great. A frost so great as seldome had been seene in Ireland,' occurred in November.   *Moryson's Rebellion of Tyrone.*

1602 In January there was a 'generall scarcity of all sorts of victuals in all parts of this Kingdome. And amongst the subjects of the Pale their harvest was so unseasonable and their corne so destroyed by the weather, as numbers of subjects will undoubtedly die of famine. All manner of provisions necessarie for the maintenance of an household were, of late especially, bought at such excessive rates as well in regard of the   *Moryson's Rebellion of Tyrone.*

Date	Event and Circumstance	Authority

famine growing daily greater in Ireland by the continuall spoile of the country and the armies cutting downe of the rebels' corne for these last two years, as also in regard of the disvaluation of the mixed coyne now current . . .' 'Former mention hath been made . . . of carcasses scattered in many places all dead of famine. And, no doubt, the famine was so great as the rebell souldiers, taking all the common people had to feede upon, and hardly living there-upon (so as they besides fed not only on hawkes, kytes, and unsavourie birds of prey; but on horseflesh and other things unfit for man's feeding) . . .'

'September 12. — We found everywhere men dead of famine . . . between Tullaghoge and Toome there lay unburied one thousand dead, and that since our first drawing this year to Blackwater there were above three thousand starved in Tyrone.'

1603 'An intolerable famine prevailed all over Ireland.' *Annals of the Four Masters.*

'Almost the whole of Ireland was desolated and laid waste by famine and want of food, by reason of which many were obliged to eat dogs and cats; many perished from an insufficiency even of these. The famine seized not only upon men but brutes. Wolves coming out of the woods and mountains attacked, and tore in pieces the people enfeebled by want of food. The dogs dragged from their graves the putrid and partially decomposed bodies.' *O'Sullivan Beare's Historiae Catholicae Iberniae*

1641 For the reasons stated at . . . the introductory portion of this report, the third or *Scientific Period* here commences; and it also marks the date of a series of disasters of a political character, accompanied with and followed by several years of famine; during which time pestilential diseases raged both in the camp and among civilians with unusual intensity; among these Fever, Plague, Smallpox and Dysentery were especially destructive. The special pestilential period lasted about eleven years . . .

Sir Wm. Petty calculated that 167,000 of Irish and English in Ireland, died by the sword and famine and other hardships, during the eleven years subsequent to THE REBELLION OF 1641, and that the general loss of people in Ireland from all causes during the same period was 616,000. *Petty's Political Anatomy*

1646 'Between the 23rd of October, 1641, and the same day in the year 1652, five hundred and four thousand of the inhabitants of Ireland are said to have perished *Commercial Restraints of Ireland.*

Date	Event and Circumstance	Authority

and been wasted by the sword, plague, famine, hardship, and banishment.'

1651   During the seige of Galway by the Parliamentary forces, in 1652, and after the surrender, there was 'a famine throughout the country, by which multitudes perished. This was again succeeded by a plague, which carried off thousands, both in the town and the surrounding districts. This dreadful visitation continued for two years, during which upwards of one-third of the population of the province was swept away.'   *Hardiman's Galway.*

Alluding to the civil war, famine and pestilence, which occurred between 23rd of October, 1641, and the same date in 1652, Sir W. Petty (then Physician to the Army in Ireland and Secretary to Henry Cromwell, Lord Lieutenant), says . . . 'I guess two-thirds to have perished by war, plague, and famine;' and 'that about 504,000 of the Irish perished and were wasted by the sword, plague, famine, hardship, and banishment,' during the same period.   *Petty's Political Anatomy.*

1690   'After the departure of James from Ireland, famine and disease spread throughout the country on the approach of winter.'   *MacFarlane's History of England.*

1728   'Since I came here in the year 1725, there was almost a famine among the poor; last year [1727] the dearness of corn was such that thousands of families quitted their habitations to seek bread elsewhere, and many hundreds perished; this year the poor had consumed their potatoes, which is their subsistence, nearly two months sooner than ordinary, and are already, through the dearness of corn, in that want, that in some places they begin already to quit their habitations. And as the winter subsistence of the poor is chiefly this, scarcity drove the poor to begin with their potatoes before they were full grown, so that they have lost half the benefit of them. Oatmeal is at this distance from harvest [March, 1728] in many parts of this kingdom three times the customary price; so that this summer must be more fatal to us than the last.'   *Primate Boulter's Letters.*

'Spring mild and mostly fair; summer wet; autumn various; winter various, inclined to frost. In the winter was a scarcity of bread, and the province of Ulster suffered greatly, and intermittent fevers raged among them.'   *Rutty's Registry.*

1729   'The great scarcity of corn had been so universal in this kingdom in the years 1728 and 1729, as to expose   *Commercial Restraints.*

Date	Event and Circumstance	Authority

thousands of families to the utmost necessities and even to the danger of famine; many artificers and housekeepers having been obliged to beg for bread in the streets of Dublin. It appeared before the House of Commons, that the import of corn for one year and six months, ending the 29th day of September, 1729, amounted in value to the sum of £274,000 . . . and the Commons resolve that public granaries would greatly contribute to the increasing of tillage and providing against such wants as have frequently befallen the people of this kingdom, and hereafter may befall them, unless proper precautions shall be taken against so great a calamity. The great scarcity which happened in the years '28 and '29, and frequently before and since, is a decisive proof that the distresses of this kingdom have been occasioned by the discouragement of manufactures.'

1739   'In the beginning of November, 1739, we had a very sharp, cold, N.E. wind, and which continued for about three weeks; this was succeeded by the severest frost known here in the memory of man, which *entirely destroyed the potatoes,* the chief support of the poor; provisions of all sorts became excessive [dear], and they would have perished for want but for the generous and bountiful contributions of the public.'   *O'Halloran on the Air.*

'At the conclusion of the year 1739, there happened an exceeding cold winter, remarkable for a very severe frost, continuing till spring. From this dreadful and indescribable hard frost, there arose shortly afterwards not only a great destruction of all sorts of cattle, but a lamentable blight and calamitous rot of plants and vegetables of all kinds, for the very birds of the air and other animals used for human sustenance perished in great numbers from the excessive harshness of the cold season. And what besides more heavily aggravated the mass of lamentable calamities, those tuberous roots (commonly called potatoes), almost the continual and sole food of the poor and lower orders of the inhabitants of this kingdom, completely rotted by this most terrible and long continued frost.' He also describes the famine that ensued, and the diseases arising from 'eating the bad and corrupted roots and putrid carcasses.'   *O'Connell's Observations.*

1740   'Dysenteries made their appearance in July, as they did also at the same time at Plymouth. The dysenteries, which began in July, continued through the autumn and winter, having first begun among the   *Rutty's Weather and Seasons.*

Date	Event and Circumstance	Authority

poor [several of whom died for want], they spread to the rich. There was a great dearth of provisions this autumn, which proceeded almost to a famine in winter — *The Potatoes having failed,* whilst other provisions bore double or treble their usual price. In autumn, also, appeared an epidemic continual fever, which did not wholly cease in winter,' but continued into the next year.

'Lord Chancellor Jocelyn, writing from Ireland in the year 1741, to his brother Chancellor, Lord Hardwicke, in England, mentions the distressed state of the country at this period, owing to the *entire failure of the potato crops.'*   *Bascome's History of Epidemics.*

'1740 and '41 were years which made an impression so indelible that even after a lapse of more than half a century, I have heard the old describe them with feelings of horror.'   *Harty's Sketch of Epidemic Diseases.*

During the famine of 1740 '300,000 people were supposed to have perished.'   *Irish Farmer's Journal.*

1741   'Fed at the workhouse by the charity of his Grace the Lord Primate. etc.,' on January 10th, 2,690, and on the 12th, 2,902 persons. The corporation of Galway remitted three-fourths of their market tolls 'in order to encourage farmers to sell at a lower rate' during this period of scarcity. 'This country, abounding with flesh meat of all sorts cannot suffer much by a famine if the people will be governed by reason, and change their old way of feeding.'   *Pue's Occurences.*

... 'The misery of the poor in parts of the county of Clare, and of this county [Galway], is inexpressible, many being obliged by the extreme scarcity of provisions of all kinds to eat horses and dogs, and to steal and kill ewes . . . Wheat and oatmeal are excessive dear; potatoes, 4s. 4d. a bushel. Many through want perish daily in the roads and ditches, where they are buried.'   *Faulkner's Journal.*

June. — Deaths from starvation reported. The sickness and distress prevailed generally throughout the country; and large sums of money were subscribed both by private individuals and public bodies for the support of the poor. Large supplies of provisions arrived from America. Five hundred families of poor weavers were served with bread and meal at the Court-house, Thomas Street, Dublin, by private charity.   *Pue's Occurences.*

October. — The Lord Lieutenant, in opening Parliament . . . alluded to 'the sickness which had proved   *Common's Journal.*

Date	Event and Circumstance	Authority

so mortal in several parts of the kingdom, and was thought to have been principally owing to the scarcity of wholesome provisions.'

'Want and misery in every face, the rich unable to relieve the poor, the roads spread with dead and dying; mankind of the colour of the weeds and nettles on which they feed; two or three, sometimes more, on a car, going to the grave, for want of bearers to carry them, and many buried only in the fields and ditches where they perished. Fluxes and malignant fevers swept off multitudes of all sorts, so that whole villages were laid waste. If one for every house in the kingdom died, and that is very probable, the loss must be upwards of 400,000 souls. This is the third famine I have seen in twenty years, and the severest . . .' — *The Groans of Ireland.*

'It was computed that as many people died of want, and disorders occasioned by it, during that time, as fell by the sword in the rebellion of 1641. Whole parishes were almost desolate, and the dead were eaten in the fields by dogs, for want of people to bury them.' — *Skelton's Necessity of Tillage.*

The effects of famine continued to be felt long after the symptoms of pestilence had abated, and articles of daily food had fallen to their ordinary prices. 'Tillage in the year 1740 was sadly deficient, owing perhaps as much to the despair of the people as to their actual sufferings; but whatever the cause, the effect was the same, and the year 1741 was even worse than that which preceded it. Horses, cows, sheep, pigs, and poultry, all were struck by the plague, and perished; and the mortality of the people must have been increased by feeding on the diseased animals. There were, it is said, shoals of dead fish cast on shore, on which the people also fed, but it is not believed that such food was unwholesome. The next harvest was plentiful, and it was said that cows being very scarce, a sheep produced as much milk that year as a cow would in ordinary seasons. The year 1741 was always mentioned as *Bliadhain an air,* i.e., "the year of the slaughter." ' — *Tract on Famine.*

'In the year 1740-41 the horrors of scarcity again returned, and thousands of the poor are said to have perished of absolute want and the use of bad provisions.' — *Wakefield's Ireland.*

'The years 1740-41 were seasons of great scarcity, and, in consequence of the want of wholesome provisions, great numbers of our people perished miserably . . .' — *Commercial Restraints*

Date	Event and Circumstance	Authority
1756	. . . With the exception of the years 1757 and 1760, which were unusually dry, the seasons were characterised by an amount of moisture uncommon even in this humid climate, and storms occurred with more than general frequency. A partial famine followed, and provisions rose to a great height during 1756 and 1757. Agues were rife; diseases of the mucous membrane, especially affecting the Eyes and the bowels followed; and then an outbreak of Influenza spread with unwonted mortality over the country, and extended to the lower animals — horses and dogs in particular; Fever and Dysentery, Scurvy and Small-pox, appeared in the train of calamaties; finally, there occurred in 1763 and 1764 great inundations that destroyed much property, and formed the not unusual prelude to the destruction of the potato crop.	
1766	In spring, 1766, 'Several towns were in great distress for corn; and by the humanity of the Lord Lieutenant, Lord Hertford, money was issued out of the Treasury to buy corn for such places as applied to his Lordship for that relief.'	*Commercial Restraints.*
1782	An embargo was placed on the exportation of provisions; 'if it had not taken place there would not be more than five pounds of bread for a shilling, by Christmas day. A famine must have been the consequence.'	*Hibernian Magazine.*
1798	'From 1794 to 1798 fever, with a few exceptions, was observed to have been rather of a mild type; but the misfortunes of the latter year left as their unavoidable consequence, a melancholy succession of famine and disease.'	*Geary's Report of Limerick Fever Hospital.*
	'The effects of the rebellion were felt in death, famine, and pestilence, for two years afterwards. The next period of famine and fever happened in 1800, which arose from the vast destruction of property during the unfortunate civil war of 1798 . . .'	*Ryan's Manual Midwifery.*
1799	' . . . continued rains, attended with an unusual degree of cold, occasioned an almost general deficiency in the crops, and a consequent failure of the usual supply of nourishment to the poor, already suffering under many privations . . . The state of the poor in the principal towns of Ireland, in the years 1799, 1800-1 and 2 was wretched in the extreme.'	*Barker and Cheyne's Report.*
	. . . In October Government ordered an embargo to be laid on all vessels leaving Irish ports with potatoes,	*Hibernian Magazine.*

and 'such measures have been taken to procure a supply of bread corn from the Baltic and America, as will remove every danger of scarcity in this essential article.'

November. — 'The most melancholy accounts of the harvest arrive from all parts of the country; in many places the oats and other late corn remain on the ground not worth the reaping. Great dearth of corn apprehended. The herring fishery very abundant; nevertheless, distress had commenced among the poor at the end of the month.'   *Faulkner's Journal.*

December 24th. — The poor of the country, and Dublin in particular, are said to be perishing from the dearness, scarcity, and bad quality of all kinds of provisions, in consequence of the dreary harvest.

1800   This century opened, as the former closed, with unusual severity of weather, and great distress among the people, owing to the high price of provisions and two successive but partial Potato Failures, contemporaneous with which appeared Fever, Dysentery, Scarlatina, Ophthalmia, and Influenza — . . .

'This year the price of food has been enormous, and it is hard to say what have been the chief articles of food or what their prices. Potatoes in March or April last were scarcely to be procured for 7 or 8s per cwt. Oatmeal has been as high from May till harvest as from 37s. to 40s. per cwt. In consequence many articles of food were purchased by the gentry and resold at a considerable loss; besides oatmeal, wheat, and barley meal, American Indian meal, and rye meal, both very fine were brought down from Dublin, as also rice, and while potatoes could be procured, Scotch herrings. All these afforded seasonable relief. Nothing, however, on the failure of their usual food, pleased the people better than stirabout, made from the flour of Indian meal ground in America.'   *Frazer's Agricultural State of County Wicklow*

. . . In November, provisions were at the high prices of the spring of the year, but 'early in the following spring large quantities of Indian-corn meal, and rye flour were imported by the Government or on a bounty which served much to allay this famine.'   *McSkimin's Carrickfergus.*

'Summer unusually hot and dry, but followed by a wet autumn with deficient crops: the crops, moreover, of very bad quality: the people in a state of starvation, malignant fever continued from 1798.'   *Corrigan's Fever and Famine.*

Date	Event and Circumstance	Authority
1801	POTATO FAILURE. — 'The summer of 1801, proved remarkably dry and hot in Ireland, vegetation was obstructed, *Potatoes Failed,* and a famine was near taking place with the poor, whose chief food in Ireland is potatoes.'	*Transactions Royal Dublin Society.*
1817	'The summer and autumn were humid, cold, and ungenial, and agricultural produce, with the exception of potatoes, which were more abundant than in the former year, was almost as scarce as in 1816. We recollect to have seen, when travelling on the north road leading from Dublin, corn in sheaves rotting on the ground in the month of December, 1817. In some places the poorer classes were compelled to the sad necessity of collecting various exculents, wild vegetables, nettles, wild mustard, navew, and others of the same kind, to support life; and in places distant from Dublin wretched beings were often seen exploring the fields with a hope of obtaining a supply of this miserable food. In districts contiguous to the sea various marine plants were had recourse to for the purpose of allaying the cravings of hunger. In some districts seed potatoes were taken up from the ground, and the hopes of the future year thus destroyed for the relief of present necessity; and the blood drawn from the cattle on the fields and mixed with oatmeal, when this could be procured, has not unfrequently supplied a meal to a starving family. So general was the distress, and insufficient the supply in some distant parts of the country, that a few unhappy sufferers are said to have died of absolute want of food . . .'	*Barker and Cheyne's Report.*
1821	. . . All the newspapers of the time agree as to the fact of the unparalleled wetness of the autumn, which had the effect of souring the potato, even then of stunted growth, . . . This peculiar failure of the potato crop, which was almost confined to certain districts in the west and south, was the manifest product of a want of balance . . . at particular seasons of the year, . . . The cereal crops of Ireland were not at all injured in proportion; and hence the remarkable fact alluded to by a committee of the House of Commons, of the exports of grain 'infinitely exceeding the imports' from some of the distressed districts, at a time when the famine and pestilence prevailed most; but the potato was alone employed as food in these districts. 'The failure of 1822 in the provinces of Munster and Connaught, was owing to a continued and excessive	*The Irish Crisis.*

Date	Event and Circumstance	Authority
	humidity, which caused the potatoes to rot after they had been stored in the pits [in 1821], so that the deficiency of food was not discovered until late in the season.' — *Sir C. Trevelyan.*	
1822	. . . Extensive and alarming distress prevailed throughout the counties of Galway, Mayo, and Clare, during the spring; and famine was reported from various districts of the West. Public meetings were held to consider the state of the poor. Seed potatoes could not be procured, and what were planted were in many instances subsequently removed from the ground for food. Towards the end of April starvation was reported from Clare; and the failure in last year's potato crop was also reported from Kerry. At this period, the counties which had suffered most from the potato failure, and were now labouring under undeniable famine, were Mayo, Galway, Clare, Kerry, Limerick, and Cork. Towards the end of the month, we read:- 'Potatoes, the only support of the miserable lower orders, exceed in price any thing that can be conceived,' and are of such inferior quality as to promote disease. 'Such misery was never witnessed before in the town of Galway, whole clans pouring in from the mountains of Connemara in quest of food.' Potatoes 8d. a stone. Public meetings were again held throughout the country for the purpose of alleviating the general distress. At that in Limerick, it was recommended 'that other food be substituted for potatoes, in order to spare the supply of seed, and to avoid an article of consumption perhaps less wholesome than usual, the potato in many instances not having ripened last year.' Seed potatoes were, in many instances, given to the people — cut to prevent their being used as food. Upon the 25th of May, the distress at Skibbereen and its vicinity was 'horrible beyond description.'	*Provincial and other Public Newspapers*
	The distress is every day increasing; a woman was 'found dead in a field from starvation' in the county Mayo . . .	*Freeman's Journal.*
	. . . During the end of June and the whole of July, famine and disease spread extensively through the north-western districts. Fever prevailed particularly at Galway and in some of the small towns of Sligo, Mayo, and Clare. 'Thousands of the inhabitants of Erris [county Mayo] are subsisting on sea-weed: typhus fever and dysentery were so bad, that the living were scarcely sufficient to bury the dead. The	*Irish Farmer's Journal. Saunders News-Letter, and Freeman's Journal.*

Date	Event and Circumstance	Authority

people at Achill, it is said, perish in such numbers, that they are found on the road side lying dead. On the 22nd, we read that in Mayo, 260,000 persons were receiving public relief . . .'

'A dreadful famine came on, produced by the failure of the harvest, and especially of the potato crop. The southern and western counties suffered most. Government hastened to abate these horrors, sending over £500,000 to be placed at the disposal of Lord Wellesley and to be dispensed by him in charitable relief or in public works. Private benevolence came to the aid of national generosity; great subscriptions were raised in England and Scotland, and wherever there was an English colony or settlement, or any place where a few Englishmen were congregated, some money was raised for the suffering people of Munster and Connaught.' *MacFarlane's History of England.*

'The humidity of the season 1821, caused want of employment, which was followed by severe famine and fever in 1822. So great was the distress among the lower classes all over Ireland in 1822, that many of them removed the seed potatoes out of the earth to consume as food, — others lived on wild esculent herbs they collected out of the corn fields; and as several cattle died from starvation, their carcasses were greedily eaten . . .' *Ryan's Midwifery.*

A Committee of the House of Commons appointed to report upon the calamaties of 1822, stated that 'a pressure of distress wholly unexampled was felt in Ireland, and which led to the appropriation of large sums . . . for the purposes of mitigating, if not of averting that famine and disease which had extended to so alarming a degree in many parts of Ireland.' The districts in which the distress was found to be most urgent were the following — Cork, Kerry, Limerick, Galway, Mayo, Sligo, Roscommon, Clare, Tipperaray (part of,) Cork City, Limerick City, and Galway Town — 'containing altogether a population of 2,907,000 from which it would appear that the distressed districts were equal in extent to one half of the superficies of the country. In the districts averted to, the potato crop, which furnishes the general food of the peasantry, had failed; but there was no want of food of another description for the support of human life. On the contrary, the crops of grain had been far from deficient, and the prices of corn and oatmeal were very moderate. The calamities of 1822, may, *Report of Parliamentary Committee.*

Date	Event and Circumstance	Authority

therefore, be said to have proceeded less from the want of food itself, than from the want of adequate means of purchasing it; or in other words, from the want of profitable employment.'

Doctor Graves, who graphically described this partial famine in the west of Ireland, says 'the great increase of wretchedness eperienced by the poor throughout that district [the town and county of Galway] in the spring and summer of 1822, is still [1824] fresh in the memory of all. The general failure of the potato crop had deprived the peasantry of their principal, if not only support, and conspired with the pressure of the times to reduce them to a state of the most urgent want.' . . . Places were appointed 'in which the famished multitudes might assemble for the purpose of receiving relief — stores of provisions were collected, and food was given to every one who asked for it.' As Galway was the chief depot of these stores, thousands of distressed persons collected therein; and many were so exhausted by previous suffering that they survived their arrival but a few days. Sometimes the number fed amounted to as many as 4,000 daily . . . *Graves Report upon Fever in Galway and the West of Ireland.*

Authority: *Transactions of Association of College of Physicians in Ireland.*

1825   Bishop Doyle, in his evidence before a Committee of the House of Commons upon the condition of the poor of his diocese, Kildare and Leighlin, in this and the previous year, stated, 'that the extent and the intensity of their distress is greater than any language can describe, and that the lives of many hundreds of them are very often shortened by this great distress; it also enervates their minds, and paralyzes their energies, and leaves them incapable of almost any useful exertion. Last year was a year of much more than ordinary distress, but by no means so great as in 1822.' In answer to the question as to whether this state of distress would be one of ordinary occurrence, he replied, 'That we will have great distress every summer whilst the present state of things continues, is a matter of course; it will be greater or less in proportion as the potato crop happens to be good or otherwise.'

Authority: *Parliamentary Report on Scarcity in Ireland.*

June. — Potatoes were 8d a stone in the Ennis market, and in many parts were reported to be at famine prices. The extreme distress of the lower orders is reported from many parts of the country.

Authority: *Ennis Chronicle.*

Date	Event and Circumstance	Authority
1831	In March and April, great distress was reported from the county of Mayo. The Lord Mayor of Dublin convened a meeting at the Mansion House early in April, to collect subscriptions for the relief of the starving people of the West. Early in June another meeting was held . . . for collecting subscriptions . . . for the famished poor in Mayo and Galway. The Archbishop of Tuam [the Hon. Power Le Poer Trench] early in June, addressed the following letter to the Relief Association in Dublin:— 'Until lately I had hoped that the sore famine which prevailed had been, and would continue to be, confined to the coasts of those counties, to the islands, and perhaps in some few instances to more inland parishes; but I mourn to say that now I find every day adding to the catalogue of destitution; and that besides the hitherto afflicted districts, the ravage is extending to very much of the interior. In short, the failure of provision is daily rapidly increasing, and will continue to increase until the new crops come in.'	*Dublin Evening Mail.*
	The Secretary of the Relief Committee received 'the most heart-rending accounts of the appalling misery of the people; they were similar to those of 1822.' In May dreadful distress in Connemara; — 'Famine and fever are stalking hand-in-hand through this miserable region. There is scarce a potato planted. Thousands are starving; as a last resources, some are now bleeding their starving cows, boiling their blood and eating it.'	*Bryan's View of Ireland.*
1833	Extensive failures of the potato crop were reported to the Royal Dublin Society as having occurred in the years 1833 and 1834. The failures of 1831, 1832, and 1833 were attributed to heat and drought.	*Proceedings of Royal Dublin Society.*
1835	DISTRESS. — In the month of May reports 'were made to the Irish Government that distress had been produced by the failure of the potato crop [in 1834] in some parts of the country, particularly in the district of Erris, in the county of Mayo, Connemara, in the county of Galway, and in some portions of the county of Kerry.' . . . The distress in Kerry, Clare, the coasts of Mayo and Galway, and in particular the islands in Clew Bay and Blacksod Harbour, was very great . . . In Bearhaven, county of Cork, 'many of the poor were obliged to eat sea-weed and other things only used as human food in times of famine.' Great scarcity and famine existed in Dingle and in the island of Valentia. In June the distress was experienced severly in Clare.	*Parliamentary Report on Scarcity.*

Date	Event and Circumstance	Authority

In Oughterard great distress prevailed, and typhus fever appeared there in July. The highest price given to agricultural labourers in Clifden and the neighbourhood of Galway was 8d. a day; in some places but 5d.;— whilst potatoes were 6d. a stone, and obtained with difficulty. The scarcity and distress were felt severly during the summer in Inishturk, Clare island, the island of Achill, and also in Newport and Belmullet, county of Mayo. The county of Donegal likewise suffered, especially in the neighbourhood of Rutland, Gweedore, and Lough Swilly. 'In August, 1835, relief was given [by Government] by an issue of £3,000, in consequence of the depressed state of the poor in the west of Ireland.'

1836   CROPS. — A PARTIAL FAILURE IN THE POTATO was observed in several parts of Ireland. Great anxiety was manifested for the results of the harvest at the close of this year. 'The exorbitant prices to which every article of human food had attained at the commencement of the winter, together with the dispiriting reports which were received from many parts of the country, of the perilous state of the oat and potato crop, gave rise to anticipations of so gloomy a character, that many did not hesitate to predict a famine as extensive and disastrous as that which succeeded the year 1816.' *Irish Farmers and Gardener's Magazine.*

In August, owing to the scarcity and high price of provisions, some of the people in Donegal were said to be 'living on herbs or digging up the potatoes before they were half ripe.' The distress was particularly pressing in Sligo, where the very worst description of potatoes, fit only for swine, were 5d. a stone; but it was relieved by several cargoes of potatoes shipped from Galway. The potato failure, the scarcity, and the distress were only partial, for the agricultural reports state that the crop in Wexford turned out very well. *Dublin Evening Mail.*

1839   CROPS. — POTATO FAILURE. — In July we read, 'the potato crop has felt the blighting influence of the atmosphere.' *Dublin Medical Press.*

A general failure of the grain crop. 'The extremely wet and ungenial summer and autumn excited apprehensions throughout Ireland as to the probable effect upon the crops. There was sufficient ground for alarm, the [potato] crop being considered deficient in quantity in some districts; whilst, owing to the almost incessant rains, the quality, it was believed, would be found inferior . . .' *Report of Poor Law Commissioners.*

Date	Event and Circumstance	Authority
	'In 1839 another failure occurred; and in all the western and midland counties the average price of potatoes in July and August was 7d. a stone, and of oatmeal, 18s. or 19s. a cwt.: the former double, and the latter one-third more than the usual price at that time of the year.'	*The Irish Crisis.*
	'The most distressing accounts have reached us from several parts of the country, with regard to the privations of the poor, owing to the inclemency of the summer and autumn. The farmers are refusing the accustomed dole of food, and the cities are becoming inundated with famished paupers . . .'	*Dublin Medical Press.*
1840	DISTRESS. — Great distress prevailed amongst the poor at Abbeyleix, Cashel, and Waterford; the Liberties of Dublin were said to be in a state approaching to famine. The inhabitants of Ballinasloe were also in great destitution — several persons starving.	*Saunders' News-Letter.*
1845	The potato disease is manifest in Sligo, Mayo, and Galway. 'We admit with inexpressible reluctance the constant proofs which we receive of the wide extent to which the potato disease has reached. We are unwilling to believe that famine is likely to afflict us — but it is now as impossible as it would be criminal to supress the fact that the pestilence has spread far and wide, and has invaded our own and the neighbouring counties, which we fondly hoped were wholly safe.'	*Saunders' News-Letter.* *Cork Southern Reporter.*
	Disturbances . . . occurred in Roscommon during the month of March, 'owing to the wretchedness of the peasantry and their anxiety to raise food for the support of themselves and their starving families.'	*Freeman's Journal.*
1846	'The blight in the potatoes took place earlier [than in 1845], and was of a much more sweeping and decisive kind . . . The fields assumed a blackened appearance, as if they had been burnt up, and the growth of the potatoes was arrested when they were not larger than a marble or a pigeon's egg. Full-grown wholesome potatoes were not to be procured . . .'	*The Irish Crisis.*
	' . . . Before the end of the year the poor cottiers and labourers were utterly destitute. The calamity fell with peculiar severity on the farm servants; these were among the first victims of starvation. The price of food rose enormously: turnips were sold at 1s. to 1s. 6d. per cwt. Want and misery spread throughout the land; disease rapidly followed. The poorhouses could not contain half the applicants who anxiously sought admission — often with no other object than to	*Pim's Condition and Prospects of Ireland.*

obtain a coffin to be buried in. The dead were buried hastily — frequently without a coffin. The bonds of natural affection were loosened. Parents neglected their children — Children turned out their aged parents.' But these latter remarks apply to only a few localities in the west. By the failure of the potato crop 'the poor lost their all; many have died from want, disease, and misery.' The middle classes, from want of trade, and heavy expenditure, were in danger of becoming pauperised; and the rich of all classes suffered severely. 'Potatoes were not merely the food of the people, but in many places they supplied the place of capital and of a circulating medium.'

December. — 'A terrible apathy hangs over the poor of Skibbereen; starvation has destroyed every generous sympathy; despair has made them hardened and insensible, and they sullenly await their doom with indifference and without fear. Death is in every hovel; disease and famine, its dread precursors, have fastened on the young and old, the strong and the feeble, the mother and the infant . . .'   *Cork Examiner.*

December. — In the county Donegal — 'Nothing can describe too strongly the dreadful condition of the people. Many families were living on a single meal of cabbage, and some even, as we were assured, upon a little sea-weed.' We were told that 'the small farmers and cottiers had parted with all their pigs and their fowl; and even their bed-clothes and fishing-nets had gone, for the one object — the supply of food,' and that 'many families of five to eight persons subsisted on 2½ lbs. of oatmeal per day, made into thin water gruel — about six ounces of meal for each! That there were at least thirty families in this little town [Dunfanaghy] who had nothing whatever to subsist upon, and knew not where to look for a meal for the morrow. We visited the poorhouse at Glenties [county of Donegall] which is in a dreadful state; the people were, in fact, half starved, and only half clothed. They had not sufficient food in the house, for the day's supply. Some were leaving the house, preferring to die in their own hovels rather than in the poorhouse . . .' Mr. Forster, writing from Ballina, county Mayo, to the committee, represents the country as in 'a truly deplorable state; in one small district no less than fourteen sudden deaths occurred, in which the verdict was "death by starvation." ' 29th. — A correspondent from Kilfian parish, in that *Transactions of the Relief Committee of Friends.*

Date	Event and Circumstance	Authority

county, states, 'that from one end of it to the other, the poor are without money, food, clothing, or hope of relief; no less than eight deaths from want of food have occurred within the last week, and dysentery prevails to a fearful extent.' The same gentleman's report of the counties of Roscommon, Leitrim, Fermamagh, Donegal, Sligo, Mayo, Galway, Longford, and Cavan in the month of December in this year, and in April, 1847 states, that his examination disclosed a state of destitution and suffering which far exceeded that which had been at first supposed.

In December the committee reports on the distress at this period, as follows:— 'Whole families have been reduced to subsist on a single meal a day of cabbage, or similar vegetable food; and instances have already occurred of death from want.'

1847   . . . In the third year (1847) the disease had nearly exhausted itself, but it still appeared in different parts of the country. 'Although the potatoes sown . . . were estimated only at one-fifth or one-sixth of the usual quantity, it would have been a serious aggravation of the difficulties and discouragements under which that portion of the empire was suffering, if the disease had re-appeared in its unmitigated form . . .'   *The Irish Crisis.*

DISTRESS. — January. — Fearful distress and fever prevailed in the west and south of Ireland, especially at Roscommon, and in Skibbereen, where at this time 'the dead were buried without coffins.' In Clifden, county of Galway, the distress was fearful; '5,000 in extreme destitution trying to live on field-roots and sea-weed.' . . . At a meeting held near Westport, it was stated that 'nine-tenths of the inhabitants were in a state of starvation, having neither food nor means of procuring it.'   *Saunders' News-Letter. Freeman's Journal.*

Great destitution at Oranmore, County Galway; 'whole families are living on chicken-weed, turnip-tops, and sea-weed; they did not ask for any thing, no one spoke, a kind of insanity, a stupid despairing look, was all that was manifested.' September 21st. — The distress in the districts of Castleisland and Ballincuslane, county Kerry, since the stoppage of the relief (under 10 Vic., cap. 7) is truly appalling; 'as to the people, their mental and physical energies are paralysed, they appear stupified even to the level of the brute creation.'   *Dublin Evening Mail.*

Date	Event and Circumstance	Authority

. . . 'One third of the people had been reduced to destitution by the loss of the potato crop [in 1845-46-47], and the partial failure of the oat harvest; of these many have died . . .' — *Pim's Condition and Prospect of Ireland.*

'. . . The whole world was ransacked for supplies; Indian corn, the taste for which had by this time taken root in Ireland . . .' — *The Irish Crisis.*

. . . 'The orderly and good conduct of the peasantry and even the people generally is highly to be commended; all admit that the resignation and forbearance of the labouring classes was astonishing, when it is remembered with what rapidity the real famine encompassed them . . .' — *Reports of Relief Commissioners.*

The reports in December state — the famine is severely felt in Kerry; many deaths from starvation recorded. — *Irish Farmer's Gazette.*

1848 In May wheat looked well; the oats backwards, in consequence of the long drought, but there was not the slightest symptom of failure among the potatoes. In June the potato crop promised well, but the oats were not so prolific as expected. Up to the beginning of July the potato crop was reported healthy, 'but now the disease appeared in patches in different localities, and by the continued rain of this month the progress of the disease appeared to be hastened.' It was reported in the county of Kilkenny, also at Ashford, county of Wicklow; and in the counties of Mayo, Westmeath, Limerick, and 'in many places heretofore quite free since the change of weather from dry to wet.' Early in August there were several sharp frosts, after which the potatoes generally throughout the country appeared blackened, and the great bulk of the crop was lost. — *Dublin Evening Mail.* / *Irish Farmer's Gazette.* *Freeman's Journal.*

. . . The disease is spreading in all parts of the country, and especially in the west, but seemingly mitigated in character . . . — *Dublin Evening Mail.*

DISTRESS. — 'If we review the consequences of the late famine,' writes Dr Lalor, from Kilkenny, 'we will find that it reduced the physical and moral energies of our people to the lowest standard . . . Famine also drove [during the years 1846, 1847, and 1848,] crowds of half-famished people into our large and more wealthy towns and cities, where the means of procuring food were more abundant . . .' — *Dublin Quarter Journal.*

JANUARY. — Frightful destitution reported from Tullamore, Cloghjordon, and Athlone; and deaths from starvation in Mayo, Limerick, Cork, Athlone, — *Saunders' News-Letter.*

Date	Event and Circumstance	Authority
	Galway, Kilkenny, Waterford, and Kerry. In February, the distress in Nenagh was very great, and in the counties of Roscommon and Tipperaray horses and asses were used for food.	
1849	. . . 'The potatoes last year [1848] were almost universally blighted; and the late-sown crop never came to perfection at all. These wet and unripe potatoes, being unfit for food were kept for seed; and the crop of this year resulting from them proved weak and unhealthy, and even in May exhibited the blight on the leaves, which broke into holes.'	*Irish Farmer's Gazette.*
	DISTRESS. — 'The earlier months of 1849 were marked by a greater degree of suffering in the western and south-western districts than any period since the fatal season of 1846-7.'	*Report of Poor Law Commissioners.*
	One of the agricultural instructors, writing from Clifden, Connemara, early in March, says:— 'The state of the country here, as in many other places, is utterly hopeless, and exhibits the most horrifying picture of poverty and destitution. The neglected state of the land — the death-like appearance of the people crawling from their roofless cabins — the piercing wailings of the children forsaken by their parents, and the parents in their turn forsaken by their children — the pitiful petitions of the desponding poor . . .'	*Reports of Agricultural Instructors.*
1850	SLIGHT AND PARTIAL POTATO FAILURE. — February. A large portion of the population have been existing on the turnip for the last four months. In the absence of the potato it has proved great blessing which the people can never forget.	*Irish Farmer's Gazette.*
	August. — The potato blight has appeared in several counties, the leaves and stalks have become black and withered, but the tubers are not affected, and potatoes are selling for 4d. a stone; but a disease which has been so virulent for a period of four or five years cannot be expected to disappear suddenly.	*Irish Farmer's Gazette.*
	February 9th. — Destitution very great in Wexford.	*Saunders' News-Letter.*

Selected Sources used by William Wilde in compiling his Table of Famine

Annals of Boyle.
Annals of Camden. (W. Camden, *Britannia,* ed. R. Gough (1806))
Annals of Clonmacnoise.
Annals of Clyn. (J. Clyn, *The Annals of Ireland,* HS, T.C.D.)
Annals of Dowling.

Annals of Innisfallen.
Annals of Kilronan.
Annals of Henry of Marleburgh, (part printed in Hanmer's Chronicle).
Annals of Multifernan.
Annals of the Four Masters.
Annals of Ulster.

Anon.	*The Groans of Ireland, in a letter to a Member of Parliament* (Dublin, 1741).
F. Barker & J. Cheyne	*An Account of the Rise, Progress, and Decline of the Fever lately epidemical in Ireland,* 2 vols. (Dublin, 1821).
Edward Bascome	*A History of Epidemics and Pestilences from the earliest ages,* . . . (London, 1851).
H. Boulter	*Letters written by his excellency, Hugh Boulter, D.D., Lord Primate of all Ireland, etc* . . . 2 vols. (Dublin, 1770).
J.B. Bryan	*A Practical View of Ireland,* . . . (Dublin, 1831).
D. Corrigan	*On Famine and Fever as cause and effect in Ireland* (Dublin, 1845).
R. Cox	*Hibernia Anglicana, or the History of Ireland from the Conquest thereof by the English to the present time,* (London, 1689-90).
Dowling's Annals	*Annales Breves Hiberniae Auctore Thaddeo Dowling* MS, (T.C.D.).
Robert Frazer	*General View of the Agriculture and . . . Present State and Circumstances of the County of Wicklow* (Dublin, 1801).
W.J. Geary	'Report of St John's Fever . . . Hospital, Limerick', *Dublin Journal of Medical Science,* XI (1837).
James Hardiman	*The History of the Town and County of the Town of Galway from the earliest period to the present* (Dublin, 1820).
W. Harris	*History and Antiquities of Dublin* (Dublin, 1746).
William Harty	*Historical Sketch of the Contagious Fever Epidemic in Ireland during 1817-19* (Dublin, 1820).
John Hooker [alias Vowell]	*The Chronicle of Ireland,* 1587.
J.H. Hutchinson	*The Commercial Restraints of Ireland considered in a series of letters to a noble lord* (Dublin, 1779).
C. MacFarland	*The Cabinet History of England* (London, 1845-47).
D. MacFirbis, ed.	*Chronicon Scotorum* (MS in T.C.D.)
Samuel McSkimin	*The History and Antiquities of the County of the Town of Carrickfergus from the earliest records to the present time* (Belfast, 1811).
Fynes, Moryson	*An History of Ireland, from the year 1599 to 1603: with a short narration of the State of the Kingdom for the year 1169 to which is added a description of Ireland.* 2 vols. (Dublin, 1735).
Maurice O'Connell	*Morborum Acutorum et Chronicorum quorundam Observationes Medicales Experimentales . . .* (Dublin, 1746).

Sylvester O'Halloran	'Treaties on the Air', MS, Royal Irish Academy.
Philip O'Sullivan Beare	*Historia Catholicae Iberniae* (Lisbon, 1621).
Robert Payne	*A Brief Description of Ireland: made in . . . 1589* (London, 1590).
William Petty	*Political Anatomy of Ireland* (London, 1691).
J. Pim	*Condition and Prospects of Ireland* (Dublin, 1848).
John Rutty	*A Chronological History of the weather and Seasons, and of the Prevailing Diseases in Dublin . . . during the space of Forty Years etc.* (Dublin, 1770).
Michael Ryan	*A Manual of Midwifery, to a Summary of the Science and Art of Obstetric Medicine* (London, 1828).
T. Short	*A General Chronological History of the Air, Weather Seasons, etc.,* (London, 1749).
[Philip Skelton]	*The Necessity of Tillage and Granaries . . .* (Dublin, 1741).
Edmund Spenser	*A View of the State of Ireland* (1633).
C. Smith	*Ancient and Present State of the County and City of Cork* (Dublin, 1750).
C.E. Trevelyan	*The Irish Crisis* (London, 1848).

Transactions of the Central Relief Committee of the Society of Friends (Dublin, 1852).

E. Wakefield	*An Account of Ireland, Statistical and Political* (London, 1812).
James Ware	*The Antiquities and History of Ireland* (London, 1658).
N. Webster	*A Brief History of Epidemic & Pestilence Disease, 2 v* (Hartford, 1799).

Parliamentary Records
Journals of the House of Commons of the Kingdom of Ireland.
Parliamentary Report on Scarcity in Ireland.

Reports
Report of Agricultural Instructors.
Report of the Poor Law Commissioners.
Report of Relief Commissioners.

Journals and Newspapers
Cork Examiner.
Cork Southern Reporter.
Dublin Evening Mail.
Dublin Quarterly Journal of Medical Science.
Dublin Medical Press.
Ennis Chronicle.
Faulkner's Journal.
Freeman's Journal.
Hibernian Magazine.
Irish Farmer's Gazette.
Irish Farmer's Journal.
Irish Farmers and Gardener's Magazine.

Proceedings of Royal Dublin Society.
Pue's Occurences.
Saunders' News-Letter.
Transactions of Association of College of Physicians of Ireland.
Transactions of the Royal Dublin Society.

References

1. M.J. Cullen, *The Statistical Movement in Early Victorian Britain: The Foundations of Empirical Social Research* (New York, 1975).
2. *The Census of Ireland for the year 1841,* BPP 1843 [504], IV.
3. *The Census of Ireland for the year 1851,* Part V, Tables of Deaths, vol. 1, Brit. Parl. Papers 1856 [2087-I], XXIX, p.2.
4. P. Froggatt, 'Sir William Wilde and the 1851 Census of Ireland', *Medical History,* vol. 9 (1965), p.306.
5. *The Census of Ireland for the year 1851,* pp.2-3.
6. *Ibid.,* p.3.
7. *Ibid.*
8. B. Jennings, ed., *Wadding Papers,* IMC (Dublin, 1953), pp.344-5.

2

WEATHER, FAMINE, PESTILENCE AND PLAGUE IN IRELAND, 900-1500

Mary C. Lyons

Any examination of weather, famine, plague and pestilence in Ireland in the middle ages is an awkward matter. However, it is possible, using all available annalistic sources, to reconstruct much of what occurred. In no instance is the material as comprehensive as that available to Titow from the account rolls of the Bishopric of Winchester,[1] nor are there any extant runs of court rolls recording payments of heriot that can be used as a check on this data.[2] Precise quantification is impossible. Certain trends are clear, both from the annals, and in the case of the thirteenth and fourteenth centuries, from fluctuations in the price of grain and livestock,[3] but the local consequences of famines, or of visitations of the Black Death cannot be seen other than in oblique terms. Despite these limitations, a detailed chronology can be constructed using the annalistic sources, and its effectiveness can be enhanced by applying additional controls. It is in this context that Baillie's dendrochronological indices for Belfast and Dublin,[4] and Titow's harvest profiles for the Winchester estates in the thirteenth, fourteenth and fifteenth centuries have been used.

What emerges from this broad examination of weather, famine and plague in Ireland is that the demographic base was subject to severe erosion in the late thirteenth and early fourteenth century. Famines interspersed with economic crises, political unrest, invasion and exceptionally bad weather, marked the end of a period of demographic expansion. Population growth had ceased, and an effective decline set in long before the first visitation of the Black Death in 1348. Recurrent outbreaks of bubonic plague in the course of the fifteenth century appear to have contained what might otherwise have been a more comprehensive demographic recovery. In this paper I shall attempt to place what appears to have been the catastrophic demographic decline in Ireland during the final years of the thirteenth century and the first half of the fourteenth century within the context of a general overview of demographic and agrarian economic trends as reflected in annalistic evidence. I am fully aware that any overview will, of its nature, tend towards a certain amount of simplification, and the blurring of fine detail. This is unavoidable. A further problem complicating any examination of medieval social history in Ireland is the fact that the lordship, and the Gaelic regions to an even greater extent, were areas on the fringe, marginal in all senses of the word. This is, however, an issue of such broadness that all one can do is to draw attention to its magnitude, and to the inherent capacity for it to cause unusual variations which are really only reflected in other marginal lordships and kingdoms.

The Annalistic Sources

Two types of annals have been used in the compilation of the chronological table, Gaelic annals, which provide a more or less continuous narrative for the entire period covered, and Anglo-Irish annals, most of which only begin to incorporate data concerning weather, famine and disease from the mid-thirteenth century onwards, and the most detailed of which all terminate in the mid or late fourteenth century. Because of the disparity of these sources, I shall give a brief overview of regional bias and of the provenance, in so far as that can be determined, of the groups of annals used.

Gaelic Annals

Most of the extant Gaelic annals are not contemporary. Many were compiled in the sixteenth or early seventeenth century from bodies of annalistic material then surviving. The most comprehensive of these, the *Annals of the Four Masters,* was compiled as a team project between 1632 and 1636.[5] Apart from the *Four Masters,* all of the other northern and western annals are non-contemporary, though at a remove. The earliest of these, the *Annals of Ulster,* ends in 1510, and is in a single hand up to 1489.[6] Both the *Annals of Connacht* and the *Annals of Loch Cé* were probably derived independently from the same archetype or archetypes.[7] Of the two, *Connacht* is the more detailed, covering a period from 1224 to 1562 whereas *Loch Cé* begins in 1014 and ends in 1590. The disparity between accounts in these two annals, despite their common descent, shows that the process of compilation also involved a process of critical and selective editing.

If this process of editing in any way reflects a change in attitudes to Gaelic kingship, it may well have had an important influence in excluding material concerning weather and crop fertility. In a society where the local or regional king was, on his inauguration, wedded to the septal lands,[8] such accounts performed the additional function of providing a critique of the quality of his kingship. One of the clearest early expressions of this principle is to be found in the *Twelve secular abuses* of the Hiberno-Latin father known as Pseudo-Cyprian. The reign of the *rex iniquus tyranus* is clearly linked to instances of famine, crop failure, unrest and civil war.[9] The most blatant annalistic instance of such linkage occurs in the *Four Masters'* account of the death of Edward Bruce in 1318

> Edward Bruce, the destroyer of Ireland in general . . . was slain by the English . . . And no achievement had been performed in Ireland for a long time before, from which greater benefit accrued to the country . . . for during the three and a half years that this Edward spent in it a universal famine prevailed to such a degree, that men were wont to devour one another.[10]

However, this was a unique record of the end of the Bruce Invasion and as such raises important questions. The account occurs in a series of annals that more or less disregards weather, famine and disease in Ireland for a good third of the fifteenth century. Weather coverage in other main Gaelic annals is also less comprehensive for the fifteenth century than for other periods. Does this reflect an actual change in climate, or a change in attitudes to kingship either amongst the original annalists compiling contemporary accounts, or amongst the sixteenth and seventeenth century copyists?

Something of the copyists' editorial chain can be seen if one examines weather coverage in the *Annals of Inisfallen,* a series of southern medieval annals, and in two sets of translated annals, Duald MacFirbis's fragmentary fifteenth century annals, and the *Annals of Clonmacnoise.* Translation of its nature should not involve editorial work or selectiveness, and contemporary annals will reflect contemporary recording practice.

From the mid-thirteenth century onwards, *Inisfallen* is a contemporary chronicle.[11] Up to the cessation of its main group of annals in the 1320's, the hands are contemporary.[12] In general its coverage of weather, famine and plague is extensive. Its concluding entries in this group provide the best annalistic evidence concerning the impact of the agrarian crises of the mid 1320's in Ireland.

MacFirbis's translation was compiled for Sir James Ware from Gaelic annals surviving in 1666.[13] It covered the 1440's, the 1450's, and the early to mid 1460's and is the main, and frequently the only source recording weather and incidents of famine and plague in Ireland during that period. MacFirbis clearly translated without excluding, or without excluding much of significance from his original or originals. This material was presumably known to Michael Clery and the other compilers involved in the production of the *Four Masters,* yet is excluded from their work. Similar in both structure and tone to MacFirbis's annals, the *Annals of Clonmacnoise* were translated by Conell Magoeghan in 1627, and survive in a 1684 copy of the 1627 original.[14] Both were translations, rather than new synthetic complications, and each each contained significant amounts of data relating to weather, famine and disease not recorded in other Gaelic sources.

By the late sixteenth century, regional Gaelic kingship had effectively been tamed.[15] Direct English intervention in the affairs of specific Gaelic dynasts had become increasingly effective, and Gaelic lords either adapted to the changing conditions, or were forced into revolts of desperation like Shane O'Neill. The idealised concept of the ruler married to his septal lands had become irrelevant. It is therefore not unlikely that while later compilers and transcribers of annals would have included material relating to the military affairs of specific septs, material pertaining to the judgmental function of the Gaelic historian in relation to the quality of kingship would have been omitted if not sufficiently spectacular.

Anglo-Irish Annals

By comparison with the Gaelic annals the narrative scope of the Anglo-Irish annals is a fairly limited thing. Although many include brief retrospective introductory sections, extensive accounts only begin in the thirteenth century. The three main series, the *Annals of St Mary's*, the *Annals of John Clyn* and the *Annals of New Ross*, all terminate in the fourteenth century. Dowling and Grace's annals provide continuous coverage, with a south-eastern bias, into the fifteenth century.

The *Annals of St Mary's* were associated with Dublin's Cistercian foundation. It is unlikely that any of the extant recensions of these annals represents the autograph, but all are clearly derived from that original archetype.[16] There are four main textual groups. The most important of these, Bodleian MS, Laud 526, preserves a narrative from 1162 to 1370.[17] A less complete text, spanning the period from 1070 to 1427, with two lacunae, 1222-1307, and 1317-1360, is preserved in Trinity College, Dublin.[18] Two early fourteenth century fragments of the chronicle are held in the British Library,[19] and notes compiled from the chronicle for Sir James Ware are still extant.[20] Similarities between the Laud 526 entries and the entries in *Clyn* indicate that both annalists probably used a common source for the period from 1270 to 1320, this being a contemporary Anglo-Irish chronicle which is now lost. Much of the pre-1250 material in all four surviving recensions of *St Mary's*, and of *Clyn*, appear to be stock entries concerning general European history drawn from a single chronicle, or, perhaps, from a series of brief universal chronicles.

Although Clyn's narrative is continuous for the entire period up to 1349, the chronicle is only a useful independent source from the mid-thirteenth century onwards. Like the compiler(s) of *St Mary's*, Clyn relied for his early material on brief entries from a universal chronicle, and the initial historical entries are scattered.[21] The early material was being used to expand the narrative retrospectively. It is for the period in which he, or others whom he knew, lived that additional material of importance concerning weather, famine and plague occurs. The impression given by the text itself is that the project of compilation might even have been conceived and executed in 1348, with the earlier material being given as a matter of course to provide an introduction for the recording of the Black Death. In a fatalistic concluding apologia Clyn described himself as *inter mortuos mortem expectans,*[22] and this despair is the most logical *raison d'être* for the work itself.

The other Anglo-Irish annals used in the compilation of the table are the *Annals of New Ross*, Dowling's *Annals* and Grace's *Annals of Ireland*. Of these, only the *Annals of New Ross* are medieval, providing a continuous narrative from 1265 to 1346, with two later entries for 1467 and 1480.[23] Grace and Dowling are later compilations. Like Clyn, Grace was a native of Kilkenny. The Annals were probably compiled between 1537 and 1539[24] The initial entry is for 1074, and coverage of both the twelfth and the fifteenth centuries is weak. Thady Dowling, Chancellor of the diocese of Leighlin, died in 1628.[25] His *Annals* were thus probably compiled in the first two decades of the seventeenth century. While they begin with some ninth and tenth century material, the main sequential narrative does not begin until 1170. It concludes in 1600.

Thus, the Anglo-Irish sources used are similar in scope, if not in period range and area, to the Gaelic annals. Their coverage of weather, famine and disease in the late thirteenth and early fourteenth centuries is more detailed than that of the Gaelic annalists, reflecting the more severe impact of these crises on a grain-based manorial economy already facing difficulties in adjusting to the effective collapse of the war economy boom in grain exports to Wales, Scotland and the French theatre of war.

Comparative and Dendrochronological Data

No detailed work has yet been undertaken on weather conditions in either the Scottish border lands or the Welsh marches. However, Titow's work on the estates of the bishopric of Winchester provides some data which may be compared with Ireland for nearly three centuries of the period under examination.[26] The importance of this data as a control cannot be understated. Annalistic data are always problematic. There are occasions when a major, or apparently major, calamity will be noted only in a single group of annals. The scope and range of the disaster will thus be unclear. Variations in climate are such that the conditions noted might be the result of a localised micro-climate. In addition to these problems, the tendency of annalists to concentrate on the spectacular, and possibly to spectacularise the mundane cannot be ignored. A continuous series of data, such as that in the Winchester estate accounts, can thus furnish a useful supplement. In as much as both the weather conditions and the annual yield are analysed, they provide a more sensitive tool for measuring the impact of weather and crop failure at a local level. The main problem in using Winchester as a control for Ireland is that while it is probably valid for the south and east,[27] it may not be so apt a control for the north and west and for extreme marginal land in Leinster. Both in terms of terrain and climate, conditions in Ulster were probably closer to those prevailing in Scotland.

Dendrochronological data provide a further control on annalistic evidence. Oak is a slow growing tree with an annual growth rate closely related to weather conditions, in particular to the amount of rainfall in any given year. Baillie's examination of oak samples from Belfast and Dublin sites provide master chronologies and an index for much of the period under examination in this paper. There is a continuous chronology for Belfast from 1001,[28] while the Dublin material provides chronologies from 855 to 1306, and from 1357 to 1550.[29] In a year of precisely average rainfall, the index generated will be 100: drier weather will generate an index number lower, and wet weather an index number higher than this base.

While general trends are most apparent in the dendrochronological data, such evidence, together with annalistic material, also indicates the importance of micro-climate. It is clear from accounts in the *Annals of Ulster* that the years at the end of the first decade of the tenth century were years of extremely wet weather.[30] No Belfast oak samples cover this period but those from Dublin do. These indicate that rainfall in the Dublin area in the years in question was well below average.[31] Similarly, while the same overall trends can be seen in both the Dublin and Belfast chronologies, the severity or extremities of changes varies in the two regions. There are occasions on which both chronologies diverge completely.

Weather, Famine and Plague in Ireland, 900-1500

The closing years of the thirteenth century and the entire fourteenth century saw a series of demographic reverses unlike anything that preceded, or was to follow this period. Climatic changes in the late thirteenth century, coupled with a series of severe weather related famines in the first quarter of the fourteenth century, had already had a significant impact on the demographic base before the first outbreak of bubonic plague.

The interaction between weather, crop failure, disease and famine in the tenth, eleventh and twelfth centuries will be examined briefly, and compared with the reverses of the late thirteenth and fourteenth centuries. Fifteenth century developments will then be analysed in the context of this decline and contraction of population that occurred in the previous century. Little of this analysis can be supported by hard facts concerning actual known mortality rates in given localities. There are no extant court rolls for the crucial periods. In the context of the Black Death, it is, however, possible to use the rent concessions stemming primarily from the impact of the plague on the royal manors of the Vale of Dublin, and some precise listings of waste tenements on Elizabeth de Clare's estates in the early 1350's, to gauge effect, without obtaining any precise quantification of mortality. As the patterns of demographic decline emerging in late thirteenth and fourteenth century Ireland were by no means unique, it can be assumed in broad terms that known rates of mortality both in England and on the Continent reflect the probable course of crises, such as the great northern European famine of 1315-18, and the Black Death in Ireland.

The Tenth Century

With the exeption of 912 and 913 in Ulster, rain does not seem to have played a significant part in promoting disease among either humans or livestock.[32] While the annalist felt it necessary to record these conditions, no direct association was made with murrain or crop failure. That they were recorded at all implies that there must have been some adverse effect but the omission of the effect from the narrative indicates that this was of minimal importance. Problems relating to cold seem to have been the most serious adverse weather conditions recorded by the annalists. Thus, the mortality recorded in the *Annals of Clonmacnoise* in 917 was probably one of the classic winter diseases like typhus, and would have been associated with the cold conditions recorded in the *Annals of Ulster* and the *Annals of Inisfallen* in the same year. Similar conditions are reflected in the 955 entry in the

Annals of Clonmacnoise. Occasional famines were recorded without any explanatory commentary, and one instance of an apparent outbreak of anthrax among humans and cattle was recorded in 993.

A number of important features emerge from the annalistic accounts. The first is the degree to which occurrences of bad weather were isolated instances relating to a single year. A second important feature is the number and distribution of these instances. If one excludes accounts of weather which had no apparent effect on livestock, crops or humans, there were only nine potential disasters: less than one incident every ten years. A further factor to be taken into account is five exceptionally good autumns, indicated by records of exceptional yields of mast or fruit. The scope of disaster was thus always contained, and potentially mitigated.

The Eleventh Century

By the eleventh century a new factor had emerged in the recording of weather conditions. Tenth century accounts had not been concerned with conditions likely to damage grain crops or with actual damage to these crops. The first instance of evidence of this concern is an entry in the *Annals of Inisfallen* for the year 1012 which states that much of the corn crop had to be abandoned because of heavy rain. This probably means that rain fell in late summer or early autumn, causing lodging (i.e. laying the corn flat). The increasing importance of cereal crops in Ireland was what ultimately lay behind the distaster of the late thirteenth and early fourteenth centuries. Four other eleventh century entries, all from the *Annals of Inisfallen,* record either damage to, or exeptional yields of grain. By the close of that century tillage had become an increasingly important element in the food base in southern Ireland and so the extent of any severe damage to crops was a matter of sufficient importance to merit inclusion in the major extant local annals.

As with the tenth century, the main type of bad weather recorded affecting humans and animals was exeptional cold in winter or a prolonged cold snap stretching into spring. However, the emphasis in these accounts lies on the impact of the conditions in question on livestock and birds. There is only one specific link between these conditions and human mortality. The hard winter in Ulster in 1046-7 led to famine, and famine-related mortality. Two outbreaks of murrain were associated with good yields of mast in 1057 and 1088. These were probably cases of internal anthrax resulting from the proliferation of anthrax bacilli in surface water retained on drought hardened soil.

Dry autumns and conditions leading to good harvests occurred on a fairly regular basis throughout the century. There were nine such instances, three of which occurred before 1050 and six in the second half of the century. This distribution of good years would have done much to mitigate the impact of recurrent cold winters. It would also have meant that any check to demographic growth in the century would only have been short term, as damage to the food base would never have been so great as to interfere with natural rates of demographic replacement.

The Twelfth and Early Thirteenth Centuries

One of the distinguishing features of Irish twelfth century weather was a series of six windstorms in 1107, 1115, 1137, 1146, 1178 and 1191. While some damage to cattle and humans occurred, the most spectacular damage was to trees and woodland. The number of severe winters declined, and there were only three instances of exceptional snow and frost recorded. The major feature of the century weather was the number of good harvests, and corresponding lack of famine, disease and murrain. There were only three potential checks to demographic growth: the unspecified illnesses noted in the *Annals of Inisfallen* in 1113 and 1173, and the famine and famine-related narrative of plague and disease in *Mac Carthaigh's book* in 1117. As there were nine recorded good harvests, and a possible tenth good harvest in 1129, a year of drought, spread evenly throughout the century, conditions conducive to considerable demographic expansion prevailed.

The annals do not indicate any severe weather conditions during the first half of the thirteenth century, except during the 1220s. Though this particular crisis did not cause any lasting damage to the expanding food base or impose any major check on demographic expansion, it was a preview of the type of crisis that was to wreak havoc in the early years of the fourteenth century. None of the crop failures or famines of previous centuries had lasted for more than a single season. The 1220's were the first case of recorded cumulative mortality. It is clear from the Winchester data that the reason for this prolonged crisis was the series of wet autumns of 1224, 1225 and 1227. However, it turned out to be an isolated episode. There is evidence of exceptionally good weather in Ireland in the mid 1250's, and of the sustained expansion of the royal manors of the Vale of Dublin during the first half of the century. The farms of all these manors rose consistently between 1212 and 1262.[33]

It is clear from the annalistic accounts that there was no significant check to demographic growth in Ireland prior to the 1270's. At no time were there prolonged famines, or periods of bad weather spanning two or more consecutive years, with the exception of the 1224-7 crisis. The fact that the normal death rate was not being compounded by cumulative excess mortality is what distinguishes it from patterns established in the following century.

The Crucial Downturn: 1270-1348

The frequency with which famine conditions prevailed in Ireland increased sharply after 1270, culminating in the great famine of 1294-6. The first practical manifestation of the effects of deteriorating climate can be seen in the increase in the incidence of raids mounted by the Irish of the Leinster mountains on the royal manors of the Vale of Dublin and the efforts in the mid 1270's to curb this threat.[34] However, matters may have been even worse than is apparent, as local crises known from other sources were not recorded in either the Anglo-Irish or Gaelic annals. Thus, the extreme drought experienced on the lands of the lordship of Carlow in 1285 and 1286,[35] which resulted in a severe sheep murrain, is only known through the survival of estate accounts in the Ministers' Accounts series. Receipts from the farm of Chapelizod Manor in 1292 indicate that the manorial mill had been destroyed by flooding in 1292.[36]

While there is little surviving evidence of the causes of the great famine of 1294-6 and there is also an unfortunate lacuna in the Winchester series at this point, the initial reason seems to have been a crop failure in the first of these three years. Clyn's account of 1294 mentions a severe storm in August which destroyed grain. This episode is repeated in the *Annals of New Ross*. A number of other events combined to exacerbate the situation. The lordship was in a state of near civil war for a large part of the famine, due to the capture of the Red Earl by John Fitz Thomas.[37] Both the Liberty of Kildare and the neighbouring O'Connors Faly were in a state of ferment. Raids and counter-raids were frequent and destructive. These years also saw extensive purveyance for the war in Scotland, which can only have worsened the shortage of grain.[38] Some measure of political stability returned to the lordship following the 1295 settlement between Richard de Burgh and John Fitz Thomas.[39] The continuing severity of the famine is underlined by a 1295 entry in the fragmentary marginal annals of the Liber Niger of Christ Church Cathedral.[40] In it the annalist states that the famine was so great that paupers ate the corpses of those hanged at the cross-roads.

The worsening conditions of the early fourteenth century apparent from the surviving data from the Bishopric of Winchester were also prevalent in

Ireland. A murrain associated with a dry summer, similar to that which affected the Carlow and Wexford Bigod lands in 1284-6, occurred in Connacht and elsewhere in 1302. Following that, the three year famine of 1308-10, with its far-reaching effects on the Winchester manors, had a similar impact in Ireland.

Initially the situation passed unnoticed in the Anglo-Irish annals, but stormy, wet weather, which flattened the crops and created marshy conditions, and a great murrain of cattle were noted in the 1308 entries of both the *Annals of Loch Cé* and the *Annals of Connacht*. The effects of the famine may thus have been more severe in western regions because of greater dependence on animal husbandry, or simply because the eastern part of the country may have escaped the worst of the rain. No mention is made in any of the annalistic entries of the crisis in 1309, but by 1310 the effects of the famine were severe in Dublin. The entry in the *Annals of St Mary's* referred to a great shortage of grain, while Grace quoted the astonishingly high price of 20s. for a bushel of wheat. If, as is likely, Grace was confusing the crannoc and bushel measure, this was still an exceptionally high price for wheat. Considerable amounts of grain were also purveyed for Scotland in these years.[41]

The sequence of annalistic entries seems to indicate that the famine followed a course identical to that reflected in the Winchester data. Widespread crop failure and murrain in 1308 was followed by a year in which there was a relatively good harvest. The next year, 1310, was a year of exceptional scarcity, the harvest of 1309 having failed to compensate for that of 1308. The subsequent failure in 1310 thus had cumulative disaster proportions.

It is also significant that the early years of the fourteenth century saw a marked increase in the frequency of raids on manors in the Vale of Dublin. A vacancy of a little under a year after the death of archbishop Richard de Ferrings in October 1306 was to combine with the *de facto* vacancy occurring during the brief archipiscopate of his successor, Richard de Havering. Though placed in possession of the temporalities of the see, de Havering was never consecrated, did not come to Dublin, and resigned the see late in 1310.[42] Like the bishops of Cloyne, and possibly other bishops in marcher areas of the lordship,[43] the archbishops of Dublin probably had special, or at any rate more cordial relations with their Gaelic neighbours than would royal officials functioning in those lands during a vacancy. Instability caused by a series of vacancies and absentee prelates undermined this sort of arrangement. The concurrence of de Havering's absence and the 1308-10 famine thus de-stabilised the Vale of Dublin in a particularly serious way, given that the archipiscopal manors of Castlekevin and Ballymore were crucial points in the defence of the south county. It is in this context that the economic rationale of Gaveston's campaigns in O'Bryne and O'Toole country becomes clear.[44] As an operation in damage containment and limitation, his tactical advances may have won a brief respite from raiding for more vulnerable royal manors like Saggard and Bray. The worsening climatic conditions would have made the option of raiding these exposed manors attractive to the Leinster mountain Irish, who were dependent on marginal land.

The great north European famine of 1315-18 followed two significant famines in Ireland, those of 1294-6 and 1308-10. The sequence of events is well known.[45] There were three exceptionally wet years, during which heavy summer and autumn rains caused massive and repeated crop failures. In the final extant entry for the fourteenth century, that of 1315, the annalist of Loch Cé related that the year saw diseases, famine, murders and intolerable bad weather. Similar references are to be found in that year's entries in both the *Annals of Connacht* and the *Annals of Clonmacnoise.* Purveyance for the Scottish war had absorbed the available surplus grain in the years preceding the famine, and had actually continued into 1315.[46] There were few reserves with which the crop failure of the autumn could have been mitigated. In addition, the Bruce Invasion began in the summer of 1315 and lasted for the duration of the famine, greatly exacerbating it.

It has been asserted that Edward Bruce followed a conscious policy of destruction in the lordship.[47] His winter campaign of 1315-16 in Meath and Kildare certainly bore the hallmarks of a scorched earth policy. However, it should be noted that any large body of men living off the land would have created similar havoc, and that considerable damage was done to archipiscopal property at Swords by the passage of the Red Earl's army on its way northward to engage the Scots.[48] The dislocation caused by the invasion, coupled with local Gaelic attempts to capitalise on the disturbed conditions, such as local risings and raids on exposed manors, must have ensured that Ireland experienced some of the most severe effects of the famine.

The Gaelic annalists devoted little time to describing the effects of the famine, other than to mention in global terms its severity and to note that it and the Bruce Invasion were co-terminus. The interest lay rather in the dynastic wars of Thomond and Connacht, which received fresh impetus as a result of the invasion, and the diversion of the lordship's already thinly stretched resoures. However, the Anglo-Irish annals, and in particular the *Annals of St Mary's,* recorded both the chronology of the famine and the movement of prices. According to the St Mary's annalist, wheat was fetching 8s. a crannoc by the spring of 1316. After Easter, the recorded price had risen to 11s. a crannoc. By this time there was clearly widespread expectation of another crop failure in the coming autumn. The entry for the following year quoted the price of wheat as 23s. a crannoc, and that of oats as 16s. a crannoc, reporting also that men of substance had become beggars, corpses were being eaten and that women were eating their own children.

Famine conditions prevailed well into the summer of 1318, though the early price of 16s. a crannoc noted in *St. Mary's* may indicate the expectation of a relatively good harvest. In fact the harvest was early and good, the annalist reporting that because of it the price of wheat and oats fell respectively to 7s. and 5s. a crannoc. This progression in price movement is remarkably similar to that seen in the Winchester accounts.

While there is no evidence of the murrain of sheep prevalent in England in 1315-17, it should be noted that the annals most likely to record such a catastrophe, the Gaelic annals, were more concerned with the outcome of the Bruce Invasion and the various dynastic wars then in progress. It is highly unlikely that Ireland escaped. A noticeable drop in the price of sheep occurred at that time, and was followed by the characteristic rise in prices that occurs once the initial glut of dead meat is absorbed by the market and by the shortage of animals caused by the decimation of flocks and dislocation of normal breeding patterns.[49]

The effects of the famine of 1315-18 cannot be divorced from the cumulative effects of the crop failures of the 1320's and 1330's, and the cattle murrains of the 1320's. As with visitations of the Black Death, the cumulative effects on mortality were as important as the immediate effects in precipitating decline. Although it is unlikely that the impact of 1315-18 crisis would have been sufficient of itself to ensure that direct cultivation of demesnes by the lord's *famuli* and hired labourers was abandoned, or limited in favour of leasing demesne, but taken with subsequent crises, it could only have served to reinforce this trend.

A major cattle murrain which occurred in England in 1319-20,[50] did not affect Ireland until 1321. Its effects were widespread, meriting mentions in the two western annals, and in the *Annals of Inisfallen*. None of the annalistic sources refer to the cause of the murrain, though it is likely from evidence concerning crop failure in England in 1321, that it was accompanied by a summer drought, and was therefore probably some form of anthrax. Barley, a crop which needs a certain amount of moisture to mature, was severely hit in that year,[51] and evidence from the Winchester manors also indicates a long dry summer. This murrain recurred in Ireland in 1324 and 1325 under similar circumstances.

The mid 1320's crisis concluded with a crop failure reported in all of the western annals and in the *Annals of Ulster* in 1328. This may only have been of regional significance, as it was not mentioned by any of the Anglo-Irish annalists. It appears to have been caused by a long, hard winter and difficult spring. The Connacht annalist stated that the crops grew up 'white and blind', while the *Annals of Ulster* described crops and fruit withered by thunder and lightning.

While the famine of 1330-2 was severe, it may have been confined to Leinster and the south west, as it was not recorded in any of the Gaelic annals. The most likely Gaelic source for such an entry, the *Annals of Inisfallen,* cease in 1325, with the exception of some very fragmentary material for the fifteenth century. Massive spring floods caused spectacular damage in Trim and Drogheda, while the harvest was delayed by the wet summer. Grace wrote of the famine as continuing into 1333, and *St Mary's* indicates that wheat may have been diseased. If grain price data for the years in question may be taken as an indication of severity, this famine must have been on a par with the great famine of 1315-18, and may have been slightly more severe than the famine of 1308-10.[52]

There is evidence of further possible demographic loss in the late 1330's. Both 1338 and 1339 were years of hard winters. Snow, frost, high winds and flooding caused extensive damage in 1338, a year which also saw a severe mortality of sheep recorded in the *Annals of Connacht* and in the *Annals of Clonmacnoise.* This weather continued into 1339, by which time mortality amongst both cattle and sheep would have damaged breeding potential. The difficulties were further exacerbated by a crop failure in the autumn of 1339. Apart from these economic problems, the lordship was politically unstable throughout the 1320's and 1330's. The spread of bastard feudalism, apparent in the Statutes of 1297, 1310 and 1322,[53] the keeping of indentured retinues of kerns and idlemen, and the activities of over-mighty magnates like Maurice fitz Thomas, the first earl of Desmond, and his Gaelic and Anglo-Irish followers like Brian Bán O'Brian and the Tobin family,[54] simply made matters worse, especially in the south and south west. Fitz Thomas' reign of terror continued well into the 1340's. This, then, was the state of the lordship of Ireland in the years immediately preceding the first visitation of the bubonic plague.

The Black Death

Although the Black Death was not of itself a classic crisis of subsistence, its impact on the population of Ireland cannot be divorced from that of preceding famines. The demographic base, already weakened by a succession of famines, was vulnerable. In the context of this cumulative

mortality, the impact of a new disease, one to which immunity was difficult
to acquire, cannot be underestimated. In terms of sheer mortality rates, its
impact was infinitely greater than that of any famine, and like the famines of
the first three decades on the fourteenth century, it was a recurrent
phenomenon.

It is all too easy, relying on Clyn's account of the Black Death, to see the
visitation of 1348-9 as a cataclysmic event from which the population of
Ireland never fully recovered. This is where any annalistic account will be
at its weakest: the spectacular will always be emphasised. The impact of
1348 cannot be denied, but where accounts survive, as for Elizabeth de
Clare's lands, or where other administrative records are still extant, as for
the royal manors of Saggard, Crumlin and Newcastle Lyons, a far less well
defined picture is apparent.

Elizabeth de Clare, both in her own right as one of the de Clare heiresses,
and through an accumulation of her de Burgh and de Verdun dowers, held
lands in almost every part of the lordship. Her receivers accounted regularly
and their accounts were closely scrutinised.[55] The evidence of these
accounts is that mortality and dislocation stemming from the outbreak of
1348 varied considerably on a regional basis. General dislocation can be
seen in the change in accountancy practices in 1350-1, a year in which half-
yearly as opposed to annual accounts were rendered by the receivers,[56]
probably to give Elizabeth a chance to monitor the situation more closely.
The actual receipts over the 1350's indicate the regionalised impact of the
plague. While recovery in Ulster was relatively swift,[57] the situation in
Connacht was more volatile. Areas like Clancoscry suffered badly, whereas
Strothir remained relatively profitable despite the plague and localised
warfare.[58] Recovery on Kilkenny manors like Ballycallan and Palmerstown
merely appears to have been temporary.[59] This might be taken to indicate
that areas in Leinster were more severely hit by the plague than more
remote regions, further from ports and the main centres in which the plague
was endemic.

There are problems in using this type of account to give a form of indirect
quanification of demographic loss and recovery. These can be seen in the
case of Elizabeth de Clare's Tipperary manor of Lisronagh. By 1340 the
annual income from Lisronagh stood at £34-6-6.[60] In 1348-9, the receiver
answered for only £15-9-1.[61] By 1352-3 the receiver answered for £34-8-0
and income for the manor did not fall below £30 until 1356-7.[62] Land waste
pro defectu tenecium was listed in both the 1350-1 accounts, and the 1351-2
account. In the first half of 1350-1, from Easter to Michaelmas 1350, 720
acres were waste.[63] By the following year only 565 acres were waste.[64] This
indicates that a certain portion of the recovery was due to re-alignment of
holdings, rather than local replacement of deceased tenantry.

The impact of the Black Death on the royal manors of Dublin does not appear to have attained crisis proportions until the 1360's. In July 1362 the Seneschal of Demesne was ordered to lease plague vacated lands to any willing to hold them in Crumlin, Saggard and Newcastle Lyons.[65] This initiative failed, and in Michaelmas 1363 reeves and receivers were informed by the Council that it did not intend to take any further action respecting land cultivated prior to the pestilence.[66] By 1365, the Council found it necessary to reduce rents considerably,[67] but despite these reductions, reeves of Newcastle Lyons were still seeking substantial allowances at the Exchequer for approximately 107 acres of waste.[68]

Admittedly the crisis on the royal manors was the result of cumulative plague mortality. There had also been a history of chronic indebtedness, and of raiding by the Irish, particularly in the case of the two biggest manors, Saggard and Newcastle Lyons.[69] However, these moves to reduce rents were being made in the 1360's and early 1370's, and not in the immediate aftermath of the plague in 1348-9 or in the 1350's, in response to petitions from the tenantry.[70]

Outbreaks of the Black Death listed in the annals for the remainder of the fourteenth century seem to indicate that Ireland escaped the *mortalité des enfants* of 1350.[71] There were four further visitations in 1361, 1370, 1383, and 1398. A later continuation of Clyn gives a slight variant on this sequence, stating that outbreaks of the plague occurred in 1362, 1373, 1382, and 1391.[72] With the exception of the 1391 outbreak all of these are fairly close to instances recorded in other chronicles.

The impact of the later visitations is impossible to quantify. As was the case with the early fourteenth century crises of subsistence, this impact would have been cumulative, so much would have depended on demographic replacement rates which cannot now be established. Between visitations these may have been fairly swift, as the remainder of the century saw only one serious crop failure, that of 1397, which seems to have been localised in Munster. However, if the Black Death was endemic in any particular locality, scaled down mortality would have continued between major outbreaks. Despite this factor, demographic decline and erosion had probably levelled out by the beginning of the fifteenth century.

The Fifteenth Century

Although the fifteenth century was essentially a period of recovery in Ireland, this recovery was probably initially based on a redistribution of wealth among a diminished population, and a shift in focus from a grain based to a cattle based economy. The actual demographic recovery was probably a much slower process than the economic recovery manifested in the proliferation of new tower houses,[73] the building of additions to churches, and new friaries.[74] Moreover, the population was building up an immunity to bubonic plague, and as this collective immunity developed, the severity of plague mortality diminished. There were eight outbreaks of plague in Ireland in the course of the century. However, three of these, the visitations of 1446, 1447 and 1448 could be seen as a single visitation similar to that of 1348-50. The other occurrences, 1419, 1439, 1466, 1478 and 1489, were well spaced throughout the century. Despite the increased resistance to the virus, this recurrent pattern curbed the rate of demographic replacement.

Patterns of crop failure and famine reverted to those of the centuries preceding the late thirteenth and early fourteenth centuries. None of the ten famines recorded in the annals lasted for more than a year, and the actual severity in any given instance does not appear to have equalled any of the great famines. Some, such as that of 1439, which also coincided with a plague year, and that of 1491, were directly associated with wet weather. In 1491 the problem was probably a wet autumn as the dendrochronological indices for that year are low, with an index of 71 from the Dublin samples, and 91 from the Belfast samples. A low index coupled with known harvest failure due to wet weather point to the fact that the damage occurred after the peak periods of growth. Two other crops, those of 1445 and 1462, are associated with summer droughts. The first of these was also accompanied by murrain, almost certainly anthrax. Though it is impossible to be categorical, the crop failures of 1434, 1461 and 1497 were probably the result of wet weather. The evidence in these cases is dendrochronological only, and is not reflected in any of the annalistic accounts.

This dispersal of crises, and decrease in the severity of their impact indicates that some form of recovery was in progress. What cannot be gauged is the extent to which this recovery would have brought population levels up to anything approaching those of the pre-1270 demographic base.

Conclusion

The subsistence crises of the years from 1270 to 1348 in Ireland had severely weakened the demographic base prior to the first outbreak of the Black Death. From the tenth century up to 1250, there was unchecked, or relatively unchecked demographic expansion, conditions in the twelfth century being particularly conducive to this trend. Following the Malthusian paradigm, the population expanded to, and then slightly beyond the limits of the food base, with inevitable results, given the worsening in climatic conditions in the late thirteenth century. On the basis of evidence from marginal lands, Postan postulated stagnation in population growth prior to the Black Death.[75] Whatever the general validity of this hypothesis, it is clearly valid in the case of Ireland. However, Ireland was a marcher lordship where political stability was a matter of the difference between the march, the blatant march and the land of war, so that forces other than the purely economic would have contributed to the problems experienced in the late thirteenth and early fourteenth centuries. However, despite the caveat, it is clear that the demographic base in Ireland was vitiated by a series of crises, including the Black Death, in the course of the late thirteenth and fourteenth centuries, and recovery, when it occurred, could only have been slow.

References

1. Cf. J.Z. Titow, 'Evidence of Weather in the Account Rolls of the Bishopric of Winchester, 1209-1350', *Economic History Review*, Second Series, XII (1959-1960), 360-407, and 'Histoire et climat dans levêché de Winchester (1350-1450)', *Annales, E.S.C.* 25e année, 2 (1970), 312-50. The article which he wrote in collaboration with M.M. Postan, 'Heriots and Prices on the Winchester Manors', *Economic History Review*, Second Series, XI (1958-1959), 392-411, examined in detail the effects of the 1308-10 famine using listings in heriots received.

2. The earliest known manorial court roll to have survived in Ireland is one from the early fifteenth century for the manor of Kilcrone, a transcript of which is preserved in E. Curtis' edition and calendar, *Calendar of Ormond Deeds*, (Dublin, 1935-43), No. 439.

3. See M.C. Lyons, 'Manorial Administration and the Manorial Economy in Ireland, c.1200- c.1377' (hereafter 'Manorial Ireland') (unpublished Ph.D. thesis Trinity College, Dublin, 1984), vol. 2, pp. 90-140. Annual averages of the price of wheat and oats from 1252-1374 are given on pp. 117-118.

4. M.G.L. Baillie, 'The Belfast Oak Chronology to A.D. 1001', *Tree-ring Bulletin*, 37 (1977), 1-12; idem 'Dublin Medieval Dendrochronology', *Tree Ring Bulletin*, 37 (1977), 13-20. Both articles contain detailed chronologies of indices presented in tabular form appended to this article.

5. The compilation of the annals is fully described by the editor, J. O'Donovan in the introduction to vol. 1 of 7 vols. *Annals of the Kingdom of Ireland* (Dublin, 1854). O'Donovan's manuscripts of the Four Masters are those held by T.C.D. and the R.I.A.

6. S. Mac Airt and G. Mac Niocaill, eds., *The Annals of Ulster (to A.D. 1131)* (Dublin 1983). The main text of the annals used in T.C.D. MS H.1,8. Evidence concerning hands is presented on p. ix of the MacAirt and Mac Niocaill edition. The earlier edition of the entire corpus comprising the annals, W.M. Hennessy and B. McCarthy, eds., *The Annals of Ulster*, 4 vols (Dublin, 1887-1901), has been used for all post 1131 material cited in the chronological table appended to this article.

7. For an account of the textural recensions and relationships of the western Gaelic annals see B.W. O'Dwyer, 'The Annals of Connacht and Loch Cé and the Monasteries of Boyle and Holy Trinity', *Proc. R.I.A.* LXXII (1972) Section C, 83-101.

8. A typical example of this form of inauguration rite is that described by Giraldus Cambrensis in *The History and Topography of Ireland*, Translated by J.J. O'Meara (Harmondsworth, 1982), pp. 109-110. The symbolic mating of the ri with a white mare, and subsequent ritual slaughtering and eating of the mare is clearly a bonding of king, sept and septal lands.

9. S. Hellman, 'Pseudo-Cyprianus de XII abusivis saeculi', Texte und Untersuchingen zur Geschichts der altchristlichen *Literatur*, 34 (Leipzig, 1910), pp. 52-3.

10. J. O'Donovan, ed., *Annals of the Kingdom of Ireland* (Dublin, 1854) vol. 3, entry for 1318.

11. S. Mac Airt, ed., *The Annals of Inisfallen* (Dublin, 1951). The manuscript from which the text is drawn is in the Bodleian Library MS Rawlinson B 503.

12. See Ibid. pp. xxx-xli, where Mac Airt discusses the hands and the contemporaneity of the annals from the mid-thirteenth century onwards.

13. A printed text of these fragmentary annals is given in O'Donovan's edition of the *Annals of the Kingdom of Ireland* (Dublin, 1854), vol. 4 as appended additional material footnoting the narrative of the years 1443-68. The autograph of MacFirise's 1666 translation of Sir James Ware is scattered through B.L. Cod. Claren, tom 68, Ayscough 4799 and Plut. C. xv E. O'Donovan depended mainly on an early copy of the annals, T.C.D. MS F. 1, 18.

14. Murphy, ed., *The Annals of Clonmacnoise . . . from the earliest period to A.D. 1408 translated into English A.D. by Conell Mageoghagan* (Dublin, 1896). The original translation is probably no longer extant, and the 1684 copy from which Murphy's text is drawn is T.C.D. MS F. 3, 19. See also S. Sanderlin, 'The Manuscripts of the Annals of Clonmacnoise', *Proc. R.I.A.* LXXXII (1982), Section C. No. 5.

15. Cf. G.A. Hayes-McCoy, 'The Completion of the Tudor Conquest and the advance of the Counter-reformation, 1571-1603', in T.W. Moody, F.X. Martin and F.J. Byrne, eds., *A New History of Ireland* (Oxford, 1976), p. 140.

16. A discussion of the relationship between the extant manuscripts of *St Mary's Annals* is to be found in J.T. Gilbert, ed., *Chartularies of St Mary's Abbey Dublin* (Dublin, 1884), vol 2, pp cxi-cxli. The St Mary's entries given in the chronological table appended to this article are mainly based on those in Laud 526, but include material from the other three texts edited by Gilbert in the *Chartularies*, vol. 2, along with Laud 526.

17. Bodleian Library MS Laud 526.

18. T.C.D. MS E. 3, 11.

19. B.L. Add. MS 4792.

20. B.L. Add. MS 4787, ff 30-34, and T.C.D. MS F. 1, 18.

21. R. Butler, ed., *The Annals of Ireland by Friar John Clyn . . . and Thady Dowling . . . together with the Annals of Ross* (Dublin, 1849), pp. 1-39. The manuscript from which the text is drawn forms part of the computational and annalistic material in the Ussher collection T.C.D. MS E. 3, 20.

22. Ibid. p. 37.

23. Ibid. pp. 42-6. These annals are also preserved in T.C.D. MS E3, 20.

24. R. Butler, ed., *Jacobi Grace Kilkenniensis, Annales Hiberniae*, (Dublin, 1843), pp. v-vi. The manuscript from which Butler worked is also preserved in T.C.D. MS E. 3, 20.

25. R. Butler, ed., *The Annals of Ireland by Friar John Clyn . . . and Thady Dowling . . . together with the Annals of Ross* (Dublin, 1849), pp. 1-66 (second sequence of pagination). The manuscript from which this text is drawn is also in T.C.D. MS E. 3, 20.

26. Titow's weather articles, *vide supra*, n. 1, span the period 1209-1450.

27. Conditions in these areas, though marginal and marcher in nature were by no means as sever as those prevailing in the north, west and south-west of Ireland. Regional conditions and patterns of landholding are examined in considerable detail by M.C. Lyons, 'Manorial Ireland', vol. 1, Chapter V.

28. M.G.L. Baillie, 'The Belfast Oak Chronology . . .', 10.

29. M.G.L. Baillie, 'Dublin Medieval Dendrochronology', 18.

30. See the chronological table appended to this article.

31. The indices in question were 109 for 912, and 73 for 913.

32. For all annalistic references to famine, plague, pestilence and crop failure cited in the text of this article hereafter see the chronological table appended.

33. See Table of Chapter 1 in M.C. Lyons, 'Manorial Ireland', vol. 2, p. 1. As an example of the increase in farms, that of Saggard rose from £30 in 1212 for a half-year to be fixed at an annual rate of £112 8s 4d. in 1261-2.

34. Ibid. vol. 1, p. 13.

35. P.R.O. SC 6 1237/16, 1237/17, Carlow accounts in which loss of revenue from the borough's meadow is ascribed to drought. For an indication of the severity of the murrain see Tables II, V and VII of Chapter III (livestock on the manors of Fothered, Ballysax and Old Ross), M.C. Lyons, 'Manorial Ireland', vol. 2, pp. 19, 22 and 24.

36. This occurred in 1292. Pipe Roll 21 Ed. I *Deputy Keepers Reports* (P.R.O.I.), vol. 37, p. 52.

37. For a full account of this incident see A.J. Otway-Ruthven, *Medieval Ireland* (London, 1968), pp. 211-14.

38. See J.F. Lyons, 'Ireland's Participation in the Military Activities of the English Kings in the Thirteenth and Fourteenth Centuries', (unpublished Ph.D. thesis, London, 1955) (hereafter cited as J.F. Lydon, 'Ireland's Participation in English Military Activities'), p. 154.

39. A.J. Otway-Ruthven, *Medieval Ireland*, p. 211.

40. A. Gwynn, 'The Black Book of Christ Church', *Analecta Hibernica*, 16 (1946), 337.

41. See M.C. Lyons, 'Manorial Ireland', vol. 1, p. 350, and J.F. Lydon, 'Ireland's Participation in English Military Activities', pp. 281-3.

42. See M.C. Lyons, 'Manorial Ireland', vol. 1, p. 338.

43. Ibid.

44. Ibid.

45. An account of the famine is given by H.S. Lucas, 'The Great European Famine of 1315, 1316 and 1317', *Speculum*, V (1930), pp. 343-77.

46. Mem. Roll 13-4 Ed. II, P.R.O.I. Ex 1/2, mm 33-33d. These accounts indicate that purveyors were active between May 1315 and March 1316.

47. J.F. Lydon, 'The Bruce Invasion of Ireland', *Historical Studies,* IV (London, 1963), pp. 112-3.

48. R. Frame, 'The Bruces in Ireland 1315-8', *Irish Historical Studies,* 19 (1974), 8-10, and also Mem. Roll 9 Ed. II, (P.R.O.I. R.C. 8/10, p. 422), for a detailed account of this damage.

49. M.C. Lyons, 'Manorial Ireland', vol. 2, pp. 134-5.

50. I. Kershaw, 'The Great Famine and Agrarian Crisis in England 1315-22', *Past and Present,* 59 (1973), 14, 24-6.

51. Ibid. p. 15.

52. M.C. Lyons, 'Manorial Ireland, vol. 2, pp. 117-8.

53. The texts of these statutes are given in H. Berry, ed., *Statutes, Ordinances and Acts of Parliament of Ireland, King John to Henry V* (Dublin, 1907).

54. See G.O. Syales, 'The Rebellious First Earl of Desmond', in J.A. Watt *et.al.,* eds., *Medieval Studies presented to A. Gwynn S.J.* (Dublin, 1961), pp. 203-29; idem, 'The Legal Proceedings against the First Earl of Desmond', *Analecta Hibernica,* 23 (1966), 1-47.

55. M.C. Lyons, 'Manorial Ireland', vol. 1, pp. 143-6.

56. Ibid. p. 137.

57. Ibid. vol. 2, pp. 46-52, for abstracts of all of the receivers' accounts for Elizabeth de Clare's Ulster dower lands.

58. Ibid. vol. 2, pp. 53-7 for the Connacht receivers' accounts, and vol. 1, pp. 153-4 for a discussion of the difficulties in Clanoscry, and pp. 155a-6 for a description of Strothir.

59. Ibid. vol. 2, pp. 66-71 for the receipts of the Kilkenny manors from 1333-60.

60. Ibid. vol. 2, pp. 59; P.R.O. SC 6 1239/16.

61. Ibid. vol. 2, pp. 59; P.R.O. SC 6 1239/21.

62. Ibid. vol. 2, pp. 61; P.R.O. SC 6 1239/28 in this year the receiver answered for two years' arrears totalling £28 3s. 10d.

63. P.R.O. SC 6 1238/13.

64. Ibid.

65. Mem. Roll 35-6 Ed III, P.R.O.I. R.C. 8/28, pp. 157-8.

66. Mem. Roll 37-8 Ed III, P.R.O.I. R.C. 8/28, pp. 309-10.

67. Mem. Roll 38-9 Ed III, P.R.O.I. R.C. 8/28, pp. 679-80.

68. Mem. Roll 48-9 Ed III, P.R.O.I. R.C. 8/31, pp. 124-7.

69. M.C. Lyons, 'Manorial Ireland', vol. 1, pp. 40-1.

70. P.R.O. SC 8 file 118 (5882). This is an undated petition from the tenants of the royal manors which probably post dates the first visitation of the Black Death. See also M.C. Lyons, 'Manorial Ireland', vol. 1 pp. 18-9 for a discussion of this petition.

71. This was a secondary outbreak occurring in the spring of 1350. See P. Ziegler, *The Black Death,* (Harmondsworth, 1970), pp. 207-8.

72. R. Butler, ed., *The Annals of Ireland by Friar John Clyn,* p. 38.

73. This spate of defensive building is covered in A. Davin, 'Tower House of the Pale', (unpublished M.Litt. thesis, Trinity College, Dublin, 1982), and C. Cairns, 'The Tower Houses of County Tipperaray', (unpublished Ph.D. thesis, Trinity College, Dublin, 1984).

74. The fifteenth century boom in ecclesiastical building is covered in H. Leask, *Irish Churches and Monastic Buildings* (Dundalk, 1978), vol. 3.

75. M.M. Postan, *The Medieval Economy and Society* (Harmondsworth, 1975), p. 38 is a fairly typical assertion of his general position.

APPENDIX

*Annalistic References: Weather, Harvest Failure and Plague in Ireland 900-1500
together with comparative data*

Year	Comments	Source	D.D.T.R.I. *[13] Dublin	Belfast
909	A murrain of cows.	Ulster.[7]	78	
912	A dark and rainy year.	Ulster.	109	
913	A dark and rainy year.	Ulster.	73	
917	Great Plague in Ireland.	Clonmacnoise.[6]	*96*	
	Snow and extreme cold — unnatural ice, lakes and rivers frozen solid. Death to cattle, birds and salmon.	Ulster.		
	A mortality of cattle and birds.	Inisfallen.[8]		
919	A year of scarcity and hunger.	Inisfallen.	87	
935	An abundance of oak mast — good autumn?	Ulster.	97	
937	A mighty wind.	Inisfallen.	126	
945	Severe frost — lakes and rivers frozen solid.	Ulster.	88	
950	An abnormally great mast crop.	Ulster.	114	
951	A mortality of bees. Great outbreak of leprosy and dysentery in Dublin.	Ulster.	74	
954	A great murrain of cattle.	Ulster.	120	
955	Great dearth of cattle. Many diseases in Ireland because of great frost and snow at beginning of year.	Clonmacnoise.	138	
959	A bolt of fire passed South-West through Leinster killing people and flocks as far as Dublin.	Four Masters.[12]	96	
960	Lightning destroyed swans and barnacle geese on the Liffey.	Four Masters.	88	
963	Intolerable famine — a father would sell his children for food.	Four Masters.	128	
967	A good year for fruit — eight sacks from the foot of one tree.	Four Masters.	104	
975	Very bad weather in this year.	Clonmacnoise	95	
981	An abnormal mast crop.	Ulster.	83	
985	Abundance of mast in this year and to the end of next.	Inisfallen.	95	
986	Great mortality in Clonmacnoise.	Clonmacnoise	122	
987	Sickness which caused mortality before men's eyes in east of Ireland. Commencement of the murrain of cows — the *Maelgarbh*, which never came before.	Four Masters.	109	

* D.D.T.R.I. Dendrochronological Data Tree Ring Indices

Year	Comments	Source	D.D.T.R.I.*	
			Dublin	Belfast
975	Very bad weather in this year.	*Clonmacnoise.*	95	
981	An abnormal mast crop.	*Ulster.*	83	
985	Abundance of mast in this year and to the end of the next.	*Inisfallen.*	78	
986	Great mortality in Clonmacnoise.	*Clonmacnoise.*	122	
987	Sickness which caused mortality before men's eyes in east of Ireland. Commencement of the murrain of cows — the *Maelgarbh,* which never came before.	*Four Masters.*	109	
993	A great mortality of people and cattle.	*Ulster.*	87	
1005	The Ulaid abandoned their land on account of scarcity and scattered through Ireland — famine localised in north?	*Inisfallen.*	98	74
1007	Great frost and snow January to Easter.	*Four Masters.*	107	41
1008	Severe snow and frost — January to Easter.	*Ulster.*	123	49
1010	A very hot summer and a fruitful a u t u m n .	*Ulster.*	109	60
1011	Abundance of nuts? Good Autumn?	*Inisfallen.*	89	61
1012	Great downpour of rain — much of corn crop abandoned — ? Wet autumn?	*Inisfallen.*	92	52
1015	Most of churches in Munster vacated — scarcity and dissension.	*Inisfallen.*	114	71
1016	A great wind in autumn — broke down houses and woods.	*Inisfallen.*	77	85
1017	A great pestilence in Ára. Many people died.	*Inisfallen.*	78	89
1021	A great shower of wheat in Ossory (Could this be a garbled version of Clonmacnoise plus Four Masters 1022?)	*Loch Cé*[4]	95	122
1022	Great shower of hail in summer — it killed an infinite number of cattle — thunder and lightning.	*Clonmacnoise.*	84	116
	Great showers of hail fell in summer plus thunder and lightning so that man and beast were destroyed in Ireland.	*Four Masters.*		
1023	Great drought from January to May.	*Inisfallen.*	100	158

* D.D.T.R.I. Dendrochronological Data Tree Ring Indices

Year	Comments	Source	D.D.T.R.I.*	
			Dublin	*Belfast*
1028	Great snow in Lent — 3 days plus 3 nights. Men and cattle kept to their houses.	*Inisfallen.*	97	104
1033	A great murrain of cattle.	*Inisfallen.*	93	99
1037	Prodigious tempests and great moisture.	*Clonmacnoise.*	97	136
	Very wet stormy weather this year.	*Ulster.*		
1038	Abundance of acorns so that even young pigs were fattened.	*Clonmacnoise.*	95	118
	Very great fruit so that the last pigs farrowed were fattened.	*Four Masters.*		
1045	Universal retribution in Ireland this year and the crops were destroyed.	*Inisfallen.*	127	154
1047	Snow December 1046 — March. Caused death of people, cattle, sea-beasts and birds.	*Ulster.*	123	132
	Great snow — February-March. The like never seen before.	*Inisfallen.*		
1048	Snow, December 1047 — March. It caused destruction of cattle, beasts, birds and sea-beasts. Famine in Uladh, Ulidians proceeded into Leinster (?misdated — see Ulster and Inisfallen?)	*Four Masters.*	113	142
1051	Inclement weather — loss of corn, milk, fruit and fish — wet summer and autumn? Theft prevalent.	*Four Masters.*	127	112
1052	A violent wind 21st December. It broke down houses and woods.	*Inisfallen.*	103	107
1057	Abundance of mast. Murrain of cattle and pigs etc.	*Inisfallen.*	91	85
1063	Colic and lumps in Leinster. Scarcity of provisions for cattle and scarcity of corn and victuals.	*Four Masters.*	86	69
1066	Such an abundance of nuts that the course of the brooks and streams were impeded.	*Four Masters.*	100	85
1075	A great crop of mast.	*Inisfallen.*	90	95
1076	Great scarcity of victuals.	*Clonmacnoise.*	99	84
1077	Violent wind in autumn damaged corn crop. Sinech — many lumps afflicted cattle and humans.	*Inisfallen.*	94	78
1085	Destruction of men and cattle so that the rich were made husbandmen.	*Four Masters.*	108	151

* D.D.T.R.I. Dendrochronological Data Tree Ring Indices

Year	Comments	Source	D.D.T.R.I.* Dublin	Belfast
1087	Great harvest of mast.	*Ulster.*	111	126
1088	Abundance of nuts and fruit. Murrain of cows. Dearth. A great wind that destroyed churches and houses.	*Four Masters.*	112	127
1091	Sappy, plentiful year of good weather.	*Loch Cé.*	89	83
	A fruitful year with good weather.	*Ulster.*		
1092	End of year, very heavy frost and snow.	*Inisfallen.*	85	89
	Great frost, ice and snow. Lakes and rivers frozen solid.	*Four Masters.*		
1093	Great fruit.	*Loch Cé.*	134	126
	Violent wind sundered grain from corn and blew down numerous trees. Great pestilence — a febrile caused death to many people.	*Inisfallen.*		
	Great snow and frost — lakes and rivers frozen solid.	*Four Masters.*		
1094	Great inclemency of weather from which scarcity.	*Loch Cé*	105	113
1095	A great pestilence in Ireland which killed a multitude of people — August 1095-May 1096.	*Loch Cé.*	116	98
	A great sickness in Ireland — many died — August 1095-May 1096.	*Ulster.*		
	Snow and heavy frost — rivers and lakes frozen solid — a great loss of cattle. Abundance of mast. A great mortality of the men of Ireland.	*Inisfallen.*		
	Great pestilence Europe and Ireland. Many died.	*Four Masters.*		
1097	Great harvest of nuts — best since 1066.	*Ulster.*	118	82
	Great harvest of nuts — best since 1066.	*Four Masters.*		
1101	The best year for corn, milk and good weather — A great mortality of cattle in the south.	*Inisfallen.*	73	63
1105	Heavy snow and great loss of cattle, sheep and pigs.	*Inisfallen.*	99	105
1107	Snow for a day and a night 14th March — a great destruction of cattle.	*Loch Cé.*	90	86

* D.D.T.R.I. Dendrochronological Data Tree Ring Indices

C

Year	Comments	Source	D.D.T.R.I.* Dublin	Belfast
	Great wind and lightning. Many men and cattle died and woods destroyed.	*Four Masters.*		
1108	A great crop of mast, much corn and other produce.	*Loch Cé.*	111	102
	A great wind 3rd September. Great harvest of oak mast. Fruitful year, plenty of corn and mast.	*Ulster.*		
	Abundance of nuts and fruit. A good year.	*Four Masters.*		
1109	Heavy rain and bad weather in summer and autumn. Fasting observed to avert its consequences. An abundance of apples.	*Inisfallen.*	103	104
	Mice ate up all the cornfields in certain parts of Ireland.	*Four Masters.*		
1112	A great crop of mast.	*Inisfallen.*	101	76
1113	A great mortality.	*Inisfallen.*	89	69
1115	Very severe weather, frost and snow Dec. 1114-Feb. 1115. Havoc of birds, cattle and people. Famine.	*Loch Cé.*	115	105
	Boisterous weather frost and snow December 1114-February 1115. Destruction cattle, men and birds — Dearth especially bad in Leinster.	*Four Masters.*		
1117	Great famine in Munster. Plague in Leinster and Munster — a great mortality in Dublin.	*McCarthy Misc.9*	113	125
1121	A great wind on the Nones of December, which caused great destruction in Ireland.	*Loch Cé.*	108	116
	A great wind on 5th December which caused great destruction to the woods of Ireland.	*Ulster.*		
	A great wind in December which caused great destruction to the woods of Ireland.	*Four Masters.*		
1129	A hot summer. The rivers of Ireland dried up, a mortality of beasts and cattle.	*Inisfallen.*	86	102
	The summer of the drought.	*Four Masters.*		
1130	A great crop of every kind of produce generally in Ireland.	*Loch Cé.*	121	128
	Great crop of every produce generally in Ireland.	*Ulster.*		

* D.D.T.R.I. Dendrochronological Data Tree Ring Indices

Year	Comments	Source	D.D.T.R.I.*	
			Dublin	Belfast
	A great crop of nut.	*Inisfallen.*		
	Great fruit upon all trees, both nuts, acorns and apples.	*Four Masters.*		
1133	A great cow mortality in Ireland.	*Loch Cé.*	80	113
	Great murrain of cows in Ireland — the *maelgarbh* — it left but small remnant of the cattle in Ireland.	*Four Masters.*		
1134	The same mortality in Ireland.	*Loch Cé.*	77	114
	Lacuna from 1132 to 1155.	*Ulster.*		
	Lacuna from 1130-1159.	*Inisfallen.*		
1137	Tremendous storm the day before Rogation Sunday — many forests and churches prostrated. A great colic disease in Ireland. Great scarcity in Connacht — Many died of it.	*Loch Cé.*	85	107
	Boysterous tempestuous winds this year, that it fell down many trees, houses . . . and other things.	*Clonmacnoise.*		
	A great wind storm in Ireland which prostrated many trees, houses, churches . . . and swept men and cattle into the sea in Magh-Conaille.	*Four Masters.*		
1140	Lacuna from 1138-1170.	*Loch Cé.*	110	150
	Strange disease of biles or patches in Munster — whereof many died.	*Clonmacnoise.*		
1146	Great wind storm 3rd December which caused a great destruction of woods in Ireland — 60 trees prostrated at Doire Cholum Chille, persons killed and smothered in church, others killed at Cill Sleibhe.	*Four Masters.*	119	96
1147	Retrospectively from 1156 entry. A great crop this year.	*Ulster.*	103	89
1153	A great famine in Munster owing to the war, and it spread throughout Ireland in all directions.	*McCarthy Misc.*	128	90
1156	Great crop throughout all Ireland — 9 years from the other great crop to this year.	*Ulster.*	115	88
	Great snow and intense frost in the winter — lakes and rivers frozen over — most of the birds of Ireland perished on account of the greatness of the snow and frost.	*Four Masters.*		

* D.D.T.R.I. Dendrochronological Data Tree Ring Indices

Year	Comments	Source	*D.D.T.R.I.*★ Dublin	Belfast
1158	Great rain in the summer from which came floods into the river of Inish, with 23 people drowned on Inis na Subh (Inishnasoo, Co Antrim).	*Four Masters.*	94	80
1172	Very bad weather which killed the greater part of the cattle of Ireland.	*Inisfallen.*	89	71
1173	A great pestilence this year which killed a large number of people.	*Inisfallen.*	87	73
1177	A very great wind came this year — large tracts of woods and huge trees prostrated; 120 trees prostrated in Derry. (? misdated).	*Loch Cé.*	79	76
1178	A violent storm this year prostrated woods, forests and very great oaks. 120 trees prostrated in Derry.	*Ulster.*	118	83
	A violent wind storm this year. Great destruction of trees. Oaks prostrated. 120 trees prostrated in Derry.	*Four Masters.*		
1179	The snow of destruction.	*Ulster.*	145	99
	Noxious snow fell this year.	*Inisfallen.*		
	(Given as 1180) Snow of venom fell this year.	*McCarthy Misc.*		
1185	Great fruit in this year.	*Loch Cé.*	107	80
1191	Violent wind storm this year. It blew down churches, houses and woods and caused great mortality of the flocks (sheep) and people of Ireland.	*Inisfallen.*	95	132
1195	A great crop of mast generally this year.	*Inisfallen.*	112	201
1199	A great crop of mast and fruit this year in Desmond.	*Inisfallen.*	111	82
1200	Good mast, fruit. (mild autumn?)	*Inisfallen.*	93	108
1201	Corn crop in Desmond laid waste. (war? bad harvest?)	*Inisfallen.*	102	114
1207	Great destruction of people and cattle this year. (rain and murrain?)	*Ulster.*	75	72
1221	A great wind.	*McCarthy Misc.*	112	110
	Summer: dry.	*Titow.*[13]		
	No calculation of yield.			
1222	A great wind throughout Ireland.	*Inisfallen.*	97	92
1224	Shower — rain.	*Loch Cé.*	82	105
	Murrain?			
	Corn reaped February. Bad harvest.			

★ D.D.T.R.I. Dendrochronological Data Tree Ring Indices

Year	Comments	Source	D.D.T.R.I.* Dublin	Belfast
	Shower — rain. Murrain?	*Connacht.*[5]		
	Autumn: wet.	*Titow.*		
	Yield deviation — 21.41%			
1225	Plague/Fever	*Loch Cé.*	72	101
	Connacht.			
	Harvest in February. Famine.	*Ulster.*		
	Winter: hard. Summer: very dry.	*Titow.*		
	Autumn: wet.			
	Yield deviation + 0.78%.			
1227	Famine/Disease Ireland.	*Loch Cé.*	99	106
	Famine/Disease Ireland.	*Connacht.*		
	Autumn: wet.	*Titow.*		
	No calculation for yield.			
1234	Hard winter. Snow December — January. Frozen rivers.	*Loch Cé.*	100	93
	Hard winter. Snow December — January. Frozen rivers.	*Connacht.*		
	Hard winter. Snow December — January. Frozen rivers.	*Inisfallen.*		
	No material for 1234.	*Titow.*		
1236	Rain.	*Loch Cé.*	110	106
	Bad weather.			
	Famine.			
	Winter: hard. Summer: very dry.	*Titow.*		
	Yield deviation + 33.42%.			
1245	Snow November-December.	*Loch Cé.*	89	85
	Snow November-December.	*Connacht.*		
	Heavy frost? Frostbite.			
	Summer: dry. Autumn: wet.	*Titow.*		
	Yield deviation + 9.66%.			
1246	Earthquake throughout the western world.	*St. Mary's.*[1]	105	80
	Summer: wet? Autumn: wet.	*Titow.*		
	Yield deviation — 13.05%.			
1247	Earthquake in Scotland and Wales.	*McCarthy Misc.*	121	92
	Summer: very dry. Autumn: dry.	*Titow.*		
	Yield deviation — 8.88%.			
1248	Earthquake in Ireland and Wales.	*Inisfallen.*	112	90
	Winter: hard, windy. Summer: very dry. Floods reported.	*Titow.*		
	Yield deviation + 23.50%.			
1249	Great crop on the trees — good autumn?	*Ulster.*	147	84
	Summer: dry?	*Titow.*		
	No yield data.			

* D.D.T.R.I. Dendrochronological Data Tree Ring Indices

Year	Comments	Source	D.D.T.R.I.*	
			Dublin	*Belfast*
1251	Thunder and lightning — floods. Cattle killed. Murrain?	*Loch Cé.*	124	116
	Thunder and lightning in summer — floods.	*Connacht.*		
	Thunder and lightning killed many cattle — murrain?	*Clonmacnoise.*		
	Rain and floods in summer — July.	*Four Masters.*		
	No data.	*Titow.*		
1252	Jan. wind prostrated houses.	*Loch Cé.*	89	86
	Summer: drought. Shannon dry — trees burnt — harvest in August.			
	Great heat — drought. Shannon dry, trees burnt. Harvest July.	*Connacht.*		
	Great drought and hot summer.	*Clonmacnoise.*		
	Hot dry summer.	*Inisfallen.*		
	Great heat and drought: rivers dry: trees burnt in summer.	*Four Masters.*		
	Winter: late winter dry. Summer very dry. Autumn: wet.	*Titow.*		
	Yield deviation + 3.66%.			
1253	Best year for nuts, mast, cattle and the produce of the earth.	*Loch Cé.*	108	71
	Best year for cattle and herbs.	*Connacht.*		
	Copious fruit on the trees — mild autumn?	*Ulster.*		
	Summer: dry.	*Titow.*		
	Yield deviation + 4.96%.			
1254	Abundance of acrons, milk etc. A good autumn and summer?	*Loch Cé.*	103	72
	Tranquil year: plenty of acorns, milk and other good things.	*Connacht.*		
	Winter: hard. Summer: dry? Late summer very wet. Autumn: wet?	*Titow.*		
	Yield deviation − 1.57%.			
1259	Common cough humans and horses — wet condition?	*Ulster.*	114	116
	Cough: humans and horses.	*Inisfallen.*		
	No data.	*Titow.*		
1262	Great destruction of people this year: plague and famine. Bad weather?	*Ulster.*	104	129
	No data.	*Titow.*		
1263	A hot summer in this year.	*Ulster*	62	93
	No data.	*Titow.*		
	Summer: very dry. Autumn: wet?	*Titow.*		
	No yield calculation.			

* D.D.T.R.I. Dendrochronological Data Tree Ring Indices

Year	Comments	Source	D.D.T.R.I.*	
			Dublin	*Belfast*
1270	Famine and scarcity in Ireland this year.	*Loch Cé.*	95	107
	Heavy fall of snow in January.	*Inisfallen.*		
	No data.	*Titow.*		
1271	Pestilence, famine and the sword chiefly in Meath.	*Grace.*[2]	102	118
	Famine/Plague in Ireland.	*Clyn.*[3]		
	Famine/Plague in Ireland.	*New Ross.*[11]		
	Winter: hard? Floods. Summer: dry? Great damage by wind.	*Titow.*		
	Yield deviation — 13.05%.			
1282	Snow — January and February.	*Connacht.*	76	102
	No data.	*Titow.*		
1284	Bad weather: January.	*Inisfallen.*	92	102
	Winter: wet? Summer: very dry. Autumn: wet?	*Titow.*		
	Yield deviation: — 10.44%.			
1285	Summer: very dry.	*Titow.*	97	113
	Yield deviation: — 13.32%.			
	Dry summer.	*Carlow Data.*[15]		
	Murrain.			
1286	Spring of the cattle plague.	*Connacht.*	113	114
	Summer: dry.	*Titow.*		
	Yield deviation: — 9.66%.			
	Dry summer.	*Carlow Data.*		
	Murrain.			
1294/6	Shortage and pestilence this year and the next three years.	*St. Mary's.*	81 94 111	102 93 93
	Scarcity and pestilence in Ireland for this and the next three years.	*Grace.*		
	Lightning and storm in August: grain destroyed. Lacuna 1295-1302.	*Clyn.*		
	Heavy snow, bad winter.	*Inisfallen.*		
1294	Great famine: a crannoc of grain selling at 7s. 6d.	*Dowling.*[10]		
	Lightning and storm in August: grain destroyed. (1294).	*New Ross.*		
	No data 1294-5.	*Titow.*		
	Yield deviation in 1296 c. + 14.88%.			
1302	Great destruction of cows and mortality of cattle this year.	*Loch Cé.*	68	135
	Great plague and destruction among cattle this year.	*Connacht.*		

* D.D.T.R.I. Dendrochronological Data Tree Ring Indices

Year	Comments	Source	D.D.T.R.I.*	
			Dublin	*Belfast*
	Summer: very dry, flooding reported. Yield deviation: + 3.13%.	*Titow.*		
1305	Great hardship early summer.	*Inisfallen.*	155	100
	Summer: very dry.	*Titow.*		
	Yield deviation: 14.1%.			
1308	Destruction of people and cattle — great inclemency of weather.	*Loch Cé.*		104
	Stormy weather — destruction of men and cattle.	*Connacht.*		
	Great murrain of cattle.	*Clonmacnoise.*		
	Autumn: long and wet.	*Titow.*		
	Yield deviation: + 2.09%.			
1310	Great shortage of grain.	*St. Mary's.*		110
	Scarcity in Ireland: wheat 20s. a bushel.	*Grace.*		
	Violent wind destroys houses etc. Great crop of masts. Good autumn?	*Inisfallen.*		
	Summer: dry. No autumn data.	*Titow.*		
	Yield deviation: − 15.67%.			
1315	Arclow, Newcastle McKinegan, Bray etc. vills burnt by O'Tooles and O'Byrnes.	*St. Mary's.*		107
	Diseases, famine, murders and intolerable bad weather.	*Loch Cé.*		
	Many afflictions, famine, storms, strange diseases and murders.	*Connacht.*		
	Summer victualling problems for both the Scots and the Earl of Ulster.	*Inisfallen.*		
	Famine.	*Four Masters.*		
	Winter, summer, autumn: wet.	*Titow.*		
	Yield deviation: − 35.77%.			
1316	Famine suffered by Scots in Offaly/ Kildare. Half-way through Lent wheat 8s. a crannoc: after Easter 11s. a crannoc.	*St. Mary's.*		110
	Lacuna from 1316 to 1413.	*Loch Cé.*		
	Famine.	*Connacht.*		
	Famine.	*Ulster.*		
	Great shortage: a crannoc of salt 40s. and elsewhere 4 marks.	*New Ross.*		
	Famine.	*Four Masters.*		
	Winter, summer, autumn: wet.	*Titow.*		
	Yield deviation: − 44.91%.			
1317	Shortage of victuals, wheat 23s. a crannoc, oats 16s. a crannoc.	*St. Mary's.*		98

* D.D.T.R.I. Dendrochronological Data Tree Ring Indices

Year	Comments	Source	D.D.T.R.I.*	
			Dublin	*Belfast*
	Country devastated by Scots and Ulstermen. Famine — corpses eaten, women eat their children.			
	Scarcity and famine in Ulster: only 300 survived. Corpses eaten, flesh cooked in skulls. Women eat their children.	*Grace.*		
	Great shortage wheat 40s. a crannoc and in some places 4 marks and more a crannoc.	*Clyn.*		
	Famine.	*Connacht.*		
	Great scarcity of victuals in Ireland this year.	*Clonmacnoise.*		
	Famine.	*Ulster.*		
	Great storms, wind, famine.	*Dowling.*		
	⅓ of a crannoc (of wheat) 23s. (sic).			
	Famine.	*Four Masters.*		
	No weather data, but some report of flooding.	*Titow.*		
	Yield deviation: − 13.05%.			
1318	Mortimer fails to pay for goods purveyed. Good early harvest — June wheat 16s. a crannoc, then 7s. and oats 5s. a crannoc by late July.	*St. Mary's.*	108	
	Great shortage from May to autumn — famine. Wheat at 20s. plus a crannoc.	*Clyn.*		
	Three years: the time of Bruce, famine and homicide — men ate one another.	*Connacht.*		
	Three years: Bruce, famine, cannibalism.	*Ulster.*		
	Great shortage in Ireland — many died. Wheat 20s. and more a crannoc.	*New Ross.*		
	Three and a half years' famine — men ate one another — Bruce Invasion.	*Four Masters.*		
	Summer: very dry. Autumn: wet?	*Titow.*		
	Yield deviation: + 32.38%.			
1321	Lacuna 1316 to 1413.	*Loch Cé.*	99	
	Great cattle plague throughout Ireland.	*Connacht.*		
	Murrain of cows throughout Ireland.	*Clonmacnoise.*		

* D.D.T.R.I. Dendrochronological Data Tree Ring Indices

Year	Comments	Source	D.D.T.R.I.* Dublin	Belfast
	A great murrain of cattle in Ireland this year.	*Inisfallen.*		
	No detailed data, but some indication of a dry summer.	*Titow.*		
1324	A great wind: 6th January. Murrain of oxen and cows in Ireland.	*St. Mary's.*		78
	Grave cattle plague in many parts of Ireland.	*Clyn.*		
	The same murrain called *Mael Domnaigh.*	*Connacht.*		
	Murrain called *Moyle Dawine.*	*Clonmacnoise.*		
	Murrain mentioned in duplicate entry.	*Ulster.*		
	Common cattle plague called Maldow.	*New Ross.*		
	Autumn: wet? Yield deviation: − 5.48%.	*Titow.*		
1325	Murrain amongst oxen and cows.	*Grace.*		87
	The cattle plague continued to rage in Ireland.	*Connacht.*		
	The murrain continued.	*Clonmacnoise.*		
	The same cattle plague.	*Ulster.*		
	Winter flooding. Summer: very dry. Yield deviation: + 28.98%.	*Titow.*		
1326	Dry summer and autumn: rivers dried up.	*Clyn.*		89
	Driest year in living memory.	*New Ross.*		
	Winter: hard, dry. Summer: very dry. Yield deviation: + 34.46%.	*Titow.*		
1327	Smallpox.	*Clonmacnoise.*		89
	Smallpox.	*Ulster.*		
	Summer: dry. Yield deviation: + 11.75%.	*Titow.*		
1328	Much thunder and lightning: fruit ruined and the corn grew up white and blind.	*Connacht.*		112
	Thunder and lightning: corn destroyed and white Murrain of people (sic).	*Clonmacnoise.*		
	Thunder and lightning withered crops and fruit. Widespread colds among people.	*Ulster.*		
	Great thunder and lightning in summer. Fruit and crops injured.	*Four Masters.*		

* D.D.T.R.I. Dendrochronological Data Tree Ring Indices

Year	Comments	Source	D.D.T.R.I.*	
			Dublin	Belfast
	Corn white and unprofitable. A cold raged second in agony to death.			
	Winter long and hard with flooding.	*Titow.*		
	Yield deviation: nil (= average).			
1330	Massive floods in spring — Boyne in spate; mills at Trim and Drogheda thrown down. Summer rain — harvest delayed. Wheat 20s. a crannoc. Oats/peas/beans 8s. a crannoc.	*St. Mary's.*		109
	Storm — Boyne floods — damage at Trim and Drogheda; rain — harvest delayed until Michaelmas — wheat 20s. a crannoc oats 8s. a crannoc.	*Grace*		
	Famine — so humid, rainy and stormy that summer and autumn were converted into winter tempests. In winter wheat sold for 13s. 4d. a crannoc.	*Clyn.*		
	Given as 1329: corn fields unreaped until Michaelmas because of bad weather.	*Four Masters.*		
	Winter: hard. Summer: wet. Autumn: wet.	*Titow.*		
	Yield deviation: + 4.18%.			
1331	Famine in Dublin area.	*Grace.*		88
	Winter: very wet. Summer: very dry.	*Titow.*		
	Yield deviation: + 6.53%.			
1332	Manses attacks young and old wheat. Before Easter wheat 22d. a peck; afterwards 12d. a peck.	*St. Mary's.*		90
	Famine in Dublin area.	*Grace.*		
	Summer: dry.	*Titow.*		
	Yield deviation: + 16.19%.			
1333	Good early harvest, wheat 6d. a peck.	*St. Mary's.*		93
	A good year.	*Grace.*		
	Summer: very dry.	*Titow.*		
	No yield data.			
1335	Heavy snow in spring killed small birds.	*Connacht.*		100
	Great snow in spring killed small birds.	*Clonmacnoise.*		
	Winter: early and dry.	*Titow.*		
	Yield deviation: + 0.52%.			

* D.D.T.R.I. Dendrochronological Data Tree Ring Indices

Year	Comments	Source	D.D.T.R.I.*	
			Dublin	*Belfast*
1338	Hard winter — skating and fires lit on the Liffey 2nd December to 10th February.	*St. Mary's.*		110
	Intense frost: deep snow 2nd December - 10th January.	*Grace.*		
	High winds, flooding mills demolished. Bad floods in Kilkenny with water reaching the alter in the Abbey.	*Clyn.*		
	Nearly all the sheep in Ireland died this year.	*Connacht.*		
	Plague hits sheep.	*Clonmacnoise.*		
	Winter: wet. Summer: dry.	*Titow.*		
	Autumn: very wet.			
	Yield deviation: + 21.93%.			
1339	Stormy and evil to man and beast. Rain, snow and ice in winter. Salt 16s. or 20s. a crannoc. Oxen and cows died — only a seventh of ewes survived, most lambs died.	*Clyn.*		120
	Cattle and winter grass suffered from storms.	*Connacht.*		
	All the corn of Ireland destroyed: general famine.	*Clonmacnoise.*		
	Frost and snow early winter — spring. Cattle died — green crops failed.	*Ulster.*		
	Winter: hard, flooding reported. Summer: dry. Autumn: wet?	*Titow.*		
	Yield deviation: − 40.73%.			
1345	Early spring tempests.	*Clyn.*		115
	Winter: wet? Autumn: wet.	*Titow.*		
	Yield deviation: + 5.48%.			
1348	Black Death.	*St. Mary's.*		103
	Black Death.	*Clyn.*		
	Black Death.	*Clonmacnoise.*		
	Black Death.	*McCarthy Misc.*		
	Winter: flooding reported. Autumn: wet.	*Titow.*		
	Yield deviation: + 5.22%.			
1349	Last entry in new hand — author died of plague in 1348.	*Clyn.*		111
	Black Death.	*Connacht.*		
	Black Death.	*Ulster.*		
	Black Death.	*Four Masters.*		

* D.D.T.R.I. Dendrochronological Data Tree Ring Indices

Year	Comments	Source	D.D.T.R.I.*	
			Dublin	Belfast
	Winter: wet, flooding. Summer and Autumn: wet. Yield deviation: − 41.25%.	*Titow.*		
1358	Heavy hail storm in Carbury in summer.	*Connacht.*	113	124
	Heavy storm in Carbury — summer hail.	*Ulster.*		
	Heavy hail storm in Carbury.	*Four Masters.*		
	Summer: dry.	*Titow.*		
	Yield deviation: + 16.1%.			
1361	Great storm 15th January.	*Grace.*	95	105
	Black Death.	*Clonmacnoise.*		
	Black Death.	*Four Masters.*		
	Summer: very dry.	*Titow.*		
	Yield deviation: + 19.4%.			
1363	A great wind which wrecked houses and sank ships.	*Connacht.*	63	102
	Great storm — houses destroyed — ships sunk.	*Clonmacnoise.*		
	Great storm — houses destroyed — ships sunk.	*Ulster.*		
	Great wind: houses destroyed — ships sunk.	*Four Masters.*		
	Winter: beginning humid?	*Titow.*		
	Yield deviation: − 9.4%.			
1370	Black Death.	*St. Mary's.*	108	92
	Black Death.	*Grace.*		
	Black Death.	*Dowling.*		
	Winter: humid?	*Titow.*		
	Yield deviation: + 14.0%.			
1383	Black Death.	*Clonmacnoise.*	118	75
	Winter: floods?	*Titow.*		
	Summer and Autumn: very dry.			
	Yield deviation: + 13.6%.			
1397	Famine — summer and autumn windy, wet and cold.	*McCarthy Misc.*	104	95
	Summer: very dry.	*Titow.*		
	Autumn: end ?humid.			
	No yield calculation.			
1398	Black Death.	*Connacht.*	109	114
	No weather observations for this year. Yield deviation: − 5.7%.			
1404	Many diseases in Ireland this year, especially the lectual sickness (? typhus)	*Connacht*	85	75

* D.D.T.R.I. Dendrochronological Data Tree Ring Indices

Year	Comments	Source	D.D.T.R.I.*	
			Dublin	*Belfast*
	Many diseases in Ireland this year — the Kingdom abounded with fevers.	*Clonmacnoise.*		
	No data.	*Titow.*		
1407	Very bad weather and loss of cattle this year.	*Connacht.*	92	68
	Foul bad weather, and a great murrain of cattle.	*Clonmacnoise.*		
	Very tempestuous weather, and a murrain of cattle this year.	*McCarthy Misc.*		
	Summer: very dry.	*Titow.*		
	No yield calculation.			
1408	Great plague in Meath this year. (Black Death).	*Connacht.*	95	76
	General plague in Meath this year. (Black Death).	*Clonmacnoise.*		
	Autumn: high winds.	*Titow.*		
	Yield deviation: − 12.2%.			
1410	Great famine in Ireland.	*Dowling.*	77	74
	Winter: end dry. Summer: very dry.	*Titow.*		
	Yield deviation: − 4.0%			
1419	The year of the hot summer. The waters, all but a few, ebbed away. Openings appeared in the surface of the ground. Leaves and grass withered. Living fire in the earth, which continued to bear its fruits long afterwards, and a great yield of every fruit and crop. Much plague in Ireland and England this year (Black Death) — fever.	*Connacht.*	67	85
	Persistent cold north winds in March and April. Summer: very dry.	Titow.		
	Yield deviation: + 11.1%.			
1420	Wolves killed many people this year. (? hard winter).	*Connacht.*	125	124
	Summer: very dry.	*Titow.*		
	Yield deviation: − 23.1%.			
1434	Famine in the summer of this year, called *samhra na mearaithne*, as no one able to recognise a friend or relative because of the greatness of the famine.	*Four Masters.*	143	152
	No reference to climate.	*Titow.*		
	Yield deviation: − 2.2%.			

* D.D.T.R.I. Dendrochronological Data Tree Ring Indices

Year	Comments	Source	D.D.T.R.I.*	
			Dublin	Belfast
1435	A very great frost so that men and laden horses walked on the chief lakes of Ireland. This frost lasted from the eve of St Andrew (29th November 1434) until after the feast of Berach (15th February 1435). The ground was not worked (during this time).	*Connacht.*	139	125
	Great frost at the end of this year [1434] It began five weeks before Christmas and lasted seven weeks after. Cattle and horses used to go on the chief lakes. Great destruction of the fowl of Ireland during the frost.	*Ulster.*		
	An unusual frost and ice — people used to traverse the lakes and rivers of Ireland on solid ice (winter 1434-5).	*Four Masters.*		
	Winter: hard.	*Titow.*		
	Yield deviation: — 13.4%.			
1439	The plague virulently in Dublin. 3,000 persons, male and female, large and small, died of it from the beginning of spring to the end of May (Black Death).	*Four Masters.*	94	86
	Winter: very humid.	*Titow.*		
	No calculation of yield.			
1443	A rany tempestuous yeare after May, so that many filthes multiplied in all the rivers . . . and much hurted both bees and sheepe in Ireland.	*Duald MacFirbis*[16]	51	93
1444	A wett summer and harvist which made all corne maltish for the most part.	*Duald MacFirbis.*	65	101
1445	A greate mortality of the cattle of Ireland; both want of victuals and dearth of Corne also in Ireland.	*Duald MacFirbis.*	71	91
1446	A hard yeare. A great pestilence in Iochtar Connacht. (? Black Death).	*Duald MacFirbis.*	74	67
1447	A great plague came at that time in the town of Ath-truim. (Black Death).	*Ulster.*	95	94
	In summer and autumn this year raged a great plague . . . a great number . . . in Meath, Leinster and	*Four Masters*		

* D.D.T.R.I. Dendrochronological Data Tree Ring Indices

Year	Comments	Source	D.D.T.R.I.*	
			Dublin	*Belfast*
	Munster died. Some say 700 priests died of the plague. (Black Death).			
	Yield deviation: − 15.1%.	*Titow.*		
	Greate ffamine in the spring of this yeare throughout all Ireland. Men were then wont to eat all manner of herbs. Greats plague in summer, Harvest and winter . . . and many more in Meath, in Munster and Leinster died . . . innumerable multitudes . . . died in Dublin. (Black Death).	*Duald MacFirbis.*		
1448	A great plague raged in Meath. (Black Death).	*Four Masters.*	85	100
	Yield deviation: − 7.5%.	*Titow.*		
	A great pestilence in Meath. (Black Death).	*Duald MacFirbis.*		
1450	Last fragment 1450.	*Inisfallen.*	74	90
	A hard warlick yeare . . . with greate stormes and loss of cattle.	*Duald MacFirbis.*		
1461	Great dearth throughout Ireland.	*Connacht.*	126	86
	Great dearth and very bad cheape (? chap — i.e. trade) throughout Ireland.	*Duald MacFirbis.*		
1462	Spring and summer very hard this year. The Galway dried up . . . and many things were found in its bed.	*Connacht.*	118	98
	Great frost in this yeare that slaughtered many stocks, and it was dissolved partly from the beginning until the ffeast day of S. Berry (15th February). Great dearth in this summer. Galway, the river so called, was made dry, whereby many good things were found.	*Duald MacFirbis.*		
1465	Exceeding great frost and snow and stormy weather . . . so that no herb green in the ground or leaf budded on a tree until the feast of St. Brendan (14th May), but a man, if he were stronger, would forcibly carry away food from the priest in church.	*Connacht.*	118	109
	An exceeding frost and fowl weather that hindereth the growth of all herbs and leaves . . . so that no such was	*Duald MacFirbis.*		

* D.D.T.R.I. Dendrochronological Data Tree Ring Indices

Year	Comments	Source	D.D.T.R.I.*	
			Dublin	*Belfast*
	seen before the feast of St. Brendan (14th May), which occasioned great famine in Silmuredhy . . .			
1466	A great plague in Dublin, in Meath and in Leinster. (Black Death).	*Connacht.*	138	132
	A great plague in Leinster, and in Dublin and in Meath. (Black Death).	*Duald Macfirbis.*		
1468	Great scarcity in Ireland . . . the result of plague, treachery, (?) murder and general war, so that a small *puitel* (?) cost 2d. in the summer.	*Connacht.*	89	117
1470	Great plague, namely *Airaing in Fir Manach.*	*Ulster.*	63	94
1471	Showers of hail either side of Baltaine (1st May) with lightning and thunder, destroying much blossom, beans and fruit in all parts of Ireland . . . At the monastery of Boyle a boat could have floated over the floor of the church. An abundant nut crop. The summer and autumn very dry and the crop early.	*Connacht.*	74	90
	Showers of hail in May . . . accompanied by lightning and thunder. Each of the hailstones measured two to three inches (in circumference), and they inflicted wounds and sores on the persons whom they struck.	*Four Masters.*		
1473	Great mortality of cattle this year.	*Connacht.*	100	89
1477	Great wind on the eve of John the Evangelist which demolished many stone and wooden buildings and crannogs in Ireland.	*Connacht.*	102	113
	A great storm on the night of St John the Baptist which destroyed . . . buildings, crannogs and many stacks.	*Four Masters.*		
1478	This was a hard niggardly year. A mighty wind on the eve of Epiphany (5th January) . . . men, cattle, trees, lake and land buildings laid low. 180 glazed windows broken in Dublin.	*Connacht.*	80	103
	Great wind came after Christmas, whereby was destroyed much cattle	*Ulster.*		

* D.D.T.R.I. Dendrochronological Data Tree Ring Indices

Year	Comments	Source	D.D.T.R.I.* Dublin	Belfast
	and whereby were broken down many monasteries, churches and houses throughout Ireland. A great plague came in a ship to the harbour of Eas-Ruadh — it spread throughout Tir Conaill, and in Fir Manach and in the province in general.			
	A great plague was brought by ship into the harbour of Assaroe. This plague spread throughout Fermanagh, Tir-Connell and the province in general (Ulster). A great plague in Ireland (Black Death). A great tempest on the night of Epiphany (6th January) — persons, cattle, trees and houses destroyed.	*Four Masters.*		
1488	A whirlwind attacks a number of persons as they were cutting turf on the bog of Tumona (Co. Roscommon), which killed one of them, and swelled the faces of the rest; four others killed by it in Machaire Connacht.	*Four Masters.*	78	80
1489	A great plague . . . so devastating that people did not bury the dead in Ireland (Black Death)? The sheep of Meath from Dublin to Drogheda ran, despite their shepherds, into the sea and did not come back.	*Four Masters*	74	84
1490	Earthquake at Shalb Gamh (Moymlagh, Killoran Parish, Sligo), by which 100 persons were destroyed . . . Many horses and cows were killed by it, much putrid fish thrown up, and a lake sprang up in the place.	*Four Masters.*	75	7
1491	Wet and unfavourable weather in summer and autumn; it resembled a deluge, so that much of the corn crops of Ireland decayed.	*Four Masters.*	87	82
1492	An unusual plague in Meath — of 24 hours duration; survivors beyond this period recovered. It did not attack infants or young children.	*Four Masters.*	89	79
1497	Great famine throughout Ireland this year.	*Connacht.*	118	100

* D.D.T.R.I. Dendrochronological Data Tree Ring Indices

Year	Comments	Source	D.D.T.R.I.* Dublin	Belfast
	Very grevious famine in Ireland . . . in Meath the peck of wheat bought for 5 ounces, the gallon of beer for 6d., the slender bundle of oats for an in-calf cow . . . the beef for a mark and the milch cow, for 2 cows in calf 1s. or more.	*Ulster*		
	Great famine throughout Ireland in this and in the following year, so that people ate food unbecoming to mention and never before introduced as human dishes.	*Four Masters.*		
1500	Continuous wet weather from the feast of the Cross in autumn (1499) to the feast of St. Patrick — it injured husbandry especially the wheat.	*Ulster.*	108	95

Notes on Chronological Table

1.	St. Mary's.	See textual references 16-20.
2.	Grace.	See textual reference 24.
3.	Clyn.	See textual reference 21.
4. & 5. Loch Cé and Connacht.		See textual footnote 7. The printed texts used in the compilation of this table are A. Martin Freeman ed., *The Annals of Connacht* (Dublin, 1944) and W.M. Henessy ed., *The Annals of Loch Cé* (London, 1848-52), 2 vols.
6.	Clonmacnoise.	See textual reference 13.
7.	Ulster.	See textual reference 6.
8.	Inisfallen	See textual reference 11.
9.	McCarthy Misc.	S. O'hInnse ed., *Miscellaneous Irish Annals* (Dublin, 1947).
10.	Dowling.	See textual reference 25.
11.	New Ross.	See textual reference 23.
12.	Four Masters.	See textual reference 5.
13.	Titow.	See textual reference 1. For the period 1220-1350 the yield deviation in percentages is calculated from the average yield for the period 1209-1350 as a whole J. Titow, 'Evidence of Weather in the Account Rolls of the Bishopric of Winchester 1209-1350', *Economic History Review*, Second Series, XII (1959-60), 361-407. J. Titow, 'Histoire et climat dans l'évêché de Winchester (1350-1450)'. *Annales E.S.C.* 25, (1970), 312-343.
14.	D.D.T.R.I.	See textual reference 4.
15.	Carlow Data	SC 6 1237/16, 1237/17, PRO.

* D.D.T.R.I. Dendrochronological Data Tree Ring Indices

16. Duald MacFirbis   See textual reference 13. These annals were also published separately by J. O'Donovan, 'The Annals of Ireland from the year 1443 to 1468, translated from the Irish by Dudley MacFirbis, for Sir James Ware in the year 1666', *The Miscellany of the Irish Archaeological Society*, I (1846), 198-302.

3

MEAL AND MONEY: THE HARVEST CRISIS OF 1621-4 AND THE IRISH ECONOMY

Raymond Gillespie

The importance of the closely interrelated topics of weather and success or failure of the harvest is widely recognised by historians of pre-industrial societies. Considerable imagination and ingenuity have been exercised in devising ways of measuring the impact both of good and bad harvests and of climatic fluctuations on economy and society in different regions. Price movements, demographic change, commercial slumps and booms, and crime have all been analysed in the context of harvest failures and their consequences. In Ireland, however, progress in understanding these phenomena has been much slower than in other countries. Until recently early modern Ireland was seen as a predominantly pastoral economy, the Irish diet comprising mainly cattle products. The fate of the grain harvest thus appeared of marginal significance. Secondly, the sources which historians of other pre-industrial societies have used so effectively — price data and parish registers for example — either never existed in seventeenth century Ireland, or have not survived into the present century, or were destroyed in the burning of the Dublin Public Record Office in 1922.

All of these reasons for not studying the history of the grain harvest have now been considerably undermined. The Irish diet in the early seventeenth century seems to have been more varied than the passing comments of English travellers, many of whom were unsympathetic to the native Irish, might suggest. Grain certainly played a significant part in the expanding Irish trade in the early seventeenth century, perhaps up to 10 per cent by value by the 1620s. Also, despite the lack of sources of the type used by historians of other societies, it is still possible to piece together fragmentary literary evidence in order to identify whether a particular harvest was good or bad. Admittedly the results are much more impressionistic than those achieved elsewhere but given the fragmented survival of early seventeenth century material it is fortunate that even these limited results can be obtained.

From the available evidence a number of years may be identified as ones

of poor or disastrous harvests in the early seventeenth century.[1] Not
surprisingly the pattern tends to follow fairly closely the chronology of
failure in England and Scotland but there were local factors which
exacerbated or reduced the impact of the grain failure in regions of Ireland.
In the years 1601-3, for example, poor harvests were worsened by the
effects of war, especially the destruction of corn by the English army as part
of the 'scorched earth' policy then being pursued. Equally difficult years
occurred in 1629-31 and 1639-41. All of these episodes created widespread
disruption and were associated with outbreaks of disease, increased
pauperisation and emigration both to England and continental Europe. The
events of 1639-41 resulted in conditions which, when combined with fears
of religious persecution and political instability, formed the background to
the rebellion which broke out in late October 1641.[2]

There were also less serious crises. In 1607-8 there seems to have been a
shortage of grain in Ireland although it was not acute enough to arouse
much contemporary comment. The worst affected part of the country, the
west, was relieved by shipments of corn from other areas. Another crisis,
worse than that of 1607-8 although seemingly not reaching the scale of
those described above, was that of 1621-4. While these years were difficult
they did not elicit the levels of complaint or government action which
characterised the years of most severe failure. However, the crisis of these
years has a particular interest for the historian for a number of reasons. It
came after an unbroken period of eighteen years of almost uniformly good
harvests. During those years there had been considerable settlement of
Ireland by English and Scots. Confident administrations had repealed the
medieval legislation prohibiting grain exports and all seemed well. Indeed
by the early part of 1621 the main concern of landowners and government
alike was that the grain harvests were too good and that the market was
becoming glutted, causing prices to fall as a result. As the Lord Deputy
observed early in 1621 'corn is brought to little or no estimation'. The
second reason for the significance of the 1621-4 failure is that its effects are
particularly well documented. From the early 1620s the London
administration became increasingly concerned that Ireland was not
producing the revenue for the English exchequer which had been expected
as a result of the early seventeenth century settlement of the country.
Instead, Ireland was costing England money in exchequer subventions
every year. The commercial crisis of the early 1620s in England brought
increased concern about bullion flows. This focused attention on the
subventions paid to the Irish Exchequer and detailed inquiries were set on
foot into almost every aspect of Irish life. The data collected by the
Commissioners for the Reformation of Ireland, as well as the more usual

sources such as the official correspondence and estate material, provide a useful insight into the economic and social difficulties which resulted from harvest failures.

I

The first indication that something was amiss appeared in the autumn of 1621 when the harvest was below average. The earliest evidence came from Galway when in September 1621 the corporation ordered that no-one should buy corn except for his own household. To prevent stockpiling, the amount bought was not to exceed what would be required until the next harvest.[3] As a further precaution orders were made prohibiting the brewing of beer and and the distilling of *aqua vitae* should the grain price rise further. It is not surprising that the earliest concern about a grain shortage should come from the west of the country since it was most sensitive to local grain shortage. Little grain was grown within Connacht itself, the main form of agriculture there being cattle raising. The archbishop of Tuam, William Daniel, for example, noted in 1622 that the inhabitants of his diocese were 'generally given to indolence and live rather by cattle than manuring the ground by reason whereof . . . they want for the most part their daily bread'. Even in good years many parts of west Connacht were not self-sufficient in grain. A late seventeenth century tract on the life of Francis Kirwan commented of the west of Galway that 'the inhabitants . . . continued to till a few of the more loamy patches and thus cultivate a little barley and oats but agriculture of this sort did not bring them a sufficient supply of bread, for this was an article of food unheard of for the greater part of the year'.[4] The concentration on cattle left Connacht's own grain supply very vulnerable to harvest fluctuations since a partial failure which would have caused only inconvenience elsewhere might totally eliminate the small western grain crop. Furthermore, a reduction in the surplus normally available for distribution from other provinces would exacerbate the problem. By the end of October 1621 the complaints of the Galway corporation were joined by others within the province while in Munster there was concern about the lack of oats and barley for trade.[5]

The spring of 1622 brought renewed reports of difficulty. Cattle disease, a 'weakening' of the cattle, and shortage of coin joined the scarcity of grain as common problems.[6] The failure of the spring harvest made matters worse and by June when the new Lord Deputy, Lord Falkland, was preparing to come to Ireland he took the precaution of securing from the Privy Council permission to import 100 quarters of wheat for himself and his household.[7] As 1622 progressed the government became increasingly worried. The report of the commissioners appointed in March to survey the state of Ireland made dismal reading. They observed the shortage of grain in Ireland and a consequent decay in trade. They also recorded what appeared to be a predominance of grazing in the country, which they felt contributed to the corn shortage since Ireland was not producing sufficient surplus of corn to withstand a shortage. They also felt that too much grain was being used for distilling *aqua vitae,* which not only reduced the amount available for export but also discouraged the import of wine into Ireland. This lost the government valuable revenue through the impost of wines which had fallen from £14,271 in 1617 to £2,629 in 1621. The commissioners also identified a link between the harvest failure and the increasing complaints of a shortage of coin in Ireland, noting the 'scarcity of corn and consequently money'. The remedy they prescribed was the usual early modern one, of increasing control of bullion movements. Since Ireland had no mint they recommended that one should be established.[8]

Despite the growing realisation by the administration that there was a deepening crisis, it was reluctant to intervene. The failure of the autumn harvest of 1622 forced it to act. In November the export of corn was prohibited and all licences for transportation were revoked.[9] Smuggling, however, was normal in these circumstances. As Charles Moncke, the Surveyor General of the Customs, noted in 1637, the area between Portaferry and Donaghadee in County Down was where 'a great part of the corn was stolen and transported in the time of prohibition, which corn if it had been held, it would have prevented much mischief that happened'.[10] In April 1623 further measures were taken to prevent hoarding. Justices of the Peace were ordered to enquire what corn was available in their localities and any surplus was to be brought to the market. They were also instructed to report to the county sheriff every twenty days on the state of the market. Measures were to be taken against engrossers and forestallers and justices were also to send to the Council any recommendations they might have for controlling the general situation.[11] Similar measures against forestallers had been taken by some major towns earlier in the year. In September 1622 the corporation of Dublin had complained of 'great dearth that grain and corn are raised unto'. It placed restrictions on the bakers who were forestalling in the Dublin markets on pain of imprisonment during the mayor's pleasure, and forfeiture of the grain.[12] In times of harvest crisis the forestaller was seen as a social parasite. Stephen Jerome, the chaplain to the Earl of Cork, preaching in 1623, argued that harvest failure and plague were God's way of ensuring that man remained on the right road but the forestaller was not part of that divine plan. He called upon the king to 'vindicate God's glory upon drunkards, swearers, profaners of the Sabbath . . . against the cormorants that forestall the markets, enhance the price of corn, engross and so purloin from the poor'.[13]

It was not until the spring of 1623 that the full effects of the successive harvest failures in 1621 and 1622 became apparent. In May 1623 there were comments that the condition of the people in Ireland was very poor and one commentator went as far as to say that famine conditions prevailed with people dying as a result. Greater than normal cattle mortality, because of disease brought about by weather conditions and lack of fodder, was again recorded. By October another disruptive element, although not directly precipitated by the harvest difficulties, smallpox, was reported in Lismore although it does not seem to have reached epidemic proportions.[14] The grain shortage was noted by the author of the *Advertisements for Ireland,* probably written in 1623, who commented that in that year the entire corn stock of the Pale, the main grain producing area, was consumed within six months. He also noted the import of rye from the Netherlands in times of dearth.[15]

In the middle of the year the Commission for the Increase of Manufactures in Ireland provided an analysis similar to that contained in the earlier report. The Commission recorded shortage of corn, reduced inflows of coin and bullion and a general lack of tillage, which may have been more the fault of successive harvest failures than the norm of agriculture. Again the commissioners recommended restrictions on the movement of bullion, except to pay for the import of corn, and the establishment of an Irish mint.[16] In the autumn of that year came the familiar complaints against forestallers with action being taken by towns as small as Clonmel.[17]

The fate of the harvests of 1624 is unclear although in Ulster there was one report of a late harvest being threatened because of heavy rain.[18] Certainly there are fewer complaints of difficulty and by January 1625 exports of grain from Ireland were again allowed by the Privy Council, implying that the 1624 harvest had been a relatively good one. It took some time for supplies to recover fully and imports of beer from England, which had begun to rise in 1623 as the shortage of grain in Ireland had made brewing impossible, remained high into 1625.[19] Certainly the trade figures for 1625 suggest that the economy had nearly recovered fully from its temporary setback and grain exports again came high on the list of items in the Irish trade figures.

While the complaints of contemporaries can be used to establish the broad chronology of the harvest failure they are less useful in determining the effects of the crisis on the various sectors of the Irish economy. Fortunately a list of Irish exports for the period March 1621 to March 1622 has survived among the papers of the Commissioners who were instructed to inquire into the state of Ireland in 1622. By comparing it with lists from earlier in the century and a later list for 1625 we can give some insight into the events of the winter of 1621 and the early spring of 1622, when the early indications of the scale of the crisis were becoming apparent.[20] Seventeenth century statistics are at best perilous to work with but it is probably a safe assumption that if the numbers themselves cannot be trusted, the general trend they reveal is reasonably accurate. There are also some gaps in the lists. The trade of the ports of Londonderry and Coleraine is not recorded. The figures appear to be based on customs duties and these two ports were exempt from the payment of duties. Thus, oats, for example, which formed an important part of the trade of Londonderry and Coleraine, are understated as a proportion of overall trade.

Not surprisingly one of the first victims of a poor harvest was grain exports. Wheat had accounted for about 5 per cent of Irish trade by value in 1616, and was to rise to almost 10 per cent in 1625, but none was exported in 1621-2. Wheat dominated the trade when measured by value but in the overall grain trade played a much smaller part. Unfortunately since those Ulster ports which, to judge from the port books, exported considerable quantities of oats, are not recorded in the listings it is difficult to judge the total volume of grain exported. However in volume terms, wheat probably made up about half the grain exported. In contrast to the fate of the wheat exports in these years the oats trade held up well. The live cattle trade also collapsed in this year, the numbers of cattle exported falling from the 1616 level of 6,655 to 4,290 in 1621-2. In reality the fall was probably greater than these figures suggest because the cattle trade had grown significantly between the dates of the two lists. In 1625 cattle exports stood at 30,745 beasts. This is probably a better guide to what the 1621 figure should have been in the absence of depression than the figure for 1616. Other cattle products exported in 1621-2 were also lower than their 1616 levels. Barrel beef had fallen below the earlier level, to about 2,000 barrels, again at a time when the trade generally was rising. Tallow was another victim of the crisis, a particularly significant blow since a tract on the tallow trade of about 1630 estimated that tallow could form up to one-fifth of the profit of an animal.[21]

Conversely the export of hides boomed, the growth between 1616 and 1621-2 being significantly higher than that for the period 1616 to 1625 as a whole. This suggests that the difficult winter of 1621-2 had seen a significant slaughtering of cattle. There could be at least three reasons for this. First, some cattle may have been slaughtered for food at a time when bread was difficult to come by. The fall in tallow exports, however, indicates that cattle had less fat and there was probably difficulty in feeding them over the winter. Secondly, the collapse of wheat exports alongside a relatively buoyant oats trade suggests a cold wet summer in 1621 which could also have meant retarded grass growth and problems in saving hay for winter fodder. This would have created fodder problems and the grain shortage meant that grain could not be used as a substitute feed. Finally, livestock may have died from disease in the spring of 1622.[22] This is because a cold, wet summer would have increased the incidence of liver fluke and other diseases. Cattle might survive one attack but a second in the spring of 1622 would have proved fatal. There is some support for this in the pattern of sheep exports. Exports of sheepskins in 1621-2 were significantly higher than the general trend between 1616 and 1625 would lead us to expect, suggesting a slaughter of sheep. Like cattle, sheep would have been particularly prone to diseases such as fluke in a cold wet summer, especially since they were pastured on marginal land.

This pattern of harvest failure and attendant animal disease created both long and short-term problems. Most immediately it created a shortage of milk products, such as milk and cheese, which were normally plentiful in Ireland and formed an important part of the Irish diet. In the winter of 1623-4 Welsh butter and cheese had to be imported into Ireland in large quantities. On one occasion a ship arriving in Dublin carried 626 firkins of Welsh butter.[23] A longer term, and more serious, consequence was the impact of the depletion of the stock of cattle because of deaths in these years. In 1625, for example, a total ban was placed on the slaughter of cattle to conserve what by then was a small breeding stock. The recovery was slow and as late as 1628 the country was still experiencing a shortage of cattle severe enough to merit the proclamation of a fast and special prayers in Dublin.[24]

By contrast with the sectors of the trade which declined, others boomed, especially the fish trade which was centred on Munster. Both herring and pilchard exports were much higher in 1621-2 than 1616 although this may reflect the rapid growth of the industry as much as a move into fishing during difficult years. In 1616 the Irish fish trade was still in its infancy. Fishing off the Irish coast was carried on mainly by foreigners, especially the Dutch and English, although Irish landlords became increasingly interested in developing this natural resource as time progressed. Richard Boyle in Munster, for example, began to invest in fishing from 1616. Large scale fishing was often expensive — especially because of the need to buy nets and salt for curing — but Boyle made small loans to men interested in setting up in a lesser way.[25] However the rate of growth in the years immediately after 1616 was slow and Boyle by 1619 expressed himself dissatisfied with the return. The failure of the harvest probably gave the trade a considerable boost not only as a souce of food but also as a source of cash to buy food and pay rents.[26]

III

While the chronology of the harvest failure of 1621-4 and something of its impact on the various sectors of the economy is relatively easy to establish, it is rather more difficult to make an assessment of its consequences for the Irish economy and society as a whole in both the short and long term. One reason why harvest failures in Ireland were potentially more serious than in contemporary England was that grain production was much less well developed in Ireland. The best Irish grain yields were a long way behind the best English yields and the lowest Irish yields were very poor by English standards.[27] A small, although rapidly expanding, labour force, poor land quality and probably a shortage of high quality manure all contributed to this situation. Even a small divergence between Irish and other seed-grain ratios would have been significant since the reciprocal of the ratio was the amount of seed which had to be kept for the next year's sowing. Low yields meant a large proportion had to be held over. Thus even a modest failure in one year could have a serious impact in successive years. Secondly, and perhaps more significantly, Irish trade in the early seventeenth century was almost entirely dependent on unprocessed agricultural goods, especially grain and cattle. Linen and woollen cloth, for example, were almost entirely absent from Irish trade although linen yarn was exported in large quantities from the Ulster ports to England where it was turned into cloth. In 1616, for example, 5.8 per cent of all Irish trade by value was in grain and this had risen to over 10 per cent by 1625. Live cattle made up about 7.6 per cent of trade rising to almost 30 per cent by 1625.

The impact of a harvest failure, with its attendant difficulties for the livestock population outlined above, had a particularly severe effect on Irish trade. One measure of its severity was the change in the yield of the Irish customs. The English Lord Treasurer, Lionel Cranfield, recorded the customs receipts for 1620-21 as £12,461. By 1621-2, the first year of failure, they had fallen to £11,459, and by the second year of the crisis, 1622-3, the yield was down again to £10,783. However, just as the fall had been dramatic so was the recovery. As the harvest recovered so did the customs receipts. By 1623-4 they had risen to £14,776 and had risen again to £16,469 by 1624-5.[28] Useful as these figures are in giving an indication of developments in trade they provide only a partial picture which may be misleading. Since different goods had different valuations, a change in the composition of trade, without any change in overall volume, could be reflected as a change in yield. It is therefore necessary to attempt to measure the overall level of each branch of the trade, in constant prices. Secondly, as well as measuring the overall volume of trade it is necessary to look at the balance of trade, distinguishing exports from imports, two elements which are combined in the calculation of the customs yield.

Comparing the fate of the various elements in Irish trade it is possible to see the scale of the fall in exports. Betwen 1616 and 1625 the value of Irish trade for the ports for which we have data (expressed in constant 1665 prices, since there is no earlier comprehensive price series) rose by 2.3 per cent per annum. Using this trend to project forward from 1616 the value of Irish trade for the same ports should have been about £157,300, in 1621-2. The actual value in this period was £149,200, about 5.1 per cent below the projected value. While this fall in itself may not appear particularly severe it should be remembered that these figures reflect only the early months of the crisis, which had first mainifested itself in the autumn of 1621 and lasted for a further two and a half years. The effect over those years was cumulative.[29]

To resolve the problems of the changing balance of trade during the years 1621 to 1625 is more difficult since there are no reliable lists of imports. Instead it is necessary to use the customs data which provides a reliable measure of the relative values of items traded. The Irish balance of trade in the early seventeenth century was usually in surplus, the value of exports usually substantially outstripping that of imports. The 1622 Commissioners, for example, were of the opinion that the outgate part of the customs yield was usually about twice the ingate. In the case of Youghal the outgate was more than three times the ingate in 1620-1, reflecting the fact that it was one of the fastest growing ports of Munster. The effect of harvest failure was a reduction in the export yield and an increase in the import yield so that by 1622-3 the receipts from the two were almost evenly balanced. By 1624-5 the position had returned to its old level with the outgate being almost seven times the ingate.[30]

This temporary trade dislocation had at least one extremely important side effect. Ireland in the early seventeenth century had neither a mint nor any way of creating credit domestically. Its main sources of supply of specie were shipments from England and the proceeds of trade. The result was that the Irish money stock was smaller than its English counterpart in relation to the volume of economic activity it had to support and considerably more volatile. As William Petty noted in the later seventeenth century the ratio of money stock to payments, or velocity of circulation, was 1:7 in England while in Ireland it was 1:10.[31] Petty's actual figures should not be taken too seriously but as an indication of relative magnitudes they are probably correct. The reasons which Petty offered, in the later seventeenth century, for this state of affairs were similar to those posited earlier in the century: repatriation of rents by absentees, and demand by merchants, especially the East India Company, for foreign coin circulating in Ireland, and the monetary instability of sterling circulating in Ireland.

In an expanding economy, such as early seventeenth century Ireland, which relied almost entirely on coin to make payments, reliance on a favourable balance of trade and a high velocity of circulation was courting disaster. When a crisis, such as a harvest failure, reduced the volume of production in the economy, and so hit trade and encouraged hoarding of coin, the money stock fell much faster than the number and value of payments which had to be made. Rents, for example, would still be due despite a short-term harvest crisis. The substitution of imported goods for falling domestic production in a time of crisis had two immediate economic consequences. It ensured that transactions in the economy did not fall as fast as the falling supply of money, but it also drew money out of the country to pay for imports thus further reducing the supply of money.

It should have been possible, in theory, to offset the effect of a falling money stock on the price level by a reduction in the general level of transactions in the economy or an increase in the velocity of circulation in line with the changes in the money stock. However, these variables were not responsive to the short-term changes in the money supply. There is no hard evidence as to the behaviour of the velocity of circulation, it may have risen somewhat, but given the high level of velocity in good years there was little room for a dramatic increase. Price stability was not maintained; rather prices rose in response to the fall in the supply of agricultural products in relation to demand. In December 1622, for example, Richard Whitbourne wrote to Lord Deputy Falkland about provisions for the ships about to sail to the new colony of Newfoundland and noted that the prices of grain products, such as beer, bread and biscuits were higher in Dublin than in London, a reversal of the normal seventeenth century position.[32] The monetary disruption probably had some depressing effect on the extent of the price increase. This apparent contradiction between the demands from the real economy and the monetary forces at work created its own problems for the markets as we shall see below.

The possibility of compensating for coin shortages through changes in the price level assumes that even in good years the market mechanism in Ireland was perfect. This was not the case. In sixteenth century Ireland large areas of the country were still being run on the old Gaelic type of redistribution mechanism whereby surpluses were redistributed as renders to the great lords who used them in hospitality and feasting. There was, of course, some contact with merchants and trade but the degree varied from place to place and often was very limited indeed, usually associated with the hinterland of the port towns, such as Sligo and Galway in the west. Thus in the early seventeenth century the market mechanism was still rudimentary in some areas. Other social controls, such as the idea of the just price as expressed in the assize of bread and wine, together with the deflationary effect of the fall in the money stock, conspired to keep prices below the level needed to ensure that money was kept in circulation in sufficient quantity.[33]

The result of the failure of these adjustments in prices and velocity of circulation during the harvest crisis of 1621-4 meant that the supply of coin was insufficient to make the required number of payments. Consequently, complaints about the shortage of coin mounted. As the Commisioners of Ireland for the Increase of Manufactures noted in mid-1623

'the want of coin and bullion in Ireland proceeds . . . first, from the leaving off of tillage for corn, and the population being much increased in these latter times the inhabitants are in great want of it, whereas heretofore the plenty grain was such as by exporting the same, good store of coin and bullion was brought in.'[34]

The most obvious consequence of this shortage of coin was the fall in the level of transactions. Payments could not be made because of the lack of an acceptable means of exchange. Royal revenue, for example, was much slower than usual in coming in. Thus, as late as April 1624 it was noted that

the universal scarcity being such as interrupts and prevents the great diligence and industry the Vice Treasurer uses in bringing in what is due to the king because it [coin] is indeed exhausted and not to be had in the land.[35]

In the case of the feudal aid granted for the proposed marriage of Prince Charles payments were slow as one Cork collector noted 'by reason of the scarcity of money and the weakness of the cattle (which is the common distress).'[36] The problem was not restricted to royal revenues. The coin shortage and economic depression affected all sections of the community.

Landlords had severe problems in collecting rents. On the estates of Trinity College, widely scattered throughout Ulster and Munster, the arrears of rent rose from about £500, which had been the level of arrears in midsummer 1618 and 1621, to almost £700 by midsummer 1623. By 1629, when the next accounts are available, it had fallen to £580 but this was another difficult year and the figure for arrears may have been higher than normal.[37] In Connacht the Earl of Clanricard also complained of the non-collection of rent, writing to his agent in March 1624, 'I hope you will take good course for the collection of in due time all rents and arrears of rents for this last two years hath been wonderful chargeable to me and hath put me deep in debt again.' Distraint for rent, relatively uncommon in seventeenth century Ireland, was also being practised in Munster by Richard Boyle by mid-1623.[38]

Without adequate means of exchange, the problems created for markets by a reduction in the volume of produce were worsened. Richard Boyle's iron works in Munster nearly collapsed because of the failure of the market in iron during these years. Although he continued to produce iron there was no market for it and the iron was left unsold and the workmen unpaid.[39] The merchant communities of early seventeenth century Ireland were small and most of the trade was done by English or other foreigners in foreign ships. This slowing of the market meant that little business could be done and many simply left Ireland or did not come there. As Clanricard complained in mid-1623, bills of exchange were virtually unobtainable in Ireland because of the shortage of merchants trading there and he was compelled to pay high premiums to get any bills at all.[40]

Government made some attempt to rectify this problem.[41] In September 1622 copper farthing tokens were ordered to be struck to help trade. They were to be issued at par but redeemed at £1 for 21 shillings in an attempt to keep them in circulation. The proclamation was reissued in 1625. The idea was not a new one but its re-appearance at this point is significant. Another old idea, that of establishing a mint in Ireland, also made a re-appearance. There had been repeated calls for a mint in Ireland since 1603 but none had been acted upon. The 1622 Commissioners had called for a mint to ease the specie shortage as had the Commissioners of 1623. The plan nearly succeeded on this occasion and in 1623 the English Privy Council agreed to the establishment of a Dublin mint. Scales, beams and weights were purchased but the return of normal conditions meant that the project was again abandoned. The crisis brought one new initiative from the administration; a proposal to make Spanish ryals legal tender in Ireland at the rate of 4/6 but again the crisis passed before any action was taken although the plan was to resurface during the harvest crisis and trade recession of 1640-1.

Food shortages, market collapse and trade difficulties brought in their wake severe social problems. To contemporaries the most obvious and immediate was an upsurge in crime, in almost every region. In March 1622 it was reported from Munster that because of 'the likelihood of great scarcity of money and corn . . . stealing [was] more in use than I have known it these many years'. From the other end of the country in Londonderry Sir Thomas Phillips also told of an increase in crime claiming that murders and stealing were almost a daily occurrence.[42] Some attempt was made to control the worst excesses. Stolen goods being offered for sale were a continual problem and proclamations were issued in February 1624 which tried to restrict cattle dealing to markets and fairs. Butchers were likewise forbidden to buy privately.[43] What the administration feared most was that the general discontent would be seized upon by disruptive elements to incite a general rebellion and overthrow the recently established settlement of large areas of the country. In the autumn of 1622 the Lord Deputy noted that ill-affected men who had seldom been seen before now appeared with much boldness, especially the priests.[44] More clergy than usual were recorded in Ireland and in late 1623 there were reported assemblies of Catholic clergy near Cavan, Kells, Granard and Dublin.[45] Much of this activity was probably politically inspired, given the rumours of toleration which were rife as the Spanish match appeared to be moving to an inexorable conclusion. However part of this clerical activity may well have been associated with the distress. Catholic clergy were dependent for their existence on support from their flock. The diocesan clergy could at least collect the offerings for baptisms, marriages and burials which in times of crisis were valuable rights and had to be defined and defended carefully. The position of the members of religious orders was more vulnerable. For some years there had been difficulties over such rights, which were often disputed by regulars who claimed them for *ad hoc* services when they should have been paid to the parish priest. The issue reached a head in 1623, in the middle of the harvest crisis, in a dispute between the Franciscans, the largest of the orders in early seventeenth century Ireland, and the secular clergy at Drogheda over the right to collect for burials and baptisms performed.[46] Not surpisingly this increased public profile by the clergy gave rise to considerable concern. In January 1623 a proclamation was issued ordering all Catholic clergy to leave Ireland within forty days on pain of arrest and punishment, a proclamation which was repeated in January 1624.[47]

How much actual distress and dislocation there was in Ireland cannot be quantified. Not surprisingly the towns suffered worst as they were dependent for their food supplies on a surplus from the countryside, which by 1622 was almost non-existent. The admissions to freedom in Irish towns for which data survive fell dramatically with the onset of the crisis in 1622 and continued to fall until 1624 and 1625 when the economy began to recover. (See Table 1).

The reasons for this fall are complex. At least part of the explanation may be the increase in mortality which became a feature of urban life from 1622. Burials in the parish of St John's in Dublin, the only parish from which a register survives, rose dramatically to 1624 before falling back again. This

D

TABLE 1.

Admissions to freedom in Irish towns 1615-1626

	DUBLIN[1]	CORK[2]	YOUGHAL[3]	CLONMEL[4]
1615	66	2	20	
1616	78	7	20	
1617	79	15	3	
1618	70	22	18	
1619	72	10	33	5
1620	67	10	24	8
1621	76	14	13	7
1622	49	8	16	3
1623	45	8	13	0
1624	68	1	15	5
1625	63	15	31	7
1626	72	19	22	8

Sources:

1. Brendan Fitzpatrick, 'The municipal corporation of Dublin 1603-40' (Ph.D., University of Dublin, 1984), Appendix V.
2. Richard Caulfield ed., *The Council Book of the Corporation of Cork* (Guildford, 1879).
3. Richard Caulfield ed., *The Council Book of the Corporation of Youghal* (Guildford, 1878).
4. N.L.I. Ms. 19171. Clonmel Corporation Book.

does not appear to have been a purely local Dublin phenomenon. The fee book of the Limerick physician, Thomas Arthur, who travelled widely throughout the country, recorded the years 1622-4 as being unusually busy ones.[48] Unfortunately Arthur was more concerned to record his fees than his diagnoses and only a few cases are noted in detail. Spotted fever was diagnosed in October 1622, diarrhoea in 1623 and peripneumonia and pleuritis also in that year. None of these can be linked specifically with a shortage of food and are more likely to be associated with the cold wet summers but nevertheless contributed to the general disruption of these years. There is no pronounced seasonality in Arthur's consultations but the register of St John's in Dublin, as shown in Table 2, suggests that burials in the period April to September 1624 were markedly higher than the preceding six months. It is clear, however, that Ireland escaped the plague which hit England in 1624 and 1625 and seems to account for much of the distress caused in Scotland during these years. Irish theologians, nevertheless, feared a visitation as a punishment for wrong doing.[49] There is no evidence for large numbers of deaths from starvation, as has been suggested for some of the marginal areas of northern England.[50]

TABLE 2.

Burials in St. John's Parish, Dublin

	1620	1621	1622	1623	1624	1625	1626
J.	—	4	1	1	5	1	2
F.	1	1	—	3	2	1	2
M.	1	—	—	2	2	7	3
A.	—	1	—	1	3	0	3
M.	—	1	1	2	5	4	2
J.	—	1	3	1	3	2	2
J.	1	—	5	4	2	1	2
A.	—	—	2	2	4	1	—
S.	1 –	—	2	3	2	2	3
O.	1	3	—	3	3	4	1
N.	2	1	—	—	3	2	1
D.	2	2	2	5	2	4	1
Annual Totals	9	14	16	27	36	29	22

Source: James Mills ed., *The Registers of St. John the Evangelist, Dublin, 1619-1699* (Dublin, 1906).

However the incidence of mortality cannot fully explain the pattern of admissions to freedom in the main towns. In the case of Dublin, where it is possible to break down the admissions to freedom according to right of admission, it appears that certain groups were more affected by the crisis than others.[51] The numbers applying for freedom by special grace or by right to marriage to a freeman or woman were relatively little affected by the crisis, and indeed increased in some cases, whereas the greatest fall was in the numbers seeking freedom by apprenticeship. Also, of those seeking freedom by right of being the child of a freeman the fall was greater among sons of freeman than among daughters. It seems that it was the younger elements, especially young males and first generation migrants to the city, who were most affected by the crisis. Perhaps they moved out of the city seeing their future prospects reduced by the commercial stagnation which accompanied the harvest crisis. Whether their exit was balanced by an influx of the poor from the surrounding countryside hoping for some means of subsistence is unclear. Certainly there were no complaints of such an influx from contemporaries nor, unlike later crises, were there complaints of large scale movements of Irishmen to England or to the Continent. It may be that the crisis was not severe enough to promote 'subsistence' migration but was sufficiently disruptive to encourage 'betterment' migration.

IV

All these effects were of course regional. The local extent of the crisis depended on a wide range of variables — local differences in weather, the balance between arable and pastoral in regional economies, the distribution of wealth, the pattern of trade and the extent of monetisation and commercialisation of the local economy. Not surprisingly it was in the areas which relied heavily on grain for both food and trade that the impact was most pronounced. In the main these were concentrated in the east and south of the country. In the case of Dublin two of the largest items in its trade, wheat (10.3 per cent by value), and cattle (13.7 per cent) were those worst hit by the crisis. The fall in the value of Dublin trade in 1621 over that of 1616 was in excess of 20 per cent and the 1621 trade was more than 40 per cent lower than 1625. Dublin was also hit badly because the bulk of its trade was with England which also experienced harvest difficulties in these years. There was a certain resistance in western England to the import of Irish cattle. It was believed in England that such imports were having an adverse effect on the economy there.[52]

The effect of Dublin's economic and trade collapse is clearly seen in the movement of the values of benefices in its hinterland. In the dioceses of Meath, Leighlin and Ardagh the average value of a Church of Ireland living fell between 1615 and 1622.[53] By contrast, in the west of the country the overall effect of the crisis seems to have been more muted. In some of the western dioceses, such as Killaloe, Limerick and Ardfert, the average value of livings actually rose between 1615 and 1622.

This relative prosperity of the west during the difficult years of the early 1620s is also reflected in the exports of the western ports. The trade of towns such as Galway, Sligo, Limerick and the smaller ports of Kerry stood up well. In some cases their trade increased as a proportion of Irish trade in the early 1620s compared with the figures for 1616. This occurred despite the fact that the general trend of their share of trade was downward in the early seventeenth century. The explanation of this was that although the western part of the country was more vulnerable to fluctuations in grain supply, because of its insufficient production of grain, the fact that it was less commercialised than the east insulated it from the worst of the monetary disruption. This would have lessened the economic impact of the crisis in the west. In the east it was these monetary problems, brought about by coinage and trading difficulties which exacerbated the problems caused by the grain shortage. A second factor, also easing the monetary problems in the west, was that western trade was predominantly with continental Europe rather than with England as was the case with the east of the country. The depression of the English economy in the early 1620s, which affected the trade of the eastern part of Ireland, had less of an impact in the west.[54]

V

As a result of improved harvests in 1624 and 1625 the economy quickly recovered from the short-term effects of the crisis of 1621-4. But there was a significant longer term effect on Irish society. Many of those who had migrated to Ireland in the early seventeenth century had done so with the intention of speculating in cheap Irish land. This took many forms depending on the social level at which it took place. Landlords, for example, were drawn mainly from those who were declining on the social scale, such as younger sons, or alternatively those concerned to make a quick profit. Both groups saw great gains to be made in Ireland within a few years because of rising land values and increasing rentals. Lesser men also took advantage of cheap land and the shortage of good quality tenants in Ireland to obtain large holdings at modest rents. For all speculators and adventurers, Ireland appeared as a cornucopia of land and wealth. Such a view was dependent on almost continual economic expansion in order to maintain and boost confidence. These expectations seemed to be daily rewarded. Substantial immigration from 1603 boosted the labour supply which in turn increased production. Changes in economic and social organisation saw much of this surplus brought into markets and sold both locally and into a wider world through trade. The result was an export boom specialising in cattle which, in terms of European price trends, was more profitable than grain. The trade boom was further fed because domestic demand was weak. Although many settlers had large estates few had the movable wealth to indulge in excessive conspicuous consumption. Instead, rising landlord incomes were used for the building boom which also characterised early seventeenth century Ireland.[55]

The crisis of 1621-4 was the first significant setback to this picture of an ever expanding economy. There had been no significant harvest problems since those of 1603-4 and most settlers had arrived after that experience. The bubble had burst in 1622. The Lord Deputy wrote to the Privy Council in 1623 describing the disheartened planters in Ulster and the other honest men put clean out of heart.[56] One indication of the impact of the harvest crisis on the expectations of settlers is the number of grants to hold markets and fairs taken out by them. Grants of markets and fairs often involved substantial investment by landlords in infrastructure and other incentives before they would yield a significant return through market or fair tolls or the profit of market courts. Thus the expectation of profit was long-term rather than short-term. In the early years of the century this did not prevent a large number of patents to operate fairs and markets being taken out but in 1622 the number of grants made was less than half that of the previous year and fell again in 1623 and again in 1624 as demonstrated in Table 3. The harvest crisis of the early 1620s and the associated commercial dislocation meant that Ireland began to appear a less attractive area for investment and settlement. In the decades after the crisis migration slowed down. In Ulster, for example, where the number of British males had been increasing by about 13 per cent per annum between 1613 and 1622, the rate of increase between 1622 and 1630 fell to 1.2 per cent per annum. In Munster the position was similar with the growth rate in settler population falling from 9.8 per cent per annum between 1611 and 1622 to 2.5 per cent per annum between 1622 and 1641.[57]

TABLE 3.

Grants of Markets and Fairs 1615-1625

Year		ULSTER	MUNSTER	CONNACHT	LEINSTER	TOTAL
1615	Markets	3	1	—	1	5
	Fairs	1	2	—	2	5
1616	Markets	3	5	12	4	24
	Fairs	3	6	11	4	24
1617	Markets	5	—	8	5	18
	Fairs	6	—	10	7	23
1618	Markets	3	1	9	8	21
	Fairs	5	1	10	11	27
1619	Markets	4	11	10	7	32
	Fairs	5	10	10	13	38
1620	Markets	1	2	3	6	12
	Fairs	2	8	3	9	22
1621	Markets	7	8	3	10	28
	Fairs	8	5	6	8	27
1622	Markets	4	1	3	3	11
	Fairs	5	2	3	3	13
1623	Markets	1	1	—	1	3
	Fairs	3	1	2	1	7
1624	Markets	1	—	1	—	2
	Fairs	2	1	—	1	4
1625	Markets	1	2	—	—	3
	Fairs	1	2	2	—	5

Source: *Report of the Commission appointed to inquire into the State of Fairs and Markets in Ireland,* Brit.Parl. Papers, 1852-3 (1674) XLI.

Of course not all of this can be blamed on one harvest crisis. There was also the delicate political situation of 1625 created by the failure of the Spanish match, when it was feared that Ireland would bear the full brunt of the seemingly inevitable Spanish invasion. There were further severe harvest failures in 1628-32 and increasing concern in England and Scotland that the population there was being depleted by emigration. It is clear however that the crisis of 1621-4 marked the end of the golden years of the settlement of Ireland and its psychological impact should not be underestimated. After that crisis the two bogey men of the early settlers, the wolf and the woodkern, were to be joined by a third: the dislocation association with harvest crisis and trade collapse.

References

1. For the chronology of Irish harvest failures see Raymond Gillespie, 'Harvest Crises in Early Seventeenth Century Ireland', *Irish Economic and Social History,* XI (1984), pp. 5-18.

2. Raymond Gillespie, 'The end of an era: Ulster and the Outbreak of the 1641 Rising', in Ciaran Brady and Raymond Gillespie eds., *Natives and Newcomers: Essays on the Making of Irish Colonial Society* (Dublin, 1986), pp. 204-7. In table 1 on p. 206 the Ulster figure for 1641 should read 6.5 not 16.5.

3. *H.M.C., 10th Report,* Appendix 5, p. 170.

4. T.C.D., MS 2185, f. 87; John Lynch, *The Life and Death of the Most Reverend Francis Kirwan,* ed., C.P. Meehan (Dublin, 1884), p. 43.

5. N.L.I., MS 12813/2, f. 261.

6. B.L., Sloane MS 3827, f. 25.

7. *Acts of the Privy Council, 1621-3,* p. 258.

8. B.L., Add.MS 4756, ff. 30, 31, 43v, 44v.

9. R.R. Steele, ed., *Tudor and Stuart Proclamations 1485-1714* (Oxford, 1910), II, 1, no. 243.

10. B.L., Harleian MS 2138, f. 172.

11. Steele, *Tudor and Stuart Proclamations,* II, 1, no. 244.

12. J.T. Gilbert ed., *Calendar of the Ancient Records of Dublin* (Dublin, 1892), III, p. 150.

13. Stephen Jerome, *Ireland's Jubilee or Ireland's Joyes Io-paen* (Dublin, 1624), Epistle Dedicatory.

14. N.L.I., MS 12813/2, f. 314; B.L., Stowe MS 176, ff. 150-150v.

15. George O'Brien, ed., *Advertisements for Ireland* (Dublin, 1923), pp. 25, 33.

16. *Cal. S.P. Ire., 1615-25,* pp. 424-6.

17. N.L.I., MS 19171, f. 103.

18. Thomas McCrie, ed., *The Life of Mr Robert Blair* (Edinburgh, 1848), pp. 62-3.

19. *Acts of the Privy Council, 1623-5,* pp. 421, 478; P.R.O., E190/1086/3,6.

20. The lists are Kent Archives Office, MS ON 4806 (1616), P.R.O.N.I., T 2860/13/30 (1621-2); P.R.O., CO 388/85/A15 (1625). These have been valued using the prices in *Cal. S.P. Ire., 1663-5,* pp. 694-7.

21. Leeds City Library, Temple Newsham MSS I/4.

22. B.L., Sloane MS 3827, f. 25; *H.M.C., 4th Report,* appendix, p. 277.

23. P.R.O., E190/1135/3, 6.

24. Dublin City Libraries, Pearse Street, Gilbert Collection, MS 169, ff. 128, 129; Steele, *Tudor and Stuart Proclamations,* II, 1, nos. 249, 264, 271.

25. On fishing see Michael McCarthy Morrogh, *The Munster Plantation* (Oxford, 1986), pp. 155-8, 223-5.

26. For example, the case of Edward Kendall who offered to pay his rent to the Earl of Cork in October 1623 as soon as the money for his fishing came in. See N.L.I. MS 12813/2 f. 311.

27. C.H. Hull ed., *The Economic Writings of Sir William Petty* (Cambridge, 1899), I, p. 176.

28. B.L., Sloane MS 3827, ff. 198v-9; Kent Archive Office, MSS ON 6800, ON 7578, U 269; Sheffield City Library, Wentworth Wodehouse MSS, Strafford Letter Book 24/25 no. 174.

29. B.L. Add MS 4756, f. 43v; *Cal. S.P. Ire., 1615-25,* p. 184.

30. Richard Caulfield, ed., *The Council Book of the Corporation of Youghal* (Guildford, 1878), pp. 82, 95, 128.

31. Hull, ed., *Economic Writings of Sir William Petty,* I, pp. 192, 310.

32. Gillian T. Cell ed., *Newfoundland Discovered: English attempts at Colonisation, 1610-30* (Hakluyt Society, London, 1982), p. 222.

33. See for example Raymond Gillespie, 'Lords and Commons in Seventeenth Century Mayo', in Raymond Gillespie and Gerard Moran, eds., *A Various Country: Essays in Mayo History 1500-1900* (Westport, 1987), pp. 44-66.

34. *Cal. S.P. Ire., 1615-25,* p. 425. For other similar complaints see *Cal. S.P.Dom.,* 1619-23, p. 481; B.L., Add MS 11033, f. 12.

35. *Cal. S.P. Ire., 1615-25,* pp. 395, 484.

36. B.L., Sloane MS 3827, f. 25.

37. T.C.D., Mun.P/22/38, 40, 48, 49, 50, 54.

38. N.L.I., MS 3111, f. 69; MS 12813/2, f. 293.

39. N.L.I., MS 12813/2, ff. 269, 309-10, 311; Terence Ranger, 'The Career of Richard Boyle, First Earl of Cork in Ireland' (Unpublished D.Phil. thesis Oxford 1959), pp. 151-5.

40. N.L.I., MS 3111, f. 53.

41. For what follows see Raymond Gillespie, 'Peter French's Petition for the Irish Mint', *Irish Historical Studies,* 25, 100 (1987), pp. 413-420.

42. B.L., Sloane MS 3827, f. 25; D.A. Chart, ed., *Londonderry and the London Companies* (Belfast, 1928), pp. 62-3.

43. R.R. Steele, *Tudor and Stuart Proclamations,* II, 1, no. 249.

44. Bodl., Carte MS 30, f. 136; *Cal. S.P. Ire., 1615-25,* pp. 399, 423.

45. *Cal. S.P. Ire. 1615-25,* pp. 432-3, 455.

46. Brendan Jennings, ed., *Wadding Papers* (Dublin, 1953), pp. 29-58, 69-72.

47. *Cal. S.P. Ire., 1615-25,* pp. 399, 459.

48. Maurice Lenihan, ed., 'The Fee Book of a Seventeenth Century Physician', *J.R.S.A.I.,* 9 (1867), pp. 10-33, 137-47.

49. Henry Leslie, *A Warning to Israel,* (Dublin, 1625); L. Rochfort, *An Antidote to Laziness,* (Dublin, 1624); Steele, *Tudor and Stuart Proclamations,* II, 1, nos. 262, 266.

50. A.B. Appleby, 'Diseases or Famine: Mortality in Cumberland and Westmorland, 1580-1640', *Economic History Review,* Second Series, 26 (1973), pp. 403-31.

51. Brendan Fitzpatrick, 'The Municipal Corporation of Dublin, 1603-40' (unpublished Ph.D thesis, T.C.D., 1984), Appendix V.

52. *Cal. S.P. Dom., 1619-23,* pp. 291, 393, 498.

53. This is based on an analysis of the visitations of 1615, B.L., Add.MS 19836, and 1622, T.C.D., MS 550 and 1066 and 2627.

54. L.M. Cullen, 'Galway Merchants in the Outside World, 1650-1800', in Diarmuid O Cearbhaill, ed., *Galway: Town and Gown, 1484-1984* (Dublin, 1984), pp. 63-4.

55. This is based on Raymond Gillespie, *Colonial Ulster: The Settlement of East Ulster 1600-1641* (Cork, 1985); MacCarthy Morrogh, *Munster Plantation;* T.W. Moody, *The Londonderry Plantation* (Belfast, 1939), and Philip Robinson, *The Plantation of Ulster* (Dublin, 1985).

56. *Cal. S.P. Ire., 1615-25,* p. 423.

57. Based on the lower estimates in Robinson, *Plantation of Ulster,* p. 223 and MacCarthy Morrogh, *Munster Plantation,* pp. 149, 260.

4

THE GAP IN FAMINES: A USEFUL MYTH? *

David Dickson

For about eighty years centring on 1780 . . . it is not easy . . . to find contemporary accounts of deficiencies in the supply of potatoes. Disasters are often well documented, and this rarity of comment in itself, gives some foundation to the theory that a 'gap in the famines' was, in fact, a cause of population-increase. (K.H. Connell, *The Population of Ireland 1750-1845* (1950), p. 144)

During the 155 years of population buildup, which began in 1690, there were thirty-two years of hunger and seven local famines. The earliest famines . . . usually occurred in remote places that had low population densities . . . Famine conditions were more frequent after 1800, as the population increased and the margin of subsistence food safety declined.' (R.E. Seavoy, *Famine in Peasant Societies* (1986), p. 313)

These apparently conflicting modern generalisations are both based on the encyclopaedic researches of Sir William Wilde, carried out in the early 1850s into the incidence of famine, crop failure, epidemic, and meteorological aberration in Ireland during the previous millennium.[1] The range of Wilde's sources was remarkably wide — annals, early printed ephemera, medical treatises, newspapers — and where he could, he sought quantitative evidence. But his huge inventory of crises was biassed towards the recent past; nearly two-fifths of his account related to the period between 1800 and 1845. This disproportionate treatment of the early nineteenth century has provided ready ammunition for historians wishing to present the Great Famine as a Malthusian climax, coming at the end of a period of growing food-supply problems and repeated local crises.

The fact that Wilde is still a useful historical source, indeed an under-exploited one, is a measure of the gap between Irish and British demographic research. The high-resolution picture of English population change between the sixteenth and nineteenth centuries now available thanks to the work of the Cambridge Group,[2] and the somewhat more nuanced account of Scottish population change over the same period provided by Michael Flinn and his associates,[3] will never be matched in Ireland, but there are still rich veins of evidence waiting to be quarried on many aspects of the eight-fold growth of Irish population between the late sixteenth and the mid-nineteenth centuries. The challenge set by Connell's pioneering study of 1950 has only recently been taken up, and most of the attention has been focussed on the data-rich final generation of population growth.

This transformation in human numbers was not achieved for any single reason; factors relevant in the seventeenth century — for example, immigration — are not relevant in the eighteenth. And what goes far to account for population growth in eighteenth-century Ulster — the social impact of the linen industry — cannot apply to nineteenth-century Clare. The transformation was not achieved at a steady rate, nationally or regionally; Gillespie has pinpointed killer famines even in the early seventeenth-century decades of rapid immigration; and the regional impact of war in the 1640s and in 1689-91 cancelled out the natural increase of many years.

The shape of population growth in the 150 years after 1691 is now somewhat clearer than it was when Connell first tried to make sense of the available macro-demographic data, the hearth-tax returns. His model of a gradual acceleration from low seventeenth-century rates of growth, with full throttle only in the last quarter of the eighteenth century, was intellectually neat, but it overlooked the stop-start character of population change, and ignored the early decades of quite high growth in many counties which was halted and even reversed by rising death rates, falling fertility levels, or a combination of both.

A perusal of Wilde's evidence points to the strategic significance of the later 1720s and the early 1740s as years when the impetus of growth was most severely checked. The pioneering investigation of a number of Church of Ireland parish registers in Ulster by Morgan and Macafee has added some statistical precision to the abundant literary evidence (not least from Swift's pen) on the famines of the 'twenties;[4] for parts of the north-east these may have constituted the greatest food crisis of the eighteenth century.

Over the country as a whole, the crisis of 1740-1 was the worst human disaster since 1650-1, possibly since the Elizabethan conquest. Drake and, more recently, Post have examined it in a comparative European setting; the twenty-one month crisis seems to have killed between 250,000 and 400,000 people, thus implying a higher death rate and proportionately greater impact than the Great Famine itself.[5] A series of weather abnormalities through seven seasons affected each food crop and nearly all branches of farming, and this came at the same time as a war-induced recession hit cattle farmers. The absence of external food supplies — because of war and continent-wide harvest failure — made it a truly horrific conjuncture of misfortunes. Malign coincidence seems to be a necessary ingredient of all calamitous famines.

The surviving county hearth-tax returns point to strong regional variations in the mortality pattern of 1740/1: the counties in Munster and the west where recent growth had been highest suffered greatest losses.[6] The hearth-tax data also highlight the regional importance of a second harvest crisis in the mid-1740s: the 1744/5 scarcity which occurred in the economically least developed counties of north Connacht and west Ulster, where mortality was as great or greater than in 1740-1.[7]

The county house-returns provided by the hearth-tax collectors become increasingly suspect after the early 1750s. The reliability of the figures improves again in the late 1780s, but shortly after the reform of enumeration procedures a large segment of the population was exempted from the tax and therefore from the county tallies.[8] In other words, after mid-century there is no macro-demographic indicator of population change available to measure county performance — or to detect local crises. As Wilde discovered long ago, there are contemporary references to harvest failures and even 'famines' in most decades after 1745. But given the trebling of Irish population between the upsets of the 1740s and the first official census of 1821, have we any alternative but to dismiss such talk of famine as scare-mongering or at best hyperbole, and to agree with Connell that there was indeed a long 'gap in the famines'?

There are four types of evidence that may help us towards an answer: two which help to pinpoint the 'bad' years, two which offer some prospect of measuring demographic trends at the local level. The first two are time series for Dublin grain prices and national grain imports. Fig I traces the movement of the median price of wheat in the Dublin market from 1702

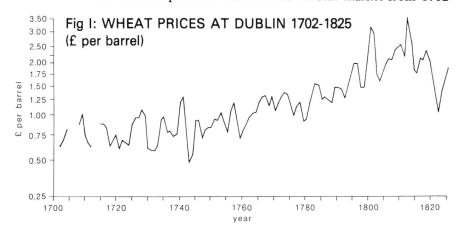

Fig I: WHEAT PRICES AT DUBLIN 1702-1825
(£ per barrel)

until 1825.[9] The long-term trend in grain prices in the first sixty years of the eighteenth century was static, reflecting the depressed character of international markets for cereals. Between the early 'sixties and the later part of the Napoleonic wars, the trend was sharply upward, again for external reasons. During the low-price phase, there were eight identifiable price peaks, some single years, some running to four years, which drastically reduced the 'normal' size of the wheaten loaf of Dubliners: 1708-9, 1715-16, 1726-9, 1734-5, 1740-1, 1745-6, 1753 and 1756-7. The Dublin market was the most tightly regulated grain market in the country, but it is likely that in the worst years (e.g. 1740 and 1756) the publicly quoted cereal prices were considerably below black-market rates. No other century-long series of food prices is extant, so how relevant to the rural food-supply situation across Ireland were the public prices delared in Thomas Street?

   Wheaten bread was not normally the food of the urban poor and was never purchased by farmer or rural labourer for family consumption. Oatmeal was the inferior urban staple diet, and before the 1780s it was still very widely consumed through most of rural Ireland, at least seasonally. Price data for oatmeal are unfortunately much less complete than for wheat.

Fig. II:
DUBLIN WHEAT AND OATMEAL PRICE MOVEMENTS
January 1782- August 1784

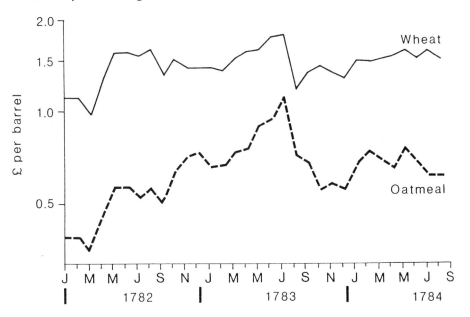

The problem is, however, less serious than it appears: in Dublin there was always a fairly strong positive correlation between the two price movements, although the price elasticity of the inferior food was naturally greater. The well-documented movement of wheat and oatmeal during the hard years of 1782-4 (Fig. II) was not dissimilar from patterns forty years earlier.[10] Eighteenth-century potato prices are much more problematical; newspaper price quotations are rare but, conventional wisdom notwithstanding, potatoes were widely traded inter-regionally, and it was a major secondary food in the towns from the 1720s. The parallel series of potato and oatmeal prices for Kilkenny city between 1769 and 1787 provides direct evidence of the close correlation between these two foodstuffs in a major urban market (Fig. III).[11] There can be little doubt that

Fig II: OATMEAL AND POTATO PRICES IN KILKENNY 1769-1787

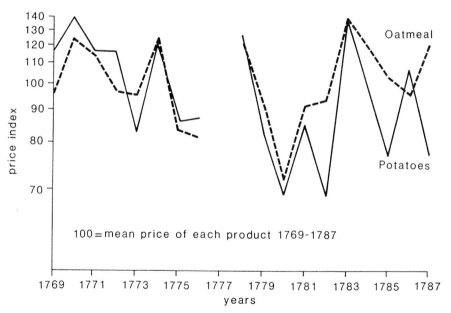

the three food markets overlapped, and that many urban consumers were price sensitive and adjusted their diets in the light of relative prices. Thus a major shortfall in potato supplies had knock-on effects on oatmeal prices and, to a smaller extent, on wheat prices, albeit largely unquantifiable ones.

In the era of rising grain prices, Dublin's years of relative shortage were the late 1760s, 1772-4, 1782-4, 1794-6, 1800-1, 1809-10, 1812-13 and 1816-18, with that of 1800-1 the most severe in terms of elevated prices. These were the periods of known economic stress at the pivot of the national economy (although they did not constitute *all* the bad years, as commercial recession caused major urban distress in 1778-9, 1792-3 and 1797). The crucial issue therefore is whether Dublin's food market and its shortcomings were insulated from the wider economy, or were a direct reflection of it.

The fluctuations in grain imports provide some clue: Ireland, from being a net exporter of cereals in the early eighteenth century, became a net importer from the 1720s, with wheat the major item and Dublin the main port of entry. Between 1722/3 and 1770/1 there was repeated and on occasions massive resort to English, Baltic and colonial American suppliers. The trade was greatest towards the end of years of local scarcity, notably 1728-30, 1735/6, 1741/2, 1745/6, 1753-5, 1757/8, 1766/7, 1769/71 and 1783-5. There was however a striking contrast between the situation in 1740/1 when despite the need, imports remained low because of the international scarcity, and 1745/6 when a record volume of over 30,000 tons of wheat was brought into the eastern and northern ports from England and Scotland, thereby averting a second catastrophe within a decade.[12] Dublin was the key distribution centre, partly because a large proportion of the grain was actually consumed within the metropolis (more than 50 per cent of the capital's cereals was being imported even in years of moderate domestic abundance); what was not bought up locally was coasted — usually northwards. Price peaks in the city were therefore likely to be lower than in the smaller urban centres, while rural access to emergency imports was far less complete. After 1758 the capital was in a doubly advantageous position: a generous parliamentary subsidy to cover the cost of transporting grain to Dublin from inland markets was successful in helping to undermine imports, and it acted as a check on grain price fluctuations in the capital. The underlying cause of the import trade had been the switch by producers in the old 'granary' districts of Dublin to fatstock and dairying production, at a time when Irish cereal farming was rarely profitable.[13]

To discover whether the years of high prices in Dublin were times of famine and elevated mortality in the countryside, we can only turn to the limited number of surviving Church of Ireland and Catholic parish registers. The problem with the former is the relatively small size of rural congregations outside Ulster, giving therefore very small numbers of observations. But in the course of an ongoing survey of such registers in Munster, rural Leinster, and Ulster, it has become apparent that activity in the Protestant graveyards was sensitive to food-price fluctuations, as measured in Dublin, even in the second half of the eighteenth century. Taking six of the unambiguous wheat-price peaks after 1750 — 1756-7, 1773-4, 1782-4, 1795-6, 1800-1 and 1816-17 — burials reached a ten-year high in a majority of the Protestant parishes sampled during two of these crises: 1756-7 (67 per cent of parishes) and 1782-4 (83 per cent); during the other four sets of bad years, a third or less of the parishes recorded their highest burials of the decade in these years.[14] This is a rather crude indication of the limited (and declining) vulnerability of Protestants to food shortages. Some Protestant clergy also registered the names of Catholic and non-conformists when they were buried in the Protestant graveyards, a practice which was more common in late seventeenth and early eighteenth centuries than later, and this complicates the interpretation of the apparent decline in the price sensitivity of 'Protestant' mortality.

What then of the unambiguously Catholic evidence? Catholic parish registers survive in much smaller quantity than do those of the Church of Ireland for the period up to 1820. The great majority that do survive record only baptisms and marriages. However these can provide indirect evidence on short-term economic stress. The impact of food-supply crises on the birth rate is well-attested; physiological, psychological and economic factors depress fertility during periods of nutritional deprivation. Mokyr has demonstrated the importance of the phenomenon during the Great Famine.[15] In this context, a short abrupt fall in baptisms can serve as a proxy for evidence of a rise, probably some months earlier, in burials in the same community.

Parish registers which are avilable for a group of eight Catholic parishes in north Leinster (Cos. Louth, Cavan and Meath) are unusual in that they include burial data from the mid- or late eighteenth century. The burials from them are plotted in Fig. IV in the form of a composite regional *mortality* index (calculated by using the procedures adopted by Michael Flinn for Scotland); a regional *baptismal* index drawing on these plus three other neighbouring parish registers is also included.[16]

The recorded burials seriously understate total Catholic deaths because children were largely or completely omitted from the registers; it is not clear what was the minimum age of deceased persons entered in the priest's register. This said, the Catholic burial trends offer some intriguing insights: the correlation with Dublin wheat prices is positive, but not strong; most price peaks are reflected (e.g. in 1774, 1783, 1794, 1800, 1808-10, 1817-18), but there are some five burial peaks which are not obviously connected with a general food crisis — notably 1762-3 when epidemics of influenza and measles seemed to have raised death rates here and far beyond these north Leinster parishes.[17]

The baptismal data in Fig. IV show a steadier trend, reaching maximum levels in the later 1780s and 1790s. Short-term reductions in the birth rate were inversely related to burials, albeit more modestly; it seems baptisms

Fig IV:
NORTH LEINSTER CATHOLIC PARISH SAMPLE
1752-1825

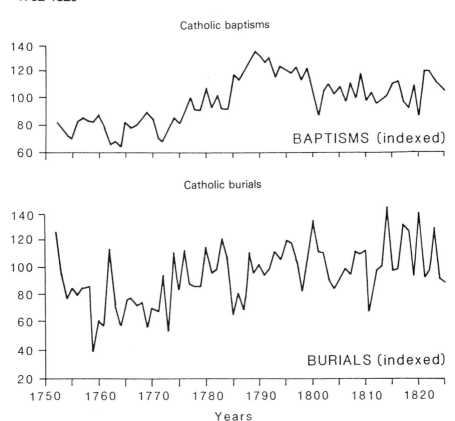

Catholic baptisms

BAPTISMS (indexed)

Catholic burials

BURIALS (indexed)

Years

fell perceptibly within a year of the burial peaks in the early 1760s (perplexing in view of the non-subsistance character of that crisis), the early 1770s, the early 1780s, in 1801, 1817 and 1819.

The strongest conclusion that can so far be drawn from the north Leinster sample is that although the years of high food prices generally coincided with above average burials and preceded years of below average baptisms, there were no devastating famines here after the 1740s. Admittedly the sample area was a highly prosperous zone, good tillage country benefitting after 1780 from the thriving trade with north-west England through Drogheda and Dundalk.[18] Rising farm incomes and abundant agricultural employment gave nearly every household sufficient reserves to ride out the hard years.

How far will other regional samples give as reassuring a picture? It is unlikely that areas of greater income inequality were as able to minimise the impact of high prices. From the English evidence of course we should expect to find a gradual weakening of the link between food prices and short-term mortality fluctuations, which Lee has shown were quite strong in England before the mid-seventeenth century, but decidedly weak in the eighteenth century.[19] Such a link was self-evidently strong in Ireland throughout the eighteenth and early nineteenth centuries: future research may permit statistical estimation. But what disappeared after the 1740s in Ireland were the general 'melt-downs' which had led to disastrous destocking of livestock, abandonment of farms, massive vagrancy and a doubling or more of normal mortality levels. Without quantitative evidence on yields, one can only assume that harvest failure in the second half of the eighteenth century was not significantly less serious than before, but that its impact was being softened. There are three developments which may have brought this about.

Rural incomes were rising fairly generally from the later 1740s, at a time of buoyant prices for most sectors in grassland farming, including the small producers of young stock. Domestic industry, notably linen and worsted spinning, were greatly extended in the third quarter of the century, and the zone engaged in seasonal linen weaving was gradually enlarged outside the core counties of eastern Ulster. One such area was Co. Sligo, and Charles O'Hara's comment of 1760 is worth repeating:[20]

> The lower class of people grow more above small accidents . . . the wetness of this season would have created dreadful apprehension fifteen years ago. At present I fear little from it. Formerly tenants had nothing to trust to but the last produce of their lands. The lower people now rely more upon their industry, which opened an access to other markets, in case of scarcity at home.

Domestic industry, the calf and pig trades, and the rising profits of oats and barley cultivation from the 1760s not only boosted rural incomes, but also helped to increase the amount of specie in circulation. Rural producers were less at the mercy of domestic food supplies.

In parts of the country however, notably the province of Munster, the labouring population grew in relative importance during this period and did not experience the full benefits of rising agricultural prices. But even they benefitted from a second development, the enlarged surplus of potatoes in normal years. The rise of a huge export trade in pork was only possible because of the expansion of potato production by smallholders for pig-feed, and this expansion gave a safety-margin over domestic needs that in the years of poor potato yields, defective oats supply, or both, could be diverted from the pig.

The relative importance of (i) rising rural incomes and of (ii) the intensification of potato cultivation in preventing a repetition of the 1740s remains controversial. Connell, Drake and Flinn among others have emphasised the central role of the potato and stressed the significance of the eighteenth-century stage in its advance, the stage when potatoes and oats were cultivated together as subsistence crops; the value of a buffer or insurance crop in protecting small-farm societies from famine is sometimes asserted as a self-evident truth, but is difficult to prove quantitatively. Cullen on the other hand has argued that it was higher incomes and savings after 1745 which moved the country 'beyond the shadow of famine'. Hard information on the pattern of potato, oats and wheat crop variation would help to resolve the issue, but in the absence of such harvest evidence, parallel price series akin to those for Kilkenny (Fig. III) offer the prospect of determining relative price movements both in the short term (to unravel the chain of causation in food crises) and in the long term (as a means of identifying *inter alia,* shifts in diet patterns). For what it is worth, the literary evidence sugests that grain 'failure' was far more prevalent than potato 'failure' in the second half of the eighteenth century, but that there were major shortfalls in potato yields in 1765-6, 1783-4 and in 1800, all times of cereal shortage. But was there a major potato failure on its own, as Wilde implied, c.1770-1, followed by a fever epidemic? Kilkenny price movements certainly hint that a rare potato-led scarcity did occur then, but parish registers, Protestant and Catholic, do not suggest serious demographic consequences.[21]

There is a third factor which, to judge by Scottish evidence, is highly relevant to the 'gap in famines' debate: the quality of the poor relief. Kelly in his work on the 1780s has emphasised its importance for Ireland.[22] In the first half of the eighteenth century the state and municipal authorities had been slow to respond to the provisioning problems created by the rapid growth of port cities. Indeed it is hard to distinguish any government policy in the 1727-9 and 1740-1 crises, other than the selective imposition of grain embargoes. At the municipal and parochial levels, the denominational exclusiveness of corporations and vestries gave rise to a rather selective approach to relief of the poor (although this varied considerably). After the establishment of city workhouses towards the beginning of the eighteenth century in Dublin and Cork, there was no move towards a poor law on English lines and little debate on the subject until the 1760s. Poor relief in the emergency years of the first half of the eighteenth century had almost completely depended on private and local charity — the written record makes much of the actions of landlords and Protestant clergy, but it was no doubt buttressed within the Catholic community by the generosity of the have-littles towards the have-nots. The beginnings of the co-ordination of emergency relief came with the introduction of voluntary relief committees funded by public subscription, which seem to have been first established for the relief of distress in Ulster in 1728-9, and were much more widespread, especially in the larger towns, in 1740-1. The co-ordination of relief reached a new administrative level in Dublin in 1740 when for the first time the workhouse was used as the centre for out-relief in the city, and all charitable donations were channelled through it. Certainly the public record of relief provision in Dublin in 1740-1 is fairly impressive and may be reflected in the surprisingly low levels of mortality recorded in the Dublin bills after the spring of 1740. However, as one pamphleteer of 1741 observed, 'daubing and patching up evils of this kind with late, and inffectual alms, is a poor, desperate necessitous expedient'.[23]

The return of very high food prices of 1756-7 created major social tensions in the port towns, and this galvanised government, parliament and local authorities to action. The comprehensive subsidy scheme for supplying Dublin with inland grain and flour, placed on the statute book in 1758, was the most dramatic innovation, but the emergency allocation of discretionary funds of £20,000 by parliament in 1757 had a more immediate impact in defusing the crisis, and the precedent was followed in 1766. The temporary prohibition of distilling in 1757 was another novelty, to be repeated in 1766 and 1783. After 1756, Belfast and other municipal authorities improved their co-ordination of relief plans, with the prospect of government-financed grain supplies coming in their direction.[24]

In the 1760s the most important development was legislation enabling the establishment of county infirmaries in 1765 under the direction of the local Church of Ireland bishops. Prior to the legislation, public hospitals had existed in only six counties; by 1770 there were twenty-one.[25] Whatever their contribution to the general level of public health, these institutions provided a new focus for organising emergency medical provision. However the legislation of 1772 enabling the establishment of county workhouses for the able-bodied poor had a less dramatic response: only Dublin, four Munster counties and three Ulster towns, built them.[26]

The disastrous grain harvest of 1782 and the destruction of the 1783 potato crop over much of the country stirred local government and voluntary bodies into unprecedented action in fund-raising, procuring imports, and distributing food outside normal wholesale channels. But at the national level, apart from a grain embargo, the government did little beyond supporting Foster's 'corn law' bill — which was intended to lubricate the commercial grain trade and to encourage exports through bounties and price supports.[27]

The larger subsistence crisis of 1800-1, coming in the wake of civil war and invasion, was tackled more energetically: Dublin Castle financed large imports of rice and maize from America and used the nation-wide army commissariat structure to reduce regional scarcities. Exchequer funds were provided in 1801 to augment by 50 per cent all voluntary subscriptions. The government's explicit concern, as it had been less openly since the 1750s, was to maintain good order in the towns.[28] Government intervention penetrated the countryside directly only in the 1816-18 and 1823-4 scarcities; there was by then a recognition that the public health of the towns could not be protected in isolation from their hinterlands. In 1817 the government introduced public works schemes, imported seed grain, and established local and national boards of health. In 1822 more careful assessment of regional food needs was introduced.[29] Public works schemes in times of crisis were a novel departure only in an Irish context — but their exclusively rural character distinguished them from European precedents.

The beginnings of a scientific interest in famine and fever in Ireland emerged in the wake of the 1817-18 fever epidemic. To writers at that period it seemed that the post-war crisis was the return of an unwelcome eighteenth-century phenomenon, and parallels were drawn with the 1720s and 1740s in particular.[30] The subsequent recurrence of crop failures in the 1820s and early 1830s reinforced the idea that a long period free from food scarcities had drawn to an end, and a variety of diagnoses, Malthusian and otherwise, were made to account for this.

It is perhaps wise to discard the notion of a national 'gap in famines' for a number of reasons. In the first place, serious dearths persisted beyond the 1740s, albeit at regional level. Secondly, there is the implication of equivalency of famine before and after the gap; yet excess mortality in the worst early nineteenth-century epidemics, those in 1800-1 and 1817-18, was calculated to have been about 40,000 deaths in each;[31] parish register analysis may reveal these to be under-estimates, but even allowing for a doubling of these figures, the rise in the excess death-rate would have been unremarkable by the standards of the 1750s. It was an indication of how far annual fluctuations of the death rate had subsided that writers in the 1820s could seriously compare the post-war epidemics with the early eighteenth-century crises. Dearth and disease in the 1810s and 1820s were far more regionally and class specific than they had ever been half a century previously, and with a far more developed infrastructure, fluctuations in the food supply even in these bad years must have been smaller in the experience of most social groups. However it is likely that *normal* standards of nutrition had worsened for the enlarged labourer/cottier section of the population by the 1810s, which would in turn have influenced the prevalence of certain deficiency diseases. The final victory of the potato as the exclusive diet of the labourer and small farmer had been achieved (outside of Ulster and parts of Leinster) by 1800. After the eclipse of oatmeal, milk and other vegetables were on the retreat. This dietary shift came as labourers' wages weakened in real terms, cereal prices rose, and potato varieties with excellent preservative qualities were introduced.[32] The narrowing of the diet had of course the effect of removing the safety-net of a second subsistence crop, although many potato-eating households depended on cereal production for cash income and had therefore an emergency food resource.

The decline in crisis mortality from the 1740s was more than the decline of famine. The as yet unexplained contraction of smallpox (and perhaps other child-killers such as 'convulsions') is part of this transformation. There was some apparent interaction between smallpox and food shortages — that was to be demonstrated once again in 1817[33] — but the general decline in smallpox can hardly be attributed to improved health or hygiene; rather its contraction removed one of the dangers arising for a population weakened by food shortages.

Finally, the demographic crises of the early and mid-eighteenth century took their rise in a more primitive, socially more homogeneous peasant society. Cattle mortality, for instance, was one of the common elements giving rise to a human mortality crisis in the first half of the eighteenth century; this indicates both the relative importance of milk in rural diets, and also the financial precariousness of small farming households. The classic indication of seventeenth and early eighteenth-century crisis was a massive rise in vagrancy, with whole families taking to the roads to beg.[34] In most parts of the country by the beginning of the nineteenth century, it was the stratum below the cattle-owning farmers who were at risk, and hunger migration was replaced by the peripatetic movement of marginal groups regularly on the road — migrant harvest workers, iterinant craftsmen, perennial beggars — whose insecurity stood in contrast to the increasingly comfortable position of the farming classes.

References

* For helping to collect much of the data reported on in this paper, I am very grateful to past research assistants Jane Massey, Carla King, Bernadette Brennan and Jane Campbell, whose work with me on Irish parish registers has been financed by grants from the Arts & Social Science Benefaction Fund, Trinity College Dublin. I am also very grateful to L.M. Cullen, Peter Campbell, S.J. Connolly, Cormac Ó Gráda and Peter Solar for sharing price data and parish register counts with me.

1. *Census of Ireland, 1851: Reports on Tables of Death* (Brit.Parl. Papers, 1856 [2087-I]XXIX), pp. 41-333; for extracts, see pp. 000.

2. E.A. Wrigley and R.S. Schofield, *The Population History of England 1541-1871: A Reconstruction* (Cambridge, 1981).

3. Michael Flinn ed., *Scottish Population History from the 17th Century to the 1930s* (Cambridge, 1977).

4. Valerie Morgan, 'A Case Study of Population Change over Two Centuries: Blaris, Lisburn 1661-1848', *Irish Economic Social History*, III (1976), 12-15; William Macafee and Valerie Morgan, 'Mortality in Magherafelt, County Derry in the Early Eighteenth Century reappraised', *Irish Historical Studies*, XXIII (1982-3), 50-60. Cf. Robert Greer, 'The Population and Economy of Two Ulster Parishes, Moira and Magheralin, in the Second Quarter of the Eighteenth Century', (unpublished B.A. dissertation, Dept. of Economic and Social History, Q.U.B., 1976), p. 21.

5. Michael Drake, 'The Irish Demographic Crisis of 1740-41', *Historical Studies VI* (1968), 101-24; John D. Post, *Food Shortage, Climatic Variability, and Epidemic Disease in Preindustrial Europe: The Mortality Peak in the Early 1740s* (Ithaca, 1985).

6. David Dickson, Cormac Ó Gráda, and Stuart Daultrey, 'Hearth Tax, Household Size, and Irish Population Change 1672-1821', *Proc.R.I.Acad.*, LXXXI C (1981), 164-8.

7. *Ibid.*, 168-9.

8. *Ibid.*, 125-50.

9. The annual means plotted in Figure 1 are based on six observations per annum at two-monthly intervals, starting as close as possible to the first week in February. For the years 1702-16, the data are more fragmentary and in a number of years the mean is based on between two and five observations only (as far as possible in different seasons). The sources used are as follows: 1702-4, 1708-12, 1715 — *Dickson's Dublin Intelligence;* 1716-18 — John Rutty, *An Essay towards the Natural History of the County of Dublin* (Dublin, 1772), ii, 424; 1718-44 — King's Hospital School Archives, Palmerstown, Co. Dublin, city toll accounts; 1745-72 — *Faulkner's Dublin Journal* (herafter F.D.J.); 1773-74 — *Dublin Gazette;* 1775-84 — *F.D.J.;* 1785-1825 — National Library of Ireland MS 4168, register of prices and quantities of corn etc. sold at Dublin markets 1785-1839.

10. Prices used in Fig. II are taken from *Dublin Evening Post*, 1782-84.

11. I am very grateful to Peter Solar for supplying the price data used in Fig. III, extracted by him from *Finn's Leinster Journal*, 1769-87.

12. *Journal of the House of Commons, Ireland*, XII, appendix pp. cccxlii-cccl, 'Account of all grain . . . imported into Ireland from . . . 1700 to . . . 1786 . . .'.

13. See Dickson, 'The Place of Dublin in the Eighteenth-Century Irish Economy', in T.M. Devine and David Dickson, eds. *Ireland and Scotland 1600-1850* . . . (Edinburgh, 1983), p. 186.

14. Results from earlier work on Church of Ireland registers were reported in my paper, 'Famine in Ireland 1700-1775', at the Famine in History Symposium, Vevey, 1981 (copies available on request). The results reported here are provisional, drawn from a data base of 33 parishes which is steadily expanding.

15. Joel Mokyr, 'The Deadly Fungus: An Econometric Investigation into the Short-term Demographic Impact of the Irish Famine, 1846-51, *Research in Population Economics*, II (1980), 237-77.

16. The parishes used in burial sample are Clogherhead (Louth), Castlerahan (Cavan), Nobber (Meath), Haggardstown (Louth), Ardee (Louth), Kells (Meath), Togher (Louth), Dunshaughlin (Meath), and Moynalty & Galtrim (Meath). With the exception of the last group of parishes these have also been used to construct the baptismal index, and in addition the baptism data from Drogheda (Louth), Lurgan (Cavan), and Ratoath (Meath) have been used. All are available on N.L.I. microfilm. I am very grateful to Peter Connell and Sean Connolly for allowing me to use the data collected by them from the Kells, Dunshaughlin, Ratoath and Nobber parish registers. For a description of the procedure used to construct the indices, see Flinn, *Scottish Population Hist.*, pp. 98-101.

17. L.M. Cullen, 'Economic Development, 1750-1800' in T.W. Moody and W.E. Vaughan eds., *New History of Ireland, 1691-1800,* iv (Oxford, 1986), p. 163.

18. John H. Andrews, 'Land and People, *c.*1780', in *ibid.,* pp. 244, 246, 260.

19. Wrigley and Schofield, *Population History,* pp. 368-77; Schofield, 'The Impact of Scarcity and Plenty on Population Change in England, 1541-1871', in R.I. Rotberg and T.K. Rabb eds., *Hunger in History* . . . (Cambridge, 1985), pp. 86-93.

20. Quoted in Cullen, 'Economic Development, 1691-1750', in Moody and Vaughan, *New Hist. Ire.,* iv, 149.

21. *Census 1851, Reports: Deaths,* p. 146; Connell, *Population of Ireland,* pp. 142-51; Michael Drake, 'Marriage and Population Growth in Ireland, 1750-1845', *Economic History Review,* 2nd ser. XVI (1963), 301-13; M.W. Flinn, 'The Stabilisation of Mortality in Pre-industrial Western Europe', *Jnl.Eur.Econ.Hist.,* III (1974), 310-11; Cullen, in Moody and Vaughan, *New Hist. Ire.,* iv, 148-50, 160-2.

22. T.C. Smout, 'Famine and Famine-relief in Scotland', in L.M. Cullen and T.C. Smout eds., *Comparative Aspects of Scottish and Irish Economic History 1600-1900* (Edinburgh, 1977), pp. 25-30; J.J. Kelly, 'Population and Famine Relief in Eighteenth-century Ireland: The Case of the 1782-4 Scarcity', (unpublished paper, 1986). I am grateful to Dr Kelly for permission to consult his paper.

23. [Rev. Philip Skelton], *The Necessity of Tillage and Granaries* . . . (Dublin, 1741), p. 37. John Rutty, *A Chronological History of the Weather and Seasons, and of the Prevailing Diseases in Dublin* (London, 1770), pp. 78-80; *Census 1851, Reports: Deaths,* p. 128; Dickson, 'In Search of the Old Irish Poor Law', in Rosalind Mitchison and Peter Roebuck eds., *Economy and Society in Scotland and Ireland 1500-1939* (Edinburgh, 1988), pp. 152-4.

24. *Census 1851, Reports: Deaths,* pp. 138-9, 143-5; Dickson, 'Old Irish Poor Law', p. 154.

25. Connell, *Population of Ireland*, pp. 274-5.

26. Dickson, 'Old Irish Poor Law', pp. 154-5.

27. Kelly, 'Population and Famine Relief', *passim*.

28. State Paper Office, Irl. OP/115/15; OP/100/3.

29. See Timothy O'Neill, 'The State, Poverty and Distress in Ireland 1815-45', (unpublished Ph.D. dissertation, N.U.I. (U.C.D.), 1971), *passim*.

30. William Harty, *An Historic Sketch of the Causes, Progress, Extent and Mortality of the Contagious Fever Epidemics in Ireland during the years 1817, 1818 and 1819* (Dublin, 1820), *passim;* F. Barker and J. Cheyne, *An Account of the Rise, Progress and Decline of the Fever late Epidemical in Ireland* (Dublin, 1821), pp. 4 *et seq.*

31. Harty, *Epidemics*, p. 21; Thomas Newenham, *A Statistical and Historical Enquiry into the Progress and Magnitude of the Population of Ireland* (London, 1805), pp. 131-32.

32. See Dickson, 'An Economic History of the Cork Region in the Eighteenth Century', (unpublished Ph.D. dissertation, University of Dublin, 1977), pp. 374-5.

33. Barker and Cheyne, *Fever*, p. 4.

34. L.M. Cullen, *The Emergence of Modern Ireland 1600-1900* (London, 1981), pp. 90-2.

5

THE GREAT FAMINE WAS NO ORDINARY SUBSISTENCE CRISIS*

Peter Solar

The proximate cause of the Irish famine of the late 1840s was a series of potato crop failures brought about by blight. This fungal disease, which appeared in North America in 1843, was first spotted in Europe in June 1845, at Courtrai in Belgium[1] It began to affect the Irish potato crop only from the late summer of 1845, so that the damage to the 1845 crop was relatively limited and was concentrated in eastern Ireland. In 1846 the blight devastated the potato crop throughout the country. While the 1847 crop was largely unaffected by disease, it was still far below normal as there was little seed left from the previous year. After the respite in 1847, the blight struck again in 1848. It was this series of disease-related crop failures with which the Irish people and the British government had to deal.

From this common starting point differences of interpretation begin to appear when the nature, causes and consequences of the Great Famine are considered. Why did these crop failures lead to so much misery, so many deaths and so much emigration? Was it simply because the Irish landed class and the British government let the Irish people starve? Or was the government faced with an impossible situation, one with which it was not equipped to cope, but to which it responded as well as could be expected? If the measures taken by Peel in 1845/6 were well considered and largely effective, why then did the Russell government prove so ineffective in 1846/7? These questions concerning the immediate impact of the potato crop failures can be answered only with a clear view of the nature of the crisis.[2] If these failures were like others that had occurred previously, in Ireland or elsewhere, then the magnitude of the human disaster and the inefficacy of relief must be seen in the context of these other crises. But if the impact of the blight was significantly more profound than that of the factors underlying other subsistence crises, then different standards are called for in assessing the course of events during the late 1840s.

The nature of the blight's impact also matters for the way in which the pre-Famine period is interpreted. Was a disaster like that of the late 1840s inevitable? Crotty seems to suggest that it was when he says that 'bearing in mind the great and growing reliance of large sections of the population on potato crops, it seems clear that famine was almost endemic in Ireland in the thirty years or so before the Great Famine.'[3] On the other hand, the general thrust of his interpretation of Irish agricultural history argues more for the irrelevance, rather than the inevitability, of the Famine by seeing it only as having accelerated demographic and agricultural adjustments already well underway.[4] Connell is less equivocal: 'given the dominance of the potato, some such disaster was all but inevitable; given the growth of population, the more it was delayed, the more malevolent it must be.'[5] The interpretation at the other extreme sees the Famine as a monumental piece of bad luck. This is implicit in Crotty's argument about the continuity of change and in Kennedy's judgment that 'in a real and tragic sense Ulster was caught in the last lap; in the absence of repeated harvest failure it might well have slipped past a Malthusian-style confrontation between people and resources.'[6]

Whether it was inevitable or not, the magnitude of the disaster has tended to direct attention to ascertaining why the pre-Famine economy was so fragile. As Cullen has put it, 'the significance of the Great Famine lies not only in the actual crisis but in the underlying vulnerability which explains why a food shortage was not a transient crisis but assumed the proportions of a major and ongoing disaster.'[7] The most systematic inquiry into the weaknesses in the pre-Famine economy is Mokyr's *Why Ireland Starved.* Mokyr goes so far as to *define* Irish poverty in terms of its vulnerability to subsistence crises. He then tries to isolate the peculiar features of the Irish economy that explain why exogenous shocks, not unlike those which affected other European countries at the time, had much more severe consequences in Ireland. The blight is seen as one such shock.[8]

Cullen, Mokyr and others who stress the vulnerability of the pre-Famine economy tend to assimilate the Great Famine to other subsistence crises. They assume that the blight-induced crop failures in the late 1840s were like those which produced distress elsewhere and at other times. While this opens up potentially fruitful comparisons with experience in other countries, it is an assumption that has not received careful scrutiny. If, however, the impact of the blight on the potato crop was significantly different from other harvest failures, then the importance accorded to rigidities or other weaknesses in the pre-Famine economy may need revision.

Likening the Great Famine to other subsistence crises does present problems in understanding its longer-term consequences. Why should a few harvest failures, however severe, lead to major changes in the composition of agricultural activity? Why did the population not only fail to recover after the Famine, as it generally did after crises elsewhere, but also continue to decline for decades thereafter? Several broad answers are possible. One is to argue, like Crotty, that the pre-Famine rural economy was already heading for its post-Famine incarnation. Another is that the changes in post-Famine Ireland are to be attributed not to the Famine but to other causes, such as the repeal of the Corn Laws or industrial expansion in Britain and America. These two answers make the Famine largely irrelevant to the long-term development of the Irish economy. A third answer, which at least gives the Famine an independent role, is to say that it somehow changed the *mentalité* of rural Ireland and so affected its demographic and economic behaviour. While there may be some truth in all of these answers, it is perhaps worth investigating whether the factors which caused the Famine did not also have longer-term implications.

This paper argues that the Great Famine was unlike other subsistence crises because the impact of the blight on the potato crop was extraordinary in two respects. First, it was unusually severe. The failures of the late 1840s were not 'normal' harvest fluctuations either in their amplitude or in their bunching. Second, the impact of the blight was not a transitory phenomenon but a persistent one. The introduction of the disease changed the environment within which Irish agriculture would be carried out until the use of anti-fungal spraying became widespread in the early twentieth century. These two distinctive features of the blight are documented in Sections I and II. Their implications for understanding the nature of the crisis of the late 1840s are taken up in Section III where rough calculations are made of the calories available to the Irish population just before and during the Famine. The paper closes with a discussion of how this way of viewing the Famine affects the interpretation of post-Famine and pre-Famine developments.

I

The potato crop failures which struck Ireland in the late 1840s were severe. Bourke has put the average pre-Famine potato yield at around 6 tons per statute acre and has estimated the yields in 1845 and 1846 at 4 and 1.5 tons. The Agricultural Statistics give the yield in 1848 as 3.9 tons.[9] Thus, in the space of four years the potato crop was short of its normal return by 33, 75 and 37 per cent. (The yield in 1847 was 7.2 tons, but this did little good since there was a great shortage of seed from the 1846 crop.) Showing how extraordinary these failures were will be the task of this section. The paucity of direct evidence on pre-Famine Irish yields means that data from other countries must be invoked to set a standard for 'normal' crop failures.

No reliable series of potato, nor indeed any other crop, yields exist for

Ireland before the Famine. The only significant body of information on harvest outcomes consists of the qualitative descriptions that regularly appeared in Irish newspapers. Those in the *Waterford Mirror* and the *Northern Whig* (Belfast) for the 1820s, 1830s and early 1840s have been thoroughly studied; those in other publications have been collected less systematically.[10] The harvest reports gave occasional quantitative indications of the deviation from an average return, particularly when the crop was very poor. In general, deficiencies were rarely described as being more than a third, for potatoes or any other crop.[11] On only two occasions was a greater shortfall mentioned. In 1811 the cereal harvest near Belfast was said to have yielded 'not half the usual produce'.[12] In 1841 the potato crop in the same area was described as 'little more than half a crop'.[13] The newspaper harvest reports pretend to no quantitative precision. Nor are they comparable to Bourke's estimates or the data in the Agricultural Statistics, for they generally refer to relatively small areas. Still, they do suggest that the 1845 and 1848 potato crop failures were extreme, yet within the range of Irish experience. The 1846 failure, by contrast, seems to be in a class by itself.

Similar conclusions may be drawn from an analysis of yield fluctuations in several western European countries during the nineteenth century. Statistics for the yields of potatoes and major cereals in France, Germany, the Netherlands, and Great Britain have been derived from the data in Mitchell's compendium. There may be problems with some of these series, but this exercise is only illustrative and, as will be seen, the conclusions do not depend on any one series.[14] The French series start in 1815; those for the other countries begin only after mid-century. It is conceivable that climatic or technological change altered the nature of harvest fluctuations between the early and late nineteenth century. The analysis which follows assumes that they did not do so in any major way.

Country series are used rather than local or regional ones, although the latter might be more plentiful and extend further back in time. One reason is simply ease of access, for this is not intended to be a major investigation of European harvest fluctuations. Another is that the potato crop failures in Ireland were widespread and should be compared to harvest outcomes over other large areas. Yields will, no doubt, fluctuate more for small areas, due to particular weather conditions and other local circumstances, but these fluctuations will to some extent cancel out across several such areas.

The object of the exercise is to determine what was a severe harvest failure in nineteenth-century western Europe. Severe is not defined absolutely, but is to be considered relative to the expected average yield in a given place at a given time. Two indicators of severity are drawn from the data. The first is simply the largest observed deficiency, as measured by the percentage shortfall from the 'normal' yield. Since most of the yield series show an upward trend, the 'normal' yield is taken to be the fitted value of a linear or logarithmic trend. The figure for largest observed deficiency in Table 1 is thus the largest negative percentage deviation from the trend. Where there is no trend, the largest deviation from the mean for the period as a whole is used.

Table 1. Nineteenth-Century Harvest Fluctuations
(percentage shortfall from 'normal' value)

		Largest Observed Deficiency	1/2000 Chance Level
FRANCE			
Wheat	1816-1913	28	46
Rye	1815-18, 1820-35	13	33
Barley	,, ,,	12	31
Oats	,, ,,	19	39
Potatoes	1817-24, 1829-44	25	41
Potatoes	1845-69, 1871-1913	36	49
GERMANY			
Wheat	1878-1913	17	24
Rye	,,	20	26
Potatoes	,,	31	44
NETHERLANDS			
Wheat	1852-1913	21	33
Rye	,,	34	37
Barley	,,	18	35
Oats	,,	18	26
Potatoes	,,	50	54
GREAT BRITAIN			
Wheat	1884-1913	14	29
Barley	,,	13	20
Oats	,,	9	19
*Potatoes	,,	18	35
IRELAND			
Wheat	1857-1913	30	34
Barley	,,	23	35
Oats	,,	20	24
Potatoes	,,	62	92

Notes: 'Largest Observed Deficiency': largest percentage deviation below fitted values of trend line (if no trend, then below series mean).
'1/2000 Chance Level': percentage deviation below fitted values of trend line corresponding to the 0.0005 level of a t-distribution based on the standard error of the trend regression (if no trend, the standard deviation of the series) and assuming 30 degrees of freedom.
* series show no trend.

Source: B.R. Mitchell, *European Historical Statistics, 1750-1970* (New York, 1976), Tables C2 and D1.

The second indicator of severity is based on an analysis of the variation in each yield series. While within a given period the largest observed deficiency may be relatively small, the entire series may be so volatile that it suggests the probability that much larger values could well have occurred instead. Similarly, a large observed deficiency in the context of a series that shows little other variation suggests that even larger deviations were improbable. The second indicator shown in Table 1 uses the standard errors of the regressions (or the standard deviations of series with no trend) and the assumption that the estimates are distributed according to the t-distribution to come up with the percentage deviation from trend (or the series mean) below which only 1/2000 of the distribution lies. One way to think about the figure of 1/2000 is that a worse harvest than that shown in the second column of Table 1 is likely to occur only once in 2000 years. This is admittedly an arbitrary cut-off: would once in 1000 years be sufficiently improbable? once in 500 years? It may be suggested that once in 2000 years sets an extreme standard and that a lower cut-off point would only emphasise the unusual severity of any harvest that exceeded this extreme value.[15]

The results for cereals show that a very bad harvest involved the loss of about a third of the normal yield. The largest observed deficiency was 34 per cent, for rye in the Netherlands. Only two other values were more than 25 per cent, those for wheat in France and Ireland. The values for the second indicator, the 1/2000 chance level, always lie above those for the largest observed deficiency, but only three are greater than 35 per cent: again wheat in France and rye in the Netherlands, but this time they are joined by oats in France. It is interesting to note that the variability of Irish cereal yields, on either measure, tended to be somewhat higher than in the other countries, and that this was particularly the case for wheat.

The results for potatoes, with the exception of those for France, all refer to a blight-infested environment. As might be expected, the variability of potato yields is greater, usually much greater, than that for cereals in each country. The French data, which have been analysed in greater detail by Mokyr, suggest that this may also have been the case before the blight appeared, though the difference in variability was smaller.[16] But the results for early nineteenth-century France are still consistent with the conclusion that a very severe failure involved a shortfall of about a third.

The extraordinary severity of the potato crop failures that occurred in Ireland in the late 1840s is now clear. The failures of 1845 and 1848, when the crops were short by about a third, were at the limits of actual nineteenth-century experience, as shown by the largest observed deficiencies in post-Famine Ireland and in other western European countries. They were also quite improbable events, on the basis of the variability that characterised harvest fluctuations in these countries. The potato failure in 1846, when three-quarters of the crop was lost, was far out of the range of actual or likely western European experience. It was in no way a 'normal' harvest failure, but was roughly twice as severe as the worst that might have been expected on the basis of recorded nineteenth-century experience in Ireland and other countries of western Europe. These conclusions depend in part, it should be recalled, on the assumption that the nature of harvest fluctuations did not change significantly from the first to the second half of the century, from which most of the data have been drawn.

That these three very severe failures took place within the space of four years must also have been highly improbable. While the nineteenth-century yield data have not been thoroughly analysed to determine the extent to which bad harvests tended to bunch together, the Durban-Watson statistics for the trend regressions, which may give some indication of whether bunching is likely to have been important, suggest that it was not.[17] If the chances of failure were largely independent from year to year, then the probability of two successive failures, as in 1845 and 1846, would simply be the product of their individual probabilities, which would turn out to be very small indeed.

One last point is worth making about the results in Table 1. The variability of potato crop yields in post-Famine Ireland was distinctly higher than in the other countries. It may be suggested that the preference of the blight for a damp climate made drastic failures more likely in Ireland. This should have depressed the average yield of potatoes relative to other crops. Table 2 shows average yields of potatoes, wheat, and oats in the 1880s for several European countries. While yields for all three crops are generally higher in Ireland than elsewhere, except Britain and the Netherlands, the Irish advantage in potato yields is distinctly less than it is for wheat and oats. The greater susceptibility of the potato crop to blight in post-Famine Ireland gives reason to think that the failures in the 1840s may have been more severe in Ireland than elsewhere in western Europe.

II

The impact of the potato blight was not only particularly severe in the late 1840s; it did not go away thereafter. Until effective treatment for the disease became available around 1900, the blight continued to devastate the potato crop at irregular intervals. The proximate cause of the Famine was thus not

Table 2. Crop Yields in the 1880s
(metric tons per hectare)

	Potatoes	Wheat	Oats
Ireland	9.2	1.84	1.70
Austria	7.7**	1.07	0.85
Denmark	7.4	2.23	1.23
France	7.5	1.19	1.10
Germany	9.7	1.47	1.37
Great Britain*	14.9	2.03	1.69
Hungary	7.8***	1.08	0.87
Netherlands	11.0	1.77	1.73
Sweden	8.2	1.40	1.29

Notes: *   1884-93
          **   1888-97
          ***   1891-1900

Where necessary, returns in hectolitres were converted to kilogrammes at the following rates: potatoes, 73 kg/hl; wheat, 75 kg/hl; oats, 45 kg/hl.

Source: B.R. Mitchell, *European Historical Statistics, 1750-1970* (New York, 1976), Tables C2 and D1.

a transitory phenomenon, but the first manifestation of a persistent change in Irish agricultural conditions. It is this aspect of the Famine that will now be documented and explored.

The most direct approach to the blight's impact is to look at the fall in potato yields. Bourke has argued for a pre-Famine average yield of 6 tons per acre on the basis of a careful analysis of a variety of contemporary sources. The Agricultural Statistics show that for the period 1847-71 the average yield was about 4 tons.[18] Thus, the gross yield fell by a third. The net yield probably fell by somewhat more. If seed was sown in both periods at the rate of 0.8 tons per acre, then the net yields would have been 5.2 and 3.2 tons, a fall of 38 per cent.

The yield statistics from the official returns, when considered in more detail, do raise a problem in the interpretation of the blight's effects. The average yield of potatoes remained fairly high until the mid-1850s, then dropped rather suddenly. The average for 1847-56 was 5.3 tons; for 1857-66, 3.1 tons. The reason for this precipitate fall, which also took place to a lesser extent in the yields of cereal crops, remains mysterious. Bourke notes that there were some changes in the procedures used to collect the yield statistics, but suggests that the major reason why yields were maintained at a reasonably high level during the late 1840s and early 1850s was the existence of a stock of soil nutrients built up by the intensive manuring that characterised the pre-Famine potato economy.[19] But why this stock should have been suddenly exhausted in the mid-1850s remains a problem.

Another approach to the impact of the blight is through the prices of Irish agricultural produce. It may be supposed that the prices of wheat and oats in Ireland were essentially determined by prices in the much larger British market. Both of these items figured prominently in Anglo-Irish trade, so one would not expect prices in the two markets to differ by much more than the costs of transport and distribution. Movements of wheat and oats prices in Belfast, Waterford and London were, in fact, highly correlated during the early nineteenth century.[20] Potatoes, by contrast, did not figure directly in trade, so that their prices may have been more independent of developments in the British market. But, as long as wheat and oats continued to be produced in Ireland, the relative price of potatoes on the average of several years (though not necessarily for any one year) ought to have approximated to their relative cost of production.

The annual prices of potatoes relative to wheat and oats at Waterford market are shown in Figure 1. The underlying indices for potato, wheat, and oats prices have 1840-5 as their reference period and are based on six price observations per year, which have been seasonally weighted over harvest years beginning with the observation for 1 October. The prices refer, unfortunately, to an urban market, but farmgate price series for nineteenth-century Ireland are rare, particularly for the pre-Famine period. The series for the Barrington farm at Fassaroe, Co. Wicklow, which begin in 1837, show relative price movements similar to those in Figure 1.[21] Prices paid by Poor Law unions for potatoes in the early 1840s and late 1850s also correspond to the trends in potato prices at Waterford, so there is reason to believe that the Waterford prices are representative of developments in the countryside.[22]

The change in relative prices that occurred in the late 1840s is manifest. Before the Famine the general picture is one of large year-to-year fluctuations around a modest fall on trend in the price of potatoes relative to cereals. Relative potato prices were particularly high in 1809/10-1811/2, 1816/7, 1821/2, and 1825/6, but rarely were more than 50 per cent of their 1840-5 average. In 1846/7 the relative price of potatoes jumped to more than double its average pre-Famine level; in 1847/8 it was more than triple! But what is interesting, for the argument here, is that the relative price of potatoes did not fall back to its pre-Famine level. Instead it remained one and a half to two times higher throughout the 1850s and early 1860s. This increase in relative price is quite consistent with the fall in the relative yield of potatoes from the early 1840s to the late 1850s.

The relative price movements tend to cast some doubt on the reality of

Figure 1

AGRICULTURAL RELATIVE PRICES AT WATERFORD, 1806/7 - 1862/3
(Sales years beginning 1 Oct.; 1840 - 5 = 1.0)

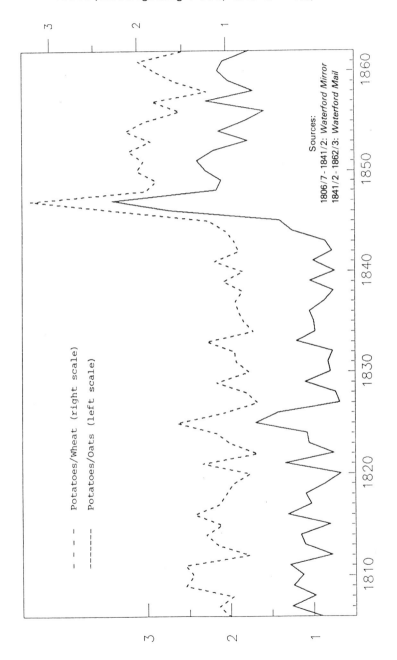

the drop in potato yields shown by the Agricultural Statistics for the mid-1850s. If yields did fall so drastically, both absolutely and relative to cereal yields, then it might be expected that the relative price of potatoes ought to have risen. Instead, if anything, it fell. Even were the medium-term supply of potatoes inelastic, which seems unlikely, the demand for potatoes would still have had to have contracted significantly in order to produce this result.

A problem in inferring the impact of the blight from both the yield and the price statistics is that changes also occurred in the Irish rural labour market over the Famine. In so far as wages rose (the sparseness of the secondary literature on Irish wages in this period makes the hypothetical necessary), it might be expected that less labour would be expended on the land, leading presumably to a fall in yields. Similarly, the relative price of labour-intensive goods, such as the potato, would rise. In fact, the increase in nominal wages appears to have been modest. On the Barrington farm, for example, labourers' wages rose from 14d. per day in the early 1840s to 18d. in the late 1850s.[23] The movement in *real* wages depends critically on the composition of the cost of living index. If potatoes form a large part, then real wages may even have fallen.

Even if the cost of labour rose over the Famine, this seems to have led primarily to a reduction in the amount of cultivation rather than to major changes in the way the land was tilled. The recent survey of Irish agricultural techniques by Bell and Watson stresses the continuity in methods during the nineteenth century.[24] On the Barrington farm the per acre labour input for the potato crop fell by only four per cent from the early 1840s to the late 1850s.[25] It might also be expected that as the cultivated acreage fell over the Famine, the land could have been rested longer and yields ought, if anything, to have risen.

The importance of potatoes as a wage good makes it difficult to separate neatly the effects of the blight from the effects of changes in the labour market. Given the reliance of the pre-Famine labourer on potatoes, an exogenous fall in their yield would translate fairly directly into an increase in the cost of labour, as measured by the land and labour-time required to sustain him. What is suggested here is that this effect dominated any further fall in yields resulting from a reduction in the labour input per acre.

The movements in yields and prices after the immediate crisis of the late 1840s can thus be seen as indicating a major role for the potato blight, as an exogenous and continuing influence, in the changes that took place in Ireland from mid-century. The introduction of this disease was not a short-term shock, but a profound and persistent change in the environment within which Irish farmers and labourers worked.

III

This paper has stressed two features of the crisis of the late 1840s: the extreme severity of the crop failures that caused it, and its significance as the first manifestation of the permanent change in Irish agriculture wrought by the introduction of the potato blight. A way to summarise and draw out some of the implications of these features is to look systematically at the food supply of Ireland on the eve of the Famine and during the Famine years.

Table 3 shows a rough account of where the Irish people got their calories in the early and late 1840s. The figures for 1840-5 are based upon estimates for the production and trade of agricultural products that are fully documented elsewhere. This is not the place to defend them, but it may be

Table 3. *Irish Food Supplies, 1840-5 and 1846-50*
(1000 m. kcal/day)

	1840-5	*1846-50*
IRISH PRODUCTION		
Potatoes	23.0	5.4
Wheat	2.7	3.1
Oats	7.6	7.7
Barley	1.2	1.7
Total Net of Seed	34.3	18.1
Oats for Horses	2.3	2.4
Total Net of Seed and Horses	32.1	15.7
USES OTHER THAN IRISH CONSUMPTION		
Distilling and Brewing	0.9	1.0
Exports	6.4	1.9
Wheat	0.6	0.4
Oats	2.1	1.0
Barley	0.1	0.1
Pork	3.6	0.4
Animal Fodder	4.5	0.2
Total Other Uses	11.8	3.1
NET DOMESTIC SUPPLIES	20.3	12.6
IMPORTS		
Wheat	0.2	1.4
Barley	0.0	0.1
Indian Corn	0.0	3.9
Total Imports	0.2	5.5
TOTAL CONSUMPTION	20.5	18.1
BALANCE OF TRADE	+ 6.2	− 3.6

Notes and Sources: See Appendix for the details of the calculations underlying this table.

noted that the estimates of Irish cereal output before the Famine are lower than those made by Ó Gráda.[26] The estimates for the late 1840s are based in part on the Agricultural Statistics, using procedures consistent with the pre-Famine estimates, and in part on some very crude estimates for 1846 output. All the estimates are described and documented in more detail in the Appendix.

Calories are, of course, only a partial measure of nutritional intake and needs. It is used here for several reasons. One is that the calculations are only illustrative and do not pretend to be a complete analysis of the nutritional consequences of the blight. While the energy content of food is only one factor in nutrition, it is still a major one. A second reason is that calories may be the most useful indicator of relatively short-term changes, such as those considered here. Third, confining the analysis to calories may understate the adverse nutritional implications of the move away from the potato.[27]

The calorie accounts deal only with the output and use of potatoes, wheat, oats, barley and maize. The products of pasture have been excluded for three reasons. First, it is much more difficult to come up with estimates for their output and consumption. Second, even crude estimates suggest that meat and dairy products were mainly exported throughout the period. Third, the calorific content of these products is quite small, so that the major changes in the calories available will be determined by what happens to potatoes and cereals.[28]

What is most striking about the results in Table 3 is the drastic fall in Irish production of calories. Net of seed for the following year's crop and of oats fed to horses, it was reduced by slightly more than a half. Both of these uses may be thought of as necessary to keep the agricultural system running. Seed and horses could conceivably have been sacrificed to current consumption (seed for potatoes was probably consumed in 1846/7), but major diversions would have meant more problems later. The fall in calories available, net of these two items, was almost entirely the outcome of the decrease in the contribution of potatoes. The fall in potato output in terms of calories was the result of three factors. One was the fall in yields owing to the blight. The other two concern the reduction in the acreage sown. The acreage in 1847 was abnormally low because of a severe shortage of seed. In other years the acreage was down from its pre-Famine level because lower yields were expected. There was only a small increase, of 10 per cent, in the output of cereals to compensate for the loss of the calories available from potatoes. (Ó Gráda's cereal output estimates would imply an 8 per cent *decrease* in calories from this source.)

These estimates suggest that there was an absolute deficiency of food in

Ireland in the late 1840s. Total pre-Famine consumption is estimated at 20.5 thousand million calories per day. Net output in the late 1840s came to only 15.7, a shortfall of 23 per cent. Thus, while changes in the entitlements to food may well have contributed to the severity of the Irish famine, the fundamental problem was that there were significantly fewer calories being produced than had previously been used for domestic consumption, let alone for other uses. It is worth emphasising that this conclusion refers to the average of *five* years' experience, which serves to highlight the persistence of the shortfall. While it was worse in 1846/7 than in subsequent years, this shortfall remained significant.

Uses of the potato and grain crops, other than for direct Irish consumption, are shown in the second part of Table 3. The first item gives the calorific equivalent of the oats and barley used in the brewing and distilling industries. Part of these industries' output was consumed in Ireland, of course, but the greater part of the calorific content of the raw materials was lost in processing, so this use has been treated separately.[29] The items for pork exports and for feeding animals (including pigs for domestic consumption) give the calorific equivalents of the potatoes fed to pigs that were exported live or as bacon and of the potatoes fed to other animals.

The calculations for the other uses of potato and cereal output show the large margin of production over domestic consumption that existed before the Famine. During the crisis a much smaller share of output went to these other uses. Nonetheless, some did, so there was an even greater shortfall in the calories available for consumption in Ireland as food in the late 1840s. Domestic supplies net of these uses were 39 per cent less than pre-Famine consumption.

It is interesting to consider the figures for other uses of potatoes and grain in terms of the traditional private and public responses to subsistence crises in Ireland. The classic private responses to deficient crops were to reduce exports and to limit the amount of fodder given to animals. Although exports of grain did continue during the Famine, they were 46 per cent below their average during the early 1840s, which made available an additional 1.2 thousand million calories per day for domestic consumption. Since cereal cultivation had increased somewhat, the fall in the share of output that was exported was even greater. Much more important adjustments were made through a reduction in the stock of pigs (and poultry) and in the use of potatoes as fodder for cattle and horses. These responses freed 7.5 thousand million calories per day. During the early nineteenth century the pig stock had served as a buffer between potato output and potato consumption. When potatoes were short, the numbers of pigs fed and exported fell significantly. But no previous crisis showed a fall in pigmeat exports at all comparable to that in the late 1840s, and the calorie accounts show how this buffer was completely overwhelmed by the severity of the potato deficiency.[30]

The traditional public responses to Irish subsistence crises were to prohibit distilling and stop grain exports. Both measures had been frequently used in the eighteenth century and both were brought into action during the severe crisis of 1800-1. Exports were never again prohibited, but distilling was suspended in 1809 and 1812-3.[31] Had these traditional public responses been used in the late 1840s, up to 2.5 thousand million calories per day might have been made available. This would have helped, no doubt, but it still came to less than a third of the short fall between domestic supplies, after allowing for the private responses to crisis, and the pre-Famine consumption level.

Rather than restrict exports or distilling, the government chose instead to rely on imports of food. The large increase in imports of wheat and maize that did take place brought the available supply of calories up to within 12 per cent of the pre-Famine level. Given the fall in population, this would suggest that *per capita* calorie consumption was maintained, or perhaps very slightly increased. This should not be taken to mean that the Irish did not starve. This analysis deals only with averages over several years, which cannot bring to the fore critical periods, such as the winter of 1846/7, when massive grain imports had not yet begun to arrive. It also abstracts from problems in the distribution of the available food: deficiencies may have been highly concentrated socially and regionally. Moreover, the analysis treats only one aspect of nutrition. The shift from the potato to grain brought with it a number of dietary imbalances. Finally, it must be recognised that population may have adjusted to the available imports rather than the other way around.

The problem with relying on imports was how to pay for them. As Table 3 shows, the Irish balance of trade, in terms of calories, shifted from a surplus of 6.2 thousand million per day before the Famine to a deficit of 3.6 in the late 1840s. Large net imports of grain were not confined to the Famine; they were one of the persistent effects of the potato blight. In the longer term cereal imports were paid for by exports of livestock and dairy products.[32] But production of these goods did not require much labour, and it was not to be expected that graziers and dairy farmers would support indefinitely a population of underemployed labourers.

IV

The Great Famine was something more than a traditional subsistence crisis. It differs from other crises not so much in its human consequences: as Lee has pointed out, mortality, while high by nineteenth-century standards, was not so extreme when compared to crises of earlier centuries.[33] The real differences were in the nature of the shock that brought on the crisis. The crop failures caused by the blight were extraordinarily severe by nineteenth-century standards. Such severity contributed, of course, to producing seventeenth-century mortality levels in the mid-nineteenth century. Moreover, the impact of the blight was not transitory, but persistent. Whereas the shocks that caused other subsistence crises may be thought of as short-term deviations from a stable underlying environment, the shock that caused the Great Famine can best be conceived of as a major and highly specific fall in agricultural productivity that took effect suddenly and with some exaggeration.

The extreme severity of the potato crop failures, given the extent of potato cultivation and consumption, had a drastic effect on domestic production of food. It has been shown how the shortfall exceeded the substantial margin that had previously existed between domestic consumption and production, and how it overwhelmed the traditional private and public responses to crisis. There can be no doubt that in the late 1840s there was an absolute shortage of food available from domestic production.

This emphasis on an absolute shortfall runs against the grain of much recent work on famines, which has stressed the maldistribution of essentially adequate total supplies of food. Sen and others have shown how changes in entitlements, resulting, for example, from changes in relative prices or employment, can lead to famine in cases where supplies of food have not been significantly reduced.[34] This approach has been fruitful and needs to be incorporated in a full analysis of the Great Famine. One of its strengths is in dealing with the effects of developments external to the economy in question. Two such developments that affected Ireland in the late 1840s were the sharp rise in cereal prices in 1846 and the commercial and industrial depression of 1847. The increase in cereal prices, arising from poor harvests in most of Europe, probably helped some Irish farmers, but also made it more costly for most of the population to substitute cereals for potatoes in consumption. The depression meant less demand for linen and other industrial goods, further reducing incomes in Ireland. The entitlements approach might also be useful in dealing with the impact of landlords' rent demands and with the roles of the poor law and private charity. But whatever the value of this approach, it should be remembered that the major change affecting the entitlements of the Irish people in the late 1840s was a direct fall in income that took the form of far fewer potatoes being harvested.

If the unusual severity of the potato crop failures helps to understand the immediate history of the Famine, the persistent effects of the blight make its longer-term consequences easier to understand. The blight significantly reduced the productivity of land and labour in Ireland: resources put into potato cultivation now produced fewer potatoes on average. If population was a function of the level of agricultural productivity, then the fall in productivity dictated a lower equilibrium population. Fewer people could be supported at the already low standard which had prevailed before the Famine. The new equilibrium population may not have been reached by the time that the immediate crisis had passed, which might help to explain why, instead of rebounding, the Irish population fell by another 11 per cent in the 1850s.

Another way of looking at the implications of the blight for the rural population begins from the role of the potato as a major wage good. The fall in potato yields that resulted from the blight made labour more expensive. This should have made the production of labour-intensive goods relatively more costly, and since Ireland was a price-taker in agricultural markets, have led farmers to a shift away from labour-intensive activities, so reducing the demand for agricultural labour and the rural population.

The move towards pasture that took place over the Famine may thus be explained in terms of changes in costs in Ireland. This avoids two major problems which confront alternative explanations that emphasise changes in demand from the British market. One is that, leaving aside potatoes and pigmeat, relative price changes from the 1830s and early 1840s to the 1850s and early 1860s were small.[35] The other is that there does not seem to have been any major move away from tillage in British agriculture before the 1860s.

Emphasis on the productivity-reducing effect of the blight thus makes it possible to see post-Famine agricultural and demographic adjustments as of a piece. This takes an important step beyond Ó Gráda's interpretation of the Famine's agricultural consequences as the product of the large reduction in the labour force, for it explains why there was no reason for the supply of labour to recover.[36]

Giving the agricultural implications of the blight a central role also makes it clear why the Famine marks a definite break in the development of the Irish rural economy. The Famine was a first, and extremely cruel, manifestation of a major regression in the conditions of agricultural production. This change could not have been foreseen. The blight struck suddenly and fiercely. Its peculiar severity might have been read from experience in North America from 1843 or in Belgium and Holland in 1845, but the disease was too new and too little understood to predict that it would have persistent effects. Even if its long-term consequences had been realised in 1845, it is still difficult to envisage how the Irish rural economy could have adapted quickly enough to such a major change to have averted disaster.

This view of the Famine sees Ireland as having been profoundly unlucky. Not all was well with the pre-Famine economy. The share of the tilled land under potatoes was far higher than in other countries. The degree to which the Irish diet was dominated by the potato argues for economic, if not nutritional, poverty. Short-term crises did take place when the potato crop failed 'normally'. The decline of rural industry and its limited replacement by modern industry reduced incomes and employment. The high level of emigration testifies to the difficulties of making ends meet in Ireland. But it would be incorrect to see in any of these features of the pre-Famine economy the signs of a crisis such as occurred in the late 1840s or of the structural changes of which the Great Famine was the first manifestation.

References

*I am grateful to Margaret Crawford for her initiative in organising the conference at which this paper was presented and for her advice on matters nutritional, to Martine Goossens for her helpful comments on the penultimate draft, and to Erik Buyst for his help in producing Figure 1.

1. This description of the blight's appearance and effects owes a great debt to the pioneering work of P.M.A. Bourke. The basic reference is his thesis 'The Potato, Blight, Weather, and the Irish Famine' (unpublished Ph.D. thesis, University College, Cork, 1965).

2. Relief policy is treated at length in M.E. Daly, *The Famine in Ireland* (Dublin, 1986) and C. Ó Gráda, *The Great Famine in Irish History* (forthcoming in the Economic History Society's *Studies in Economic and Social History* series). Unfortunately, I had neither of these valuable essays at my disposal when the first version of this paper was prepared. Both develop arguments similar to those made here, but differences of interpretation remain. I am grateful to Dr Ó Gráda for letting me see a draft of his pamphlet.

3. R.D. Crotty, *Irish Agricultural Production* (Cork, 1966), p.39.

4. Ibid., ch. 2.

5. K.H. Connell, 'The Potato in Ireland', *Past & Present*, 23 (1962), 66. Connell had surprisingly little to say about the Famine itself. The passage cited here is the echo of an equally brief and unequivocal statement in *The Population of Ireland, 1750-1845* (Oxford, 1950), p.146.

6. L. Kennedy, 'The Rural Economy, 1820-1914', in L. Kennedy and P. Ollerenshaw, *An Economic History of Ulster, 1820-1940* (Manchester, 1985), p.49.

7. L.M. Cullen, *The Emergence of Modern Ireland, 1600-1900* (London, 1981), p.250.

8. J. Mokyr, *Why Ireland Starved: A Quantitative and Analytical History of the Irish Economy, 1800-1850* (London, 1983), esp. chs. 1,9,10.

9. P.M.A. Bourke, 'The Average Yields of Food Crops in Ireland on the Eve of the Great Famine'. *Department of Agriculture and Fisheries Journal,* LXVI (1969), 26-39, and 'The Extent of the Potato Crop in Ireland at the time of the Famine', *Journal of the Statistical and Social Inquiry Society of Ireland,* XX, 3 (1959-60), 11.

10. Almost continuous series of monthly agricultural reports were published in the *Waterford Mirror* from 1819 to 1843 and in the *Northern Whig* from 1827 to 1842. These series have been analysed in detail and will be the subject of a future article. In addition, harvest reports appeared less regularly in a number of other newspapers. These have been collected less systematically over the early nineteenth century from the following publications: *Belfast Monthly Magazine, Munster Farmers' Magazine, Irish Farmers' Journal, Dublin Mercantile Advertiser.*

11. Failures of about a third were reported for the following crops: potatoes, Muskerry district, Cork, 1812 (*Munster Farmers' Magazine,* 3 Sept. 1812 (p.346)); wheat, near Doneraile, Cork, 1817 (*Waterford Mirror,* 13 Oct. 1817); wheat and oats, near Belfast, 1821 (*Irish Farmers' Journal,* Sept. 1821); oats, near Dublin, 1826 (*Dublin Mercantile Advertiser,* 28 Aug. 1826); oats, near Doneraile, Belfast and Dublin, 1828 (*Waterford Mirror* and *Dublin Mercantile Advertiser,* Sept. 1828); wheat, near Waterford, 1838 (*Waterford Mirror,* 31 Dec. 1838).

12. *Belfast Monthly Magazine,* 7 (1811), 340.

13. *Northern Whig,* 6 Nov. 1841.

14. B.R. Mitchell, *European Historical Statistics, 1750-1970* (New York, 1976), Tables C2 and D1. For a discussion of the French yield statistics, see W.N. Newell, 'The Agricultural Revolution in Nineteenth-Century France', *Journal of Economic History,* XXXIII, 4 (1973), 697-731.

15. An alternative way of presenting the results would have been to calculate the probability of a given percentage deviation, say, 33 or 75 per cent. This is somewhat less easy to do, for the relevant values would often lie off the standard tables of the t-distribution.

16. J. Mokyr, 'Uncertainty and Pre-Famine Irish Agriculture', in T.M. Devine and D. Dickson (eds), *Ireland and Scotland, 1600-1850: Parallels and Contrasts in Economic and Social Development* (Edinburgh, 1983), pp. 92-4.

17. See, for example, the analysis of U.S. crop yields in C.B. Lutterell and R.A. Gilbert, 'Crop Yields: Random, Cyclical, or Bunchy?' *American Journal of Agricultural Economics,* LVIII (1976), 521-31.

18. *The Agricultural Statistics of Ireland for the Year 1873* (Brit. Parl. Papers, 1875, LXXIX), p. lxiii.

19. Bourke, 'Average Yields', 27-32.

20. P.M. Solar, 'Growth and Distribution in Irish Agriculture before the Famine' (Unpublished Ph.D. thesis, Stanford University, 1987), ch. 2.

21. R.M. Barrington, 'The Prices of some Agricultural Produce and the Cost of Farm Labour for the past Fifty Years', *Journal of the Statistical and Social Inquiry Society of Ireland,* IX (1887), 140.

22. For example, the price of potatoes bought by Ballymoney Poor Law Union increased by 80 per cent from the early 1840s to the late 1850s (PRONI, BG 5/A/1-2, 15-22).

23. Barrington, 'Prices', 149.

24. J. Bell and M. Watson, *Irish Farming, 1750-1900* (Edinburgh, 1986), esp. chs. 2,6.

25. Barrington, 'Prices', 149.

26. C. Ó Gráda, 'Irish Agricultural Output before and after the Famine', *Journal of European Economic History*, XIII, 1 (1984), 149-65.

27. E.M. Crawford, 'Subsistence Crises and Famines in Ireland: A Nutritionist's View', pp. 198-219, below.

28. Calculations for the early 1840s show that meat and dairy prducts (excluding pigmeat) accounted for only 9 per cent of all calories produced in Ireland. A large share of this would have been exported.

29. On the basis of the grain requirements assumed for brewing and distilling and of modern nutritional analyses, it can be calculated that in brewing 69 per cent of the calorific content of the raw materials was lost and in distilling 76 per cent (see the sources given in the Appendix).

30. Solar, 'Growth', ch. 4.

31. E.B. McGuire, *Irish Whiskey: A History of Distilling in Ireland* (Dublin, 1973), pp. 183-4.

32. Solar, 'Growth', ch. 6.

33. J.J. Lee, *The Modernisation of Irish Society, 1848-1918* (Dublin, 1973), p. 1.

34. A. Sen, *Poverty and Famine: An Essay on Entitlement and Deprivation* (Oxford, 1981).

35. Solar, 'Growth', ch. 2.

36. Ó Gráda, *The Great Famine* (forthcoming).

The Calculations Underlying Table 3

The estimates for average crop output in 1840-5 are described and justified in detail elsewhere.[1] The basis upon which gross output was calculated may be summarised as follows:

Potatoes	2.1 m. acres	6.0 tons/acre
Wheat	0.6 ,,	12.5 cwt/acre
Oats	2.1 ,,	13.0 ,,
Barley	0.2 ,,	17.0 ,,

Gross output was then adjusted for seed, wastage, and use by animals along the lines described below for the 1846-50 estimates.

The estimates for crop output in 1847-50 are based upon acreages and yields given in the Irish Agricultural Statistics. For 1848 there were no returns for counties Dublin, Tipperary and Waterford, so it was necessary to make estimates for the national acreages (the average yields were used as they stood). This was done for each crop separately by adjusting the incomplete returns for Leinster and Munster upward by the ratio of the total acreage under the crop in 1849 to the acreage in 1849 for the counties that were covered in 1848.

The estimates for 1846 are far less soundly based than those for 1847-50. The best estimates are those for potatoes, which draw upon Bourke's analysis of Constabulary Reports. Here the acreage under potatoes has been taken to be 1.7 m., 20 per cent below the pre-Famine crop (this figure is justified along with the other estimates for 1840-5). The yield, again following Bourke, is put at 1.5 tons per acre.[2]

For the grain crops in 1846 the estimates are based upon contemporary comment and are necessarily very rough. Bad weather seems to have interfered somewhat with efforts to sow more wheat and barley, so the acreages under these crops have been put at their average pre-Famine levels. A Belfast market report noted, for example, that 'although the extent of the sowing [of wheat] as yet is not as large as it was last year, it is already that of a fair average season.'[3] After the harvest it was noted that 'the breadth of ground under Oats was greater than usual', so the oats acreage has been increased by 0.2 m. acres, or about 10 per cent, over its pre-Famine level of 2.1 m.[4] The yield of wheat was described as 'good in quality and yield' near Cork and 'above an average' near Belfast, so it has been set at 13.0 cwt. per acre, a bit above its pre-Famine level. Comment on the barley yield was mixed — 'fully an average crop' near Belfast, yet scarcely expected to amount to an average crop near Cork — so the pre-Famine average has been adopted. Oats clearly yielded poorly: 'decidedly short and defective in every way' near Cork and 'deficient in yield and inferior in quality' near Belfast. Their yield has been taken to be 10.0 cwt, 3 cwt below the pre-Famine average.[5]

Adjustments for seed were made on the basis of the acreages sown in the following year and the following seeding rates:

Potatoes	16 cwt/acre	Oats	1.6 cwt/acre
Wheat	1 cwt/acre	Barley	1.3 cwt/acre

In addition, the potato crop was reduced by 5 per cent to allow for wastage.

The consumption of oats by horses was calculated as follows: the stock of horses, as given in the Agricultural Statistics, was divided into farm (92 per cent) and non-farm (8 per cent) components. Farm horses were assumed to have been fed 0.5 cwt per annum: non-farm horses 1.4 cwt.

The use of grain in distilling was calculated on the assumption that 0.1664 cwt of barley and 0.0319 cwt of oats were required for each proof gallon of spirits distilled. The statistics for licit distilling were increased by a third to allow for illicit production. Licensed brewers were assumed to require one cwt of barley per barrel of 36 gallons, and private brewing was taken to be insignificant.

The figures for grain exports and imports come from the Parliamentary Papers and refer to calendar years. Trade in processed grain was converted to its unprocessed equivalent at 125 lbs wheat/112 lbs flour and 200 lbs oats/112 lbs oatmeal. The seasonal patterns of trade indicated that exports be those for the same year as the harvest and imports be those for the following year.

The estimates of pigmeat exports are described elsewhere.[6] Exports for the calendar year following the harvest have been used. It has been assumed that each pig consumed 1.5 tons of potatoes before the Famine and half a ton during the late 1840s.

The category 'feeding animals' includes potatoes fed to pigs consumed in Ireland and potatoes fed to other animals. The estimates for 1840-5 are described elsewhere. For the late 1840s the number of pigs for domestic consumption has been calculated at 70 per cent of the pig stock in the harvest year minus the number exported. These pigs were allocated 0.5 tons of potatoes each. It has been assumed that potatoes were not fed to cattle and horses in this period.

The estimates for annual output and its uses were turned into the figures for calories per day using the following conversions:[7]

Potatoes	2230 (kcal/day) / (ton/year)	
Wheat	386 (kcal/day) / (cwt/year)	
Oats	315 ,,	,,
Barley	373 ,,	,,
Indian Corn	487 ,,	,,

References for Appendix

1. P.M. Solar, 'Growth and Distribution in Irish Agriculture before the Famine' (unpublished Ph.D. thesis, Stanford University, 1987), ch. 9.

2. P.M.A. Bourke, 'The Extent of the Potato Crop in Ireland at the time of the Famine', *Journal of the Statistical and Social Inquiry Society of Ireland*, XX, 3 (1959-60), 11. Bourke's figures for the acreages in 1845 and 1846 have been adjusted downward in line with the comments made in J. Mokyr, 'Irish History with the Potato', *Irish Economic and Social History*, VIII (1981), 8-29.

3. *Mark Lane Express*, 2 March 1846.

4. *Mark Lane Express*, 5 Oct. 1846, Belfast market report.

5. *Mark Lane Express*, 31 Aug. 1846, Cork market report; 7 Sept. 1846, Belfast market report.

6. Solar, 'Growth', ch. 4.

7. These are based on figures for food composition kindly supplied to me by Dr E.M. Crawford. They come originally from R.A. McCance and E.M. Widdowson, *The Composition of Foods*, M.R.C. Series No. 297 (London, 1960) and P. Fisher and A. Bender, *The Value of Food* (Oxford, 1979).

6

THE RESPONSE OF THE MEDICAL PROFESSION
TO THE GREAT FAMINE

Peter Froggatt

I: Preface

Many historians have referred to events in Ireland in the eighteen-forties. Some have researched them in great detail. These events were momentous and horrific — 'a crisis, probably Europe's gravest in the nineteenth century'[1] — and we live today with many of their consequences. The 1841 census enumerated some 8.18 millon,[2] certainly an underestimate;[3] by late 1845 the population was probably at least 8.5 million.[4] The 1851 census enumerated some 6.5 million people.[5] At least two million, or nearly 25 per cent of the population, had disappeared, more if aborted natural growth is included. Estimating the contributions to this toll has exercised commentators since the famine itself, though modern writers accept that there were at least one million 'excess deaths'[6] while a further 1.2-1.4 million emigrated between 1846 and 1850[7] most in dubious shipping and many bearing with them to the reeking cellars of Liverpool and the hovels of Glasgow, the quarantine islands in North America and the wharfside slums of Boston, Philadelphia, New York, Quebec and Montreal, and some also to the Antipodes, the seeds of their own and their neighbours' destruction.[8] Add to this the estimated 300,000 plus 'averted births' i.e. births which did not take place because of the impact of the famine,[9] and the whole is a startling increment to the 'normal' annual attrition from death (70,000-90,000 p.a.) and emigration (50,000-100,000 p.a., 1840-1845).[10] These losses, however, are merely the tip of a vast iceberg whose hidden bulk was of sickness, internal migration, administrative and economic disruption, and social anarchy on a scale unprecedented in Europe in peacetime since the Black Death and in war not since the religious and dynastic conflicts of the seventeenth century, and in relative terms possibly not even then. In this paper I explore one detail on this enormous, tragic canvas, but a central and significant one, namely, the response of the medical profession to the famine: more accurately to the epidemics which accompanied it. I confine the period to 1845-8 since the later medical scene was influenced by the cholera epidemic of 1848-50 which was part of a general European pandemic and whose arrival in Ireland (by way of Belfast on 1st November 1848[11]) and its spread, though not its lethality, were largely independent of the famine conditions.

II: Organisation of Medical Services on the Eve of the Famine

In the mid-eighteen-forties arrangements for dealing with sickness and poverty in Ireland were remarkably comprehensive: 'the Irish poor enjoyed better medical services than their fellows in wealthier and healthier countries.'[12] Irish medicine was at its zenith and its Dublin luminaries were an impressive pantheon with Stokes, Graves, Adams, Corrigan, Colles, Cheyne, Wilde, and Jacob familiar to generations of doctors through justified and enduring eponyms. They were, however, but the brightest stars in a galaxy whose radiance ensured for Irish medicine a primacy in Europe. The two main medical journals — the (quarterly) *Dublin Journal of Medical Science*[13] and the (weekly) *Dublin Medical Press*[14] — were renowned, and during the famine were edited by two phenomenal polymaths, William Wilde (Oscar's father), and Arthur Jacob, a gifted and pungent polemicist quite up to Thomas Wakley's (of the *Lancet*) standard. Outside Dublin was the Belfast school: though small it was competent and active, and one of the best provincial schools in the Kingdom.[15] Moreover, the country was reasonably well doctored with some 2,600 qualified medical men (80 per cent physicians or surgeons and only 20 per cent exclusively apothecaries) and perhaps 1,000 others 'ministering to health'.[16] Furthermore, they covered the country and were not unduly congregated around the *salons* of the rich. The diseases they would soon face — typhus and relapsing fevers, smallpox, tuberculosis, dysentery, marasmus (starvation) and other famine disorders — were familiar being endemic in Ireland: many doctors had themselves survived dangerous infections thus adding the ultimate of personal experience to a professional one.[17] It was therefore old if dangerous friends the profession would encounter, not new or exotic ones or some half-forgotten scourge like plague. Perhaps only scurvy would be generally unfamiliar though it caused few recorded deaths.[18] Even cholera in 1848-50 was a returning if unwelcome visitor from the early eighteen-thirties, not a new face. The younger doctors also knew 'fever' well — next to consumption it was the commonest disease which crowded the teaching hospitals — and no physician seeking recognition could neglect to publish his thoughts on 'continuous' and 'intermittent' fever whether new ones or not, and no trainee could afford not to know them. It was an experienced, knowledgeable, and by contemporary standards well trained profession, which met the emergency.

But doctors require adequate institutions and ancillaries to back them. Of ancillaries I need say little; the derelicts who were the lay 'nurses' and 'attendants' in pre-Nightingale days are familiar through contemporary writings and vicious but not inaccurate squibs and cartoons. Nurses in Ireland await an historian but the lay, as distinct from those in Orders, were no doubt little better than those in Britain. On paper the medical institutions for the 'sick-poor' and 'fever' cases made an impressive reticulum, equalled in only a few countries, if at all. If often in operation ramshackle, this was because Ireland was a socially anarchic country with widespread agrarian unrest and violence, poorly policed, with ineffective local government, politically unstable, and almost designed to frustrate the best efforts of an often highly talented administration with a merited reputation as early Benthamites.[19] Above all Ireland was cripplingly poor, a poverty unambiguously described by numerous contemporaries.

The provisions for dealing with the sick fall under two heads — Medical Charities and the Poor Law — in theory distinctive, in practice during the famine to a degree interdependent especially after the 1847 Fever Act (10 Vict., c.31). Scrupulous separateness was reserved mainly for the dictates of the administration, the requirements of the legislature, and the presumptions of their vocal critics, many even within the profession, who saw in the eternal struggles for dominance in the fields of care and relief a stick with which to beat the government who they supposed were subverting the traditional freedom of the profession to run its own institutions, placing power instead in the hands of the 'bashaws of Somerset House' and their local surrogates. The role of the Poor Law is dealt with elsewhere in this book; I will just note here that by the autumn of 1846 — the start of the second successive potato crop failure — all 130 union workhouses were open, each had an infirmary of sorts, about 40 per cent had some sort of isolation building to serve as a fever hospital most of 25-60 beds,[20] and the Guardians had powers to cater for pauper fever cases over and above this.[21] By January 1847 the total fever bed complement in the workhouses (with a further 4,762 outside) was 2,454 for a total workhouse population of 101,076 inmates,[22] allegedly adequate for anything except, of course, what actually came.[23]

Medical services supplied through medical charities were on the other hand complex in organisation, control, and genesis. In the front line were the 664 dispensaries, an average of one per 12,000 of the population, though unevenly distributed.[24] Usually a small house or cabin attended by a doctor and a 'porter', they were the offspring of local philanthropy and local rates, the (pound for pound) rate support discretionary from 1805,[25] a requirement from 1837.[26] Though they provided a nationwide service of free medicine and advice, they had a structural deficiency put well by Sir George Nicholls: 'In districts abounding in rich resident proprietors a medical charity is least wanted, but subscriptions are there most easily obtained: while in districts where there are few, or possibly no, resident proprietors, the aid is most wanted but there are no subscribers and consequently there is no medical charity'.[27] He could have added other impressive debilities — patronage and nepotism in appointments, preference shown to subscribers' tenants or staff, lack of inspection and control, rudimentary (if any) records, uneven quality of care, no defined catchment area, large rural districts; and the doctors would certainly have added — low salary (£50-£120 p.a. with a national average of £71), no perks (not even a horse!), little private practice compared to their hospital colleagues, habitual risk of contracting dangerous fevers, eternally soliciting subscriptions on which their livelihood depended, and the whole seen as a wily scheme to buy cheap medical labour subsidised by the rates. Most of the officers were surgeons, few were physicians, fewer still apothecaries, but despite its deficiencies the system was a substantial administrative and medical achievement without parallel in Britain.

Behind these were the (permanent) fever hospitals — the smaller district hospitals, and the larger county ones — discharging duties under a welter of piecemeal legislation.[28] Like the dispensaries the former were part charitable, part rate-supported (to an amount not to exceed twice the subscribed fund), the outcome over a century of the robust philanthropic conscience of the gentry tempered with their equally robust fear of 'contagion'! They suffered from the deficiencies of the dispensaries especially in that being 'demand-led' they were overcrowded during epidemics when the appalling scenes inside and around their doors, and the high mortality among their inmates, made them widely hated and feared. There were 73 in 1845. Backing these were county fever hospitals, fully rate-supported, owing little to philanthropic instinct but much to sheer panic at the persistence and lethality of the fever pandemic of 1816-1820. There were 28 of these in 1845, that is 101 fever hospitals in all, whose unevenness of national spread reflected the charitable impulse, wealth and fear, of the men of property whose money supported them: none in Longford, Louth and Roscommon, one in Antrim, Leitrim, Mayo, Meath, Leix, Sligo, and Westmeath, and as many as 12 in Tipperary and 13 in Cork.[29] It would be wrong to equate them with a modern infectious disease hospital: small and poorly-equipped, often grossly overcrowded, widely seen as antechambers of death — though death had already claimed many sufferers before they could reach a fever hospital over difficult rural terrain — and with funds inadequate for expansion or even decent maintenance, they were 'inadequate for the expansion necessary to meet a sudden emergency'.[30]

There were three other categories of medical charity — lunatic asylums, county infirmaries, and general voluntary hospitals. The first played only a coincidental role in the famine; the second two should likewise since in theory they accommodated only treatable, non-contagious cases, but humanity and necessity forced many to accept fever cases at the height of the emergency, though only in 1847 did deaths in the county infirmaries exceed 1,000 mainly due to increases in fever, diarrhoea, dysentery, and dropsy, famine-related diseases sure enough but a numerical flea-bite set against the numbers dying elsewhere from true flea-bite fever![31]

For the main part rate-funded, small — average 50-60 beds — but usually adequate for normal need, the county infirmaries were the piecemeal response to voluntary Christian philanthropy bolstered by secular legislation from 1765.[32] In 1846 there were 41: five in Dublin, three in Cork, two in each of Limerick, Wicklow, and Louth, and one in each of the other counties.[33] Behind and above them were the general teaching hospitals, the gems in the Irish medical diadem. Dublin had 12 (most survived until the hospital reorganisation of the nineteen-eighties); Limerick, Waterford and Belfast had one each (the Belfast General Hospital — or Fever Hospital up to 1847 — and Dispensary, Frederick Street, forerunner of the Royal Victoria Hospital); and there was the special case of the naval hospital at Haulbowline, Co. Cork. Their bed complement was about 2,500. Though they were involved in the emergency as hospitals reflecting the disease quantum and variety in the major cities, like the county infirmaries their involvement was modest; even in 1847 the number of deaths (824 as against 546 in 1844) was unremarkable.[34] Their main importance was as theatres for the work and teaching of that eminent *coterie* which numbered some of the greatest doctors in Europe.

Though an *élite*, this *coterie* did not inhabit a Versailles world. The sufferings of the country and of their colleagues moved them deeply, and they played a prominent role in fighting disease on the ground, disseminating knowledge with the pen and in lectures, and through voluntary service on committees from hospital units up to the Central Board of Health. Some, time and again, advised and exhorted government, and in Arthur Jacob they had a ferocious polemicist of genius to carry their causes (and some of his own!) to a wide public through the columns of the *Dublin Medical Press,* which he founded and chiefly edited. These achievements have been diluted by time and distorted by events notably surrounding the 'five shilling affair' (the basic daily fee offered to doctors attending fever patients in dispensaries and hospitals). Consequently, J. O. Curran, for example, Professor of the Practice of Medicine at Apothecaries' Hall who died of typhus on 26 September 1847 contracted while attending the poor, has come down less as a doctor suffering the accepted dangers of his profession but more as a martyr for his sorely exploited profession — or to its putative pecuniary and restrictive interests — depending on viewpoint in that he contemptuously refused to accept the five shillings pittance not because it was too much but because it was too little.[35] In fact the heavy medical mortality before[36] and during[37] the famine is an eloquent testimony to the profession's commitment.

On the eve of the famine the facilities were adequate (in contemporary terms) for normal demand; by the standards of much of Europe they were lavish. The workhouses and their fever 'hospitals' had spare accommodation;[38] the district and county fever hospitals met cyclical demand by blatant overcrowding and other expedients, rarely by erecting temporary huts or sheds, and when the fever abated extra staff crept quietly away, no longer a charge on charitable or public funds.[39] Furthermore, there were the wide powers given to the Poor Law Guardians (under 6 and 7 Vic., c.92, clauses 15 and 16) in 1843 — 'smuggled in' as Jacob inevitably had it[40] — to make provision for the fevered poor outside the workhouse if necessary. And so with 101 fever hospitals, workhouses open in all 130 unions, a comprehensive if uneven dispensary network of 664 units with a back-up of county infirmaries, *élite* teaching hospitals and distinguished staff, the profession and legislators could congratulate themselves on the work of the past 40 years. They knew that fever lurked in the squalid hovels of the rural tenantry and in the foetid and crowded courts and tenements of the cities; they knew it was contagious though they did not know how or why. They knew that after a potato crop failure fever increased and spread (as the starving carried their lice and fleas across the country);[41] some, including Dominic Corrigan, who was to be highly influential, considered (in the strict sense erroneously) famine and fever to be cause and effect[42] — 'want and fever precede and succeed as cause and effect' as the *Lancet* put it.[43] They knew the danger of relying for food on a single uncertain crop, but they also knew its high nutritional value if eaten copiously so that the Irish peasantry was among the most robust, vigorous and fecund in Europe.

In the face of these potentials for disaster the profession sustained its optimism by empiricism and appeal to history: few fever pandemics had followed the numerous crop failures of the past century; and crop failures had usually been regional and limited to one season.[44] So when the editor of the *Gardeners' Chronicle and Horticultural Gazette* held up publication of the issue for September 13, 1845, to announce 'the potato Murrain has unequivocally declared itself in Ireland', the profession and government were unperturbed, indeed as unperturbed as with the earlier news of blight in Europe and England. Only when the failure was confirmed as widespread did Peel act by establishing, in November, a scientific commission to study methods of preservation of harvested healthy potatoes,[45] followed by the 'Scarcity Commission for Ireland' (called usually the 'relief commission') initially to administer the £100,000 worth of Indian corn which he had sanctioned on his own authority to prevent famine though also to prevent erosion of Poor Law principles of exclusive in-house relief.[46] Each commission had one medical member — the recently knighted Sir Robert Kane whose credentials for the former were impeccable, though those for the latter were less obvious, 'but, mainly, he is a Roman Catholic'.[47] The medical profession remained on the sidelines for several months trying to read the future from the experience of the past, but from March 1846 they were bullied and exhorted by Jacob[48] and persuaded by circumstances, as much at first medico-political as medical *per se,* onto the field which they did not vacate for several years. These circumstances are now described.

III: The Early Responses of the Profession

Initial government optimism evaporated as the potato failure became virtually nationwide and as Corrigan's 1846 tract[49] gained acceptance. Its response was the Fever Act of March 1846[50] 'to make temporary provision for the treatment of destitute poor persons afflicted with fever in Ireland', to expire on 1st September 1847. The centrepiece was to be a Central Board of Health of five commissioners with wide powers covering all fever hospitals whether under Poor Law or Medical Charities. Even before the commissioners were appointed the Fever Act was criticised by Jacob on three counts: it was unnecessary since adequate powers already existed;[51] it was subverting the Medical Charities by subordinating them to the apparatus of the Poor Law; and the three medical commissioners had been appointed without reference to the Dublin professional bodies.[52] Wakely (in the *Lancet*) and Jacob (in the *Dublin Medical Press*) emphasised, exaggerated, distorted, and cleverly played on these concerns in passages of vintage polemic, Jacob even alleging that government's new-found and precipitate fear of fever had been stimulated by false statistics which it had knowingly swallowed in order to enact an extension of its patronage.[53] To him the Act was 'a contrivance to subvert existing institutions for the purpose of transferring place and patronage to other hands . . . the faggot, unpaid, irresponsible metropolitan board, the union 'medical officer', the taxation by official ordinance, and the machinery of concentration, reveal the real object [which is to] take the fever hospitals out of the hands of the country gentlemen and the physicians and surgeons who managed them, and to transfer them to the poor-law authorities for the sake of the patronage and influence they afforded'.[54] Not everyone would have agreed — Jacob's hobbyhorse of the government stalking the medical charities was frequently ridden — but when the names of the three medical commissioners were announced (Sir Robert Kane, Sir Philip Crampton,[55] and Dr Dominic Corrigan[56]), none a nominee of a royal college or medical school, one in fact hardly practising (Kane), and two (Kane and Corrigan) Roman Catholics, Jacob had the bulk of the profession at least tacitly on his side:

> But now that [the Commissioners] are appointed, the duties to be performed do not appear of the most onerous description. We wanted no ghost to come from the grave to tell us whether or not fever was raging in Dublin much less the ghost of a still-born 'commission'. The affair is, we believe, little else than a scene of farce . . . The encouragement given by people in authority to adventurers volunteering their services as discoverers of abuses and assailants of existing institutions has had the most mischievous effect. For ten years long has one placehunter after another been endeavouring to provide for himself out of the *débris* of our medical charities . . . Perhaps [the leaked announcement] is only a feeler to ascertain whether the profession will or will not tamely submit to insult, and quietly acquiesce in the new practice of dressing up political puppets with the rags and feathers of science to fit them for popular admiration.[57]

Nor was Wakely to be outdone:

> Hardly had the last sheet of [Corrigan's] promising brochure [his 1846 fever essay][58] escaped from the press when a huxtering Board — a Board of *'Health'* — a listless triumvirate to give contagion its fling — was got up of which he was one . . . The triumvirate was totally inoperative . . . The Act a sham and an intentional sham . . . After an idle, useless existence when contagion had spread over the whole land . . . it modestly declared its existence and that it could do nothing'.[59]

And there was more, much more, from each pen, differing only in that Wakley's invective was more personalised, whereas Jacob's was aimed more at government machinations and alleged perfidy.

The beleagured Central Board of Health settled to its work at the end of March.[60] It was optimistic, which is perhaps surprising in view of Corrigan's writings on famine and fever, Routh's experience on the relief commission, and Kane's work on the ill-starred scientific commission. They were encouraged by the entrails: applications to fever hospitals though rising were mostly from women whereas in previous pandemics they had been from men; typhus seemed modest; dysentery, which was prevalent, was attributed to the hot summer; fever admissions were still below those of the 1840 epidemic which had fizzled out; everything seemed explicable in terms of temporary food shortage and internal migration. Like most who would predict the future they looked for it mirrored in the past, and they advised appropriately. But their unpopularity exposed them: attacked by Jacob, lacking the profession's confidence or the support of the medical corporations, criticised by the gentry for meddling, impotence, and extravagance (they had only 17 requests for help in five months), the Board met for the last time on 15 August — by which time its activities were confined to only four of the 130 unions[61] — and the Act was allowed to expire on 31 August even though the Commons had been informed on 16 August that 'the prospect of the potato crop this year is even more distressing than last year — that the disease has appeared earlier and its ravages are more extensive'.[62] Despite the grim outlook the board was unmourned.

This optimism was soon cruelly exposed: reports of fever multiplied as autumn progressed and the great migrations of ravenous, starving hordes of fevered scarecrows flocked to the workhouses and fever hospitals and to the reeking slums of ports and cities. Government dithered, uncertain what to do. They minimised the fever reports assuring parliament 'that the government had determined to adhere to the ordinary law as long as was possible . . . yet the country was never more free from fever in its true character than it was at present'.[63] Yet the very next day (26 January 1847) as a 'measure of precaution',[64] the Lord Lieutenant re-established the Central Board of Health under the still operative 1846 Act and with the identical membership, while new legislation was being designed which would soon be operative.[65]

Jacob exploded; not only was the 'huxtering' board to return but with the same performers, the corporations again unconsulted, the profession again slighted. In the *Dublin Medical Press* issue by issue he returned to this theme accompanied by his more personal one of the dishonourable intentions of government.

> To Sir Randolph Routh there can be no objection, except his inabilities to perform the duties, in consequence of other engagements . . . Mr Twistleton should not be there unless it [is] intended, *as we believe it is* [my italics], that the members of this board shall be the pioneers of the poor-law commissioners. As to Sir Robert Kane, we do not know what brings him there . . . To the medical profession he no longer belongs . . . and what is more, we tell him, that he never virtually belonged to it. Such homely truths may not be palatable to one

habituated to fulsome eulogy, but when we advise him to take leave of medical affairs and to part company with those engaged in the intrigues connected with them, we give him good advice. With respect to the other two . . . if the whole medical profession was searched two men of the same standing could scarcely be found less eligible for the performance of this duty . . . on no occasion [have they] kept aloof from those contentions which from time to time disturb the peace of our profession, and that neither of them is distinguished for disregard of his own interests . . . it is assumed that because men are professionally employed by people of fashion, or run after by the vulgar . . . that they are, therefore, to be considered as clever and trustworthy men of business . . . The sooner such nonsense is put out of people's heads the better.[66]

Wakley predictably was not to be outdone;[67] but opposition now broadened and in a long, measured essay, Robert Graves, one of the most illustrious Dublin physicians, entered the lists in the armour of the medical corporations, his lance at government, a dagger for Kane and Corrigan neither being a college nominee, the latter not even a Fellow of the Royal College of Physicians of Ireland, and the former hardly even a doctor!

The appointment of the present Board of Health was evidently impolitic . . . Those who found public institutions, such as the College of Physicians or the College of Surgeons, should not be the first to proclaim their inability. What is the use of having [them] if Her Majesty's ministers publicly repudiate their functions? . . . It is an act revolutionary in spirit . . . But Dr Corrigan may be excused from becoming a little giddy when he ventures into the same car as Sir Philip [Crampton] and, to the amazement of all, suddenly finds himself at an altitude so elevated that his companion, although a veteran aeronaut betrays distinct evidence of alarm.[68]

The reconvened board started energetically with a flow of directives to Poor Law Guardians and Local Health Committees: temporary wooden fever wards (or 'sheds') were to be erected offically to a prescribed plan, tents and marquees requisitioned, houses rented for fever 'hospitals', and norms for accommodation and provisioning laid down which were at once a dead letter as the temporary fever hospitals, sheds, and tents were swamped. The horrors of it all live in many eye-witness accounts sprinkled through parliamentary reports, newspapers, private publications, in the stark statistics of the census commissioners,[69] in the moving prose of some 70 doctors whose reports were collected by William Wilde in the *Dublin Journal of Medical Science,*[70] in the cutting invective of Jacob in the *Dublin Medical Press,*[71] and in the angry outbursts of outraged doctors.[72] One example must serve. In September 1846 the weekly average of patients admitted to the fever hospital at the Union, Lisburn Road, Belfast, was 20.

By January 1847 it was 55 and by April 172. A local Board of Health was established under the 1847 Fever Acts and started work on 6 May. The Union infirmary was enlarged by 90 beds, fever sheds were erected in the workhouse grounds and even a large shed beside the General Hospital in Frederick Street, the old cholera buildings were put in service, the College Hospital in Barrack Street was re-opened, and tents were set up in the workhouse grounds and in the environs of the town. By July the weekly admissions were over 600 and the total 'institutionalised' was 2,118 in a spot census on 17 July. When the epidemic ended in November and the 'normal' admission rates resumed, there had been 13,469 cases of fever admitted, 1,836 of dysentery, and 325 of smallpox with nearly 2,500 deaths all in a population of some 100,000, i.e. one in six of the population were admitted with a case mortality of 17 per cent. Add to that the countless hundreds who died outside the hospitals — in the streets, the fields, the hovels of the poor and the mansions of the rich — and extrapolate to Ireland as a whole and the enormity of the 1847 fever pandemic can be calculated if hardly credited.[73]

IV: The Profession at the Height of the Epidemic

The 'new' Fever Acts of 1847 enabled the Central Board of Health and the Poor Law Guardians to strengthen their grip on organising extra accommodation and in employing and deploying doctors: this was at the expense of local medical autonomy with more and more power channelled through the pivotal but unpopular board which continued to attract the censure and obloquy of the medical polemicists. The counter-arguments were hardly aired in the journals they controlled. There is little evidence that these political, administrative and legal niceties, worried the bulk of the country's doctors significantly in 1847: swamped by a tragedy they were powerless to prevent or even attenuate, their role mere distributors of the futile palliatives of the day, and exposed to lethal fevers and the torment of the pitiable scenes around them, they for the main part stuck conscientiously to their posts and looked to their leaders in the medical corporations as their advocates and to the Central Board for tangible recognition of their plight. They received instead from the board a stinging insult: fees for attendance on temporary fever hospitals and dispensaries (under 10 and 11 Vic. c. 22) were to be as little as 5 shillings per day, on top of any other salary, if in 'the town or district where the medical officer resides', though more generous rates were on offer 'if sent to a distant district'.[74] Moreover, though the fees were set by the Treasury and communicated by Trevelyan, 'assistant secretary' to the Treasury but its *de facto* permanent head, they were on the board's recommendation. The board were now roundly blamed for not pressing for more, more particularly Corrigan was blamed since in the profession's eyes he *was* the board by virtue of his regular attendance, authority, and influence, Kane being an absentee and Crampton largely an ornament.[75]

The profession rebuffed by the board, spurred-on by Wakley and much of the Dublin press (though not Jacob), with the inspiration of Curran's dramatic stance[76], and with the support of many of the 'medical Dublin magnates',[77] drew up in June a petition, alike temperate and dignified, addressed to the Lord Lieutenant and signed by over 1,000 physicians and surgeons, over half the country's total[78] including *inter alia* the ultra-luminaries, Stokes and Graves; Cusack, the president of the Royal College of Surgeons in Ireland; Carmichael and Wilmot, former presidents; *not* Sir Henry Marsh, late President of the Royal College of Physicians of Ireland; Wilde (but not Jacob who had mixed feelings); and such younger talent as Collins and Law. The petition basically requested 'such remuneration to be awarded to the medical officers of fever hospitals and fever districts as may be commensurate with the great value and importance of the duties required of them'.[79] Nothing came of it,[80] but the insult festered, the board, especially Corrigan, bacame ever more unpopular their every move scrutinised by their colleagues, and now watched by the newspapers (the *Nation* and the *Evening Packet* in particular) for copy as sticks to beat the government and its organ, the *Evening Post*. Much to the delight not just of Wakley, Corrigan was rejected for honorary Fellowship of the Royal College of Physicians of Ireland in November 1847 when he unwisely allowed his name to go forward under the sponsorship of Sir Henry Marsh, who in the event absented himself.[81] Government were annoyed at this slight to Corrigan and the implied slight to themselves and now outflanked the profession and had Corrigan appointed as the Queen's Physician in Ordinary in Ireland that December. This was a cue for some particularly vicious obloquy from Wakely: 'So thrives what cannot but be called professional treason . . . that while it is bad in principle for a government to reward, with bribes and honours, those medical men who are willing to set themselves in opposition to the wishes, interests, honour of their professional brethren, it is yet far worse that a profession should have within its bosom men of name and note who can stoop to grasp such temptations'.[82] We have not heard the end of Corrigan in this essay.

The unpopularity of the board, the intentions of government, and the 'five shilling affair' rumbled on in the medical press for months, but by the autumn of 1847 the profession, already battling with the rampant consequences of the second successive potato failure, were bracing themselves to face the third. The wide powers in the 'new' 1847 Fever Acts — which *inter alia* put fever expenses as a charge on the general relief fund and not on the rates, and the responsibility for provision on the relief comittees under direction from the Central Board, which had been slow to be involved at local level — were now exercised with a vengeance. Much of the central drive came from Corrigan who like his fellow commissioners worked altruistically without fee, salary, or reward of any sort: in quieter retrospect most were later to endorse the view that 'the country at large owed much to the unceasing energy and immense capacity for work which Corrigan then displayed. After a hard day's work of hospital and private practice it was no unusual thing for him to devote six or eight hours to tedious office work, receiving and answering communications from all parts of Ireland'.[83] Many local Boards of Health were established which petitioned the Central Board for temporary fever hospitals; the board either acceded on the evidence or sent medical inspectors (stigmatised by Wakley and Jacob as *protégés* of government lackeys who qualified for the largest scales of pay!) to report. In all, 576 applications were made, and 373 granted. At first tents were widely used, mostly in the rural areas: on 31 May, 35 tents and 96 'hospital marquees' — military tents of 14 beds — were dispatched by the ordnance department from their holding in Ireland of 1,528 with a reserve in England of a further 1,900. Many more were put out during the summer until by July the Board of Ordnance had to halt civilian supplies; thereafter sheds and huts were the main 'temporary hospitals' in rural areas as they had been all along in urban ones. In September these in total housed 26,378 patients and before the board was wound up in August 1850, nearly 600,000 fever patients had been treated in them — more accurately had been housed, watered and fed until they recovered or died.[84]

Such an effort required abundant manpower for extra duties as well as replacements of medical casualties. The latter were substantial: 81 medical men and pupils had died in 1843, 63 in 1844, 93 in 1845, 95 in 1846, and 192 were to die in 1847, an attrition during 1845-47 greater than 'normal' recruitment.[85] Moreover, it would require some direction of labour; the contemporary political philosophy ensured that the supply side was met by the wide powers enacted in 1847 for the board to recruit in the open market and there were mutterings of direction of government doctors from Britain if needed! Indeed, the much criticised low fees on offer would have facilitated recruitment though only by bringing in many of dubious quality.[86] Research is needed into the origins and qualifications of the 473 additional doctors appointed for fever duty up to the cessation of the Fever Acts in August 1850,[87] but from nominal lists of victims, and the realities of the situation, most were probably Irish.[88] This would only have been an issue up to the 1848 Fever Act (11 and 12 Vic., c.131) — when reappointments were transferred to the hands of the Poor Law Guardians who often forced an election to replace the incumbent with a local *protégé* — but in fact it seems to have been the practice of the Central Board up to that time to appoint *existing* dispensary or hospital doctors to take charge of fever hospitals or extra dispensaries as far as possible, and for sound reasons.[89] Jacob's obsessive concern with the Guardians' patronage was certainly not empty rhetoric, but Wakley, now pre-occupied in stepping the stony path to the (British) Public Health Act of 1848, after an initial flourish of elegant polemic fell silent:

> The triumvirate [Board of Health] was empowered to appoint medical officers to new fever hospitals or to districts requiring domiciliary attendance. And lo, forth it comes with its scale of prices [the 'five shillings'] for the greatest amount of medical ignorance coupled with the coolest medical presumption. This proclamation at the Castle mart was ineffectual . . . Whereupon the Whig government threatened, through the triumvirate, to send over a corps of State doctors from England, wisely adding another corps of sappers and miners to bury additonal dead consequent upon the coming of the former[90],

leaving Jacob to carry the fight almost single-handed, which he did coupled with an on-going tirade against government subversion of his precious medical charities! Supportive letters from doctors are scattered throughout his columns, but there is little evidence that the profession at large saw anything unduly remiss (nepotism and patronage were hardly new!) except the unremitting hazard of their daily round.

As the grim winter gave way to spring 1848 the worst seemed over. Fever in most metropolitan areas was in decline, mortality was falling, relief was on a wider scale, and though there were to be crop failures in 1848 and 1849 they were less widespread, noticeably in 1849. Famine diseases were declining also if more gradually due no doubt to reduction of susceptible individuals, successes of the Fever Acts, and many other reasons brilliantly discussed by Sir William MacArthur.[91] Many temporary fever hospitals were soon to be closed, doctors discharged, new Fever Acts passed,[92] and though fever and dysentery lingered on through 1849 and 1850 their lethality was by then attributable to past rather than current privations of their victims. The Fever Acts were finally terminated in August 1850; 'normality' had officially returned! The medical journals now turned to cholera; the medical politicians to giving advice for future legislation; the medical polemicists to upbraiding government; the profession to simply and charitably counting and honouring its dead, raising funds for bereaved medical families, reviewing the epidemic for medical lessons and medical posterity, and in the longer perspective to ensuring that the lessons were learned and acted on. The first three need not concern us; the short-term response of the profession at large does.

V: The Profession in the Immediate Aftermath

Mortality. The medical mortality was staggering. Two leading Dublin doctors, William Stokes and James William Cusack (president of RCSI, 1847) who had already reviewed 'normal' attrition,[93] organised a further survey to cover 'physicians, surgeons, diplomates of a university or chartered corporate body, apothecaries, and also pupils entrusted with the care of people particularly during the late epidemic'.[94] The mortality figures were subsequently amended upwards but remained an underestimate (Tables 1 and 2).[95] They estimated 'that during . . . the late epidemic, 500 Irish medical men, at the lowest computation, suffered from fever or other epidemic diseases contracted for the most part in discharge of public duties'. Between March 1843 and January 1848, 524 doctors and pupils died including nearly 200 in 1847, 68 per cent of these from 'fever and dysentery', compared to about 30 per cent in the 'normal' years 1843 and 1844, and all in a medical population put at only some 2,600 at any one time.[96] These statistics speak more eloquently than the harrowing reports and panegyrics which crowd the medical and lay press.

Table 1. *Numbers of Medical Men & Pupils who Died in Ireland*
26 March 1843-1 January 1848[1]

	1843	1844	1845	1846	1847	Total
Leinster	20	11	20	26	33	110
Munster	19	9	15	15	48	106
Ulster	4	9	11	20	44	88
Connaught	4	5	9	4	25	47
Unknown	2	9	10	21	30	72
Total[2]	49(74)	43(62)	65(88)	86(90)	180(179)	423(493)
Pupils[2]	3(7)	1(1)	1(5)	4(5)	11(13)	20(31)
Total[2]	52(81)	44(63)	66(93)	90(95)	191(192)	443(524)

1.   Constructed from Cusack and Stokes, *D.J.M.S.,* V (1848), p. 126.

2.   Figures in brackets are as 'adjusted' by the authors themselves [*Lancet,* (1848), p. 645].

Table 2. Deaths among Medical Men and Pupils in Ireland by Cause
26 March 1843 - 1 January 1848[1]

Disease	1843	1844	1845	1846	1847	Total
Epidemic & Contagious[2]	19(17)	11(11)	20(18)	33(30)	131(123)	214(199)
'Sporadic'	28	27	36	44	42	177
Violent or Accidental Death	1	2	1	2	8	14
Unspecified	4	4	9	11	10	38
Total	52	44	66	90	191	443
% due to 'Fever'	33	25	27.3	33.3	64.4	48.3

1. Based on combined figures in Cusack and Stokes, *D.J.M.S.* V (1848), p. 120-1.
2. Figures in brackets are deaths from 'fever'.

Medical Benevolent Fund. In 1842 Dr Kingsley of Roscrea, Co. Tipperary, established the Medical Benevolent Fund Society of Ireland ('The Society') on the lines of the (English) Medical Benevolent Fund instituted in 1836. A prudent requirement was that no disbursement could be made until the fund reached £2,000. Contributions were modest and by 1847 only some £1,600 had been raised, £500 from Dr Richard Carmichael.[97] By early 1848 the figure was £1,817[98] and by June had only just reached the crucial £2,000. The list was narrowly based: less than ten per cent (some 200) of all doctors in Ireland subscribed with some 70 from Dublin, 40 from Belfast and district, 20 from Armagh, eight from Cork, 'whilst Limerick sends us but one guinea; Waterford none; Derry none; and in a word all the remaining towns and districts of Ireland only 50'.[99] There was a further constraint: the Society's terms did not restrict payments exclusively to dependents of fever victims and so when the (London) Ladies Relief Association for Ireland wished to distribute £500 to such dependents, another vehicle — the Medical Temporary Relief Committee ('the Committee') — was formed. This comprised seven prominent medical men all members of the Society[100] and within a few weeks the £500 had been distributed, in amounts from £5 to £50, to 22 cases involving 116 persons, 17 being widows and 94 children.[101] The Ladies Association subsequently transferred a further £300 (£186-4s-7d direct to the Society to complete the £2,000, the rest to the Committee) and it appears that during 1848 the Society and the Committee disbursed over £1,000.[102] Government, who until then had refused to help the bereaved, relented, and on the personal representation of the Society's main contributor, Carmichael, it gave *ex gratia* payments of £300 each to the widows of Drs Goodison and Valentine

Flood[103] seemingly on the basis that being recipients of voluntary disbursements constituted a *prima facie* case both of need and worthiness! As Jacob presciently remarked, 'it is not unlikely that this will be made a precedent in future cases',[104] as indeed it was, and the affairs of the Society *as an issue* disappear from the press and the Medical Temporary Relief Committee was wound up. The Society continued to disburse funds to bereaved medical families swollen in number by the cholera of 1848-50, and exists to this day, in Northern Ireland as part of the Royal Medical Benevolent Fund Society.

The Epidemic Reviewed. Bare statistics were not enough; the aggregate experience and opinions of the medical survivors were gathered, collated, analysed, and placed at the disposal of the profession and posterity largely by Wilde, at 33 now at the height of his energies. He circularised a 44-item questionnaire to 'those medical practitioners . . . from whom I thought it likely [to] obtain the desired information' and published responses from over 70 replies covering 280 pages of the *Dublin Journal of Medical Science.*[105] The medical importance of this exercise is for discussion elsewhere: much formed the basis of MacArthur's classic description of the medical aspects of the famine, which is still unsuperseded, and throughout the narratives there runs a common thread of danger, tragedy, suffering on the grandest scale, yet stoicism, bravery, and human compassion expressed usually in crisp clinical terms but through which emotion inevitably breaks. It is a fitting testimony to people and profession alike. The accounts, and their influence on the reorganisation of the medical sevices, were far-reaching but are another story.

VI: Concluding Comment

MacArthur emphasises the mistaken optimism of the 1846 Board of Health in believing that the potato blight would be limited to a single year's crop, and for their misreading the medical portents that crucial summer.[106] However, their ill-prophecies made little difference. Contemporary methods of disease control involved isolating the infected, thorough cleansing of body and clothes, fumigating and limewashing houses, and controlling population movement; in short, fever Bastilles, *cordons sanitaires,* and a massive refurbishing and even rehousing programme. The fever hospitals both permanent and 'temporary' were a significant gesture towards the first, but the *cordons sanitaires,* though fitfully and locally instituted, as in Cork, were out of the question as a coherent national policy: for example, at the height of the emergency upwards of three million people were on outdoor relief which could not be organised without congregations and crowds. Refurbishing and rehousing were even more unrealistic though some unions were active in limewashing victims' homes. The bare fact is that the second successive potato failure produced a quantum leap into realms hardly even imagined and never seriously entertained, facilities were swamped though never quite drowned even though this meant on occasions turning fever patients away from 'permanent' *and* 'temporary' fever hospitals. Incredibly the administrative machinery remained basically operative, and it is unlikely that less parsimony, more vigour and foresight, and stronger central authority would have significantly reduced mortality or shortened the epidemic. This of course refers to post-famine fever; the system which ensured such a vulnerability and dealt with it in the way, on the scale, and under the political philosophy which it did, are for others to debate.

The medical profession (and its colleague disciplines) emerge with credit. They appear for the main part to have done their duty and taken their appalling casualties in best tradition. Derelictions no doubt occurred and the numerous panegyrics are hardly unbiased, but the evidence as regards at least the 'doctors', is of a committed and truly professional body of men, with renegades minimal, and if many found the traditional rural pursuits of their class overly amenable, or the competition for place too fierce to enter without benefit of 'connexion',[107] at least these amiable weaknesses pre-dated the famine and were not unduly enervating in face of the emergency. Manpower shortfall, if any, was also soon made up.

William Stokes spoke measured words some years later:

If many were lost, perhaps ignorantly, let us think of the numbers saved. We cannot be suddenly wise. Nations, as well as individuals, must purchase experience, even though the cost be serious. And whatever fault we may find with the modes adopted for relief to the sufferers in the famine of 1847, we must applaud the intention, and be grateful for the efforts that were made.[108]

References

1. P.P. Boyle and C. Ó Gráda, 'Fertility Trends, Excess Mortality, and the Great Irish Famine', *Demography*, XXIII, 4 (1986), p. 543.
2. *Report of the Commissioners appointed to take the Census of Ireland for the Year 1841* (Brit. Parl. Papers, 1843 (504) XXIV).
3. Especially of children (Boyle and Ó Gráda, *Demography*, p. 546; J. Lee, 'On the Accuracy of the Pre-Famine Censuses', in J.M. Goldstrom and L.A. Clarkson (eds), *Irish Population, Economy and Society: Essays in Honour of the Late K.H. Connell* (Oxford, 1981), p. 54; J. Mokyr, *Why Ireland Starved. A Quantitative and Analytical History of the Irish Economy, 1800-1850* (London, 1985), pp. 30 et seq., 262 et seq.

F

4. Boyle and Ó Gráda, *Demography,* p. 543.

5. *Census of Ireland for the Year 1851. Part VI, General Report* (Brit. Parl. Papers, 1856 (2134) XXXI).

6. Boyle and Ó Gráda, *Demography,* Table 8, p. 555; Mokyr, *Why Ireland Starved,* Table 9.1, p. 266.

7. W.F. Adams, *Ireland and Irish Emigration from 1815 to the Famine* (New York, 1932); Boyle and Ó Gráda, *Demography,* Table A.1, p. 560; Mokyr, *Why Ireland Starved,* p. 261 et seq.

8. O. MacDonagh, 'Irish Emigration to the United States of America and the British Colonies during the Famine', in R. Dudley Edwards and T. Desmond Williams (eds), *The Great Famine: Studies in Irish History 1845-52* (Dublin, 1956), pp. 319-88 (hereafter *Famine).*

9. Boyle and Ó Gráda, *Demography,* p. 553, The term is due to J. Mokyr, 'The Deadly Fungus: An Economic Investigation into the Short-Term Demographic Impact of the Irish Famine', *Research in Population Economics,* II (1980), pp. 246-7.

10. Modern estimates are in general accord with those of the census commissioners themselves.

11. A.G. Malcolm, *The History of the General Hospital, Belfast, and the other Medical Institutions of the Town; with Chronological Notes and Biographical Reminiscences Connected with its Rise and Progress* (Belfast, 1851), p. 133.

12. R.B. McDowell, 'Ireland on the Eve of the Famine', in Edwards and Williams, *Famine,* p. 33.

13. Founded in March 1832 by Sir Robert Kane as the *Dublin Journal of Medical and Chemical Science* it had been edited by Wilde since 1845.

14. Founded by Arthur Jacob and Henry Maunsell on 9 January 1839 as a weekly medical newspaper 'to rouse the slumbering energies of the Irish practitioner . . . and to protect the institutions of the country against the attacks of those interested in their destruction' (R.J. Rowlette, *The Medical Press and Circular 1839-1939* (London, 1939), p. 2).

15. P. Froggatt, 'The First Medical School in Belfast 1835-1849, *Medical History,* XXII (1978), pp. 237-66; 'The Distinctiveness of Belfast Medicine and its Medical School', *Ulster Medical Journal,* LIV, 2 (1985), pp. 89-108.

16. Figures from H.G. Croly, *The Irish Medical Directory* (Dublin, 1843 and 1846) and *Census, 1841,* p. 440 (Table VI).

17. J.W. Cusack and W. Stokes, 'On the Mortality of Medical Practitioners from Fever in Ireland', *Dublin Journal of Medical Science* (hereafter *D.J.M.S.*), IV (1847), pp. 134-45. The authors quantify the aphorism 'In Ireland few medical men escape fever' as 24 per cent mortality among dispensary and fever hospital doctors, 1818-1843, one in two due to typhus, compared to 10 per cent among combatant officers, 1811-1814.

18. J.O. Curran, 'Observations on Scurvy as it has Lately Appeared Throughout Ireland, and in Several Parts of Great Britain', *D.J.M.S.,* IV (1847), pp. 83-134.

19. See O. MacDonagh, *A Pattern of Government Growth 1800-1860: the Passenger Acts and their Enforcement* (London, 1961), last two chapters.

20. A union fever hospital was only mandatory if a district or county fever hospital did not exist nearby (1 and 2 Vic., c.56).

21. By removal to a fever hospital, by renting local accommodation, or by erecting temporary fever 'hospitals' (sheds or tents) in the workhouse grounds.

22. *Copies or Extracts of Correspondence Relating to the State of Union Workhouses in Ireland* (Brit. Parl. Papers, 1847 (790) LV), pp. 68-9 (hereafter *Workhouses*).

23. W.P. MacArthur, 'Medical History of the Famine', in Edwards and Williams, *Famine*, pp. 263-315 (herafter MacArthur, *History*).

24. These and other facts on dispensaries, from *Report from the Select Committee of the House of Lords on the Laws Relating to the Relief of the Destitute Poor and into the Operation of the Medical Charities in Ireland* (Brit. Parl. Papers, 1846 (694) XI-I), pp. xxv-xxxii, evidence of witnesses, appendices (hereafter *Medical Charities Commission*). Costings of dispensaries and fever hospitals through subscriptions and rates, 1845-48, are in *Abstract Return of the Number of Dispensaries, Fever Hospitals, and Infirmaries in Ireland . . .* (Brit. Parl. Papers, 1849 (561), XLIX).

25. 45 Geo. III, c.III.

26. 6 and 7 Will. IV, c.116.

27. G. Nicholls, *A History of the Irish Poor Law, in Connexion with the Condition of the People* (London, 1856), p. 127.

28. A. Jacob, 'The Five Fever Acts of Ireland', *Dublin Medical Press* (herafter *D.M.P.*), XV (1846), pp. 234-5.

29. *Medical Charities Commission*, p. xxvii; evidence of witnesses.

30. MacArthur, *History*, p. 292.

31. *The Census of Ireland for the Year 1851, Part V: Tables of Death* (Brit. Parl. Papers, 1856 (2087-II) XXX), pp. 24-5 (herafter *Census 1851, V*).

32. 5 Geo. III, c.20.

33. *Medical Charities Commission*, pp. xxviii-xxix; minutes of evidence; appendix.

34. *Census 1851*, V. pp. 2-3, 10-14.

35. See the panegyrics in the *Lancet*, ii (1847), p. 367 (by Wakley), and in *D.J.M.S.*, IV (1847), pp. 500-11 (by Wilde).

36. Cusack and Stokes, *D.J.M.S.*, IV (1847), pp. 134-45.

37. J.W. Cusack and W. Stokes, 'On the Mortality of Medical Practitioners in Ireland; Second Article', *D.J.M.S.*, V (1848), pp. 111-28.

38. *Workhouses*, 1847 (766) LV; 1847 (790) LV; 1847 (863) LV.

39. *Census 1851*, V, pp. 30-5.

40. Jacob, *D.M.P.*, XV (1846), pp. 234-5.

41. W. Harty, *An Historic Sketch of the Causes, Progress, Extent, and Mortality of the Contagious Fever Epidemic in Ireland During the Years 1817, 1818 and 1819* (Dublin, 1820), pp. 144-20.

42. D.J. Corrigan, *On Famine and Fever as Cause and Effect in Ireland: with Observations on Hospital Location and the Dispensation in Outdoor Relief of Food and Medicine* (Dublin, 1846).

43. 'Review of Corrigan on Fevers', *Lancet*, i (1846), p. 219. For a dissenting view from Corrigan's, see H. Kennedy, *Observations on the Connexion between Famine and Fever in Ireland and Elsewhere* (Dublin, 1847), and reviews e.g. in *British and Foreign Medical Review*, XXIV (1847), p. 285. Corrigan's views prevailed.

44. Twenty-four previous failures were noted by the 1851 Census Commissioners (*Census 1851*, 1856 [2087-I], XXIX, pp. 238-42).

45. The members were the chemist Lyon Playfair, the botanist John Lindley, and the Irishman Sir Robert Kane, chemist and (non-practising) physician, president-elect of Queen's College, Cork, author of *The Industrial Resources of Ireland*

(Dublin, 1844), founder of the *D.J.M.S.,* founder member of the Central Board of Health, elected FRS in 1849, and much more besides. He was much admired by Peel (See T.S. Wheeler, 'Sir Robert Kane, his Life and Work', in *The Natural Resources of Ireland* (Dublin, 1844).

46. C. Woodham-Smith, *The Great Hunger: Ireland 1845-9* (London, 1962), pp. 57 et seq. (herafter *Hunger*); T.P. O'Neill, 'The Organisation and Administration of Relief, 1845-52', in Edwards and Williams, *Famine,* p. 213.

47. Peel to Sir James Graham of 9 Nov. 1845. Cited in Woodham-Smith, *Hunger,* p. 57.

48. *D.M.P.,* XV (1846), pp. 188, 219, 234-5, 251.

49. Corrigan, *On Fever . . .*

50. 9 Vic., c.6. According to the ever-suspicious Jacob, with uninentional irony, it was 'running through parliament at railroad speed as if a pestilence was desolating the land' (*D.M.P.,* XV (1846), p. 188).

51. Jacob, *D.M.P.,* XV (1846), pp. 234-5.

52. Anon (A. Jacob), 'Famine and Fever — Cause and Effect', *D.M.P.,* XV (1846), p. 219.

53. Anon (A. Jacob), 'Progress of the Famine Fever', *D.M.P.,* XVI (1846), pp. 92-3.

54. Jacob, *D.M.P.,* XV (1846), pp. 234-5.

55. Surgeon-general, president RCSI four times (1811, 1820, 1844, 1855), baronet, Crampton was experienced in health administrative matters and stood in high favour (See C.A. Cameron, *History of the Royal College of Surgeons in Ireland and of the Irish Schools of Medicine* (Dublin, 1886), pp. 354 et seq.; 'Erinensis', in M. Fallon (ed), *The Sketches of Erinensis* (London, 1979), p. 63.

56. Imporant medical polymath later to be much honoured and respected, but in 1846 (age 43) as a Catholic very much an outsider except with the lord lieutenant who had appointed him physician-in-ordinary in 1839. (See E. O'Brien, *Conscience and Conflict: A Biography of Sir Dominic Corrigan 1802-1880* (Dublin, 1983).

57. Anon (A. Jacob), *D.M.P.,* XV (1846), p. 219.

58. Corrigan, *On Fever . . .*

59. *Lancet,* ii (1847), p. 164.

60. The non-medical members were Sir Randolph Routh, senior officer in the army commissariat and chairman of the relief commission, and Edward Twistleton, resident poor law commissioner in Ireland.

61. MacArthur, *History,* p. 290.

62. *Hansard's Parliamentary Debates* (3rd ser.). LXXXVIII (1846), p. 773. Speech of Lord John Russell.

63. *Hansard* (3rd ser.), LXXXIX (1847), p. 463. Speech of Mr Labouchere, January 25.

64. Anon (A. Jacob), 'The Famine and Fever Board', *D.M.P.,* XVII (1847), pp. 78-9.

65. 10 Vic., c.7. and 10 and 11 Vic., c.22.

66. Anon (A. Jacob), *D.M.P.,* XVII (1847), p. 79.

67. *Lancet,* ii (1847), p. 164.

68. R.J. Graves, 'Letter to the Editor of the Dublin Quarterly Journal of Medical Science, Relative to the Proceedings of the Central Board of Health of Ireland', *D.J.M.S.,* IV (1847), pp. 513-44.

69. *Census 1851*, V, *passim.*
70. W.R.W. Wilde, 'Report upon the Recent Epidemic Fever in Ireland', *D.J.M.S.*, VII (1849), pp. 64-126, 340-404; VIII (1849), pp. 1-86, 270-339.
71. Anon (A. Jacob), 'Mortality in the Medical Profession from Fever' *D.M.P.*, XVIII (1847), pp. 157-8. 'The mud walls of an old cottage, eked out with boarding, and covered with straw, formed his "fever hospital" in which nearly sixty patients were under [his] treatment at the time he contracted the disease, of which he died after a few days' illness'.
72. For example, J.O. Curran, 'Operation of the Last Fever Acts', *Ibid,* pp. 138-9.
73. Facts from Malcolm, *General Hosital,* pp. 130-1; and J.S. Reid, in Wilde, *D.J.M.S.*, VIII (1849), pp. 289 et seq.
74. Regulations printed in full in *D.M.P.*, XVIII (1847), p. 30. Wakley was typically pungent: 'carpenters, slaters and painters on the outside of the buildings [temporary fever hospitals] get 5/6 pay. There is not an assurance office in Dublin which would insure the life of one of the practising physicians at present' (*Lancet*, ii (1847), p. 26). More had been paid to the health commissioners for cholera in 1831-2, which also included Crampton!
75. In the 15 weeks from 1st April 1847, attendance at the (usually) daily meetings were: Crampton 42, Twistleton 12, Kane 2, and Corrigan 87. Crampton was often in London, Twistleton was busy as a poor law commissioner, Kane had the relief committee and University College, Cork. Corrigan was frequently the only member present (Graves, *D.J.M.S.*, IV (1847), pp. 525-7.
76. J.O. Curran, a prominent Dublin physician from Lisburn, contemptuously refused the money and instead worked gratuitously in the Dublin General Dispensary. His death from typhus in September 1847 gave him almost martyr's status (W.R.W. Wilde, 'John Oliver Curran MB', *D.J.M.S.*, IV (1847), pp. 500-11.
77. *D.M.P.*, XVIII (1847), pp. 61-2.
78. Christened 'The Irish Medical Representation' by Wakley (*Lancet*, ii (1847), p. 103). Wilde had previously called a general meeting of the profession but later cancelled it, the 'representation' being subsequently compiled.
79. The petition is printed in full in Graves, *D.J.M.S.*, IV (1847), pp. 520-1.
80. The lord lieutenant on 26 July refused in a few lines whose 'brevity is unquestionable; but it is certainly not very flattering in its manner, or condescending in its style . . . [it is] so laconic as to be actually insulting' (*Ibid,* p. 522).
81. *Lancet*, ii (1847), pp. 469, 526. The vote was 15-12. Sergeant, a supporter of Corrigan, was ousted as secretary. (See also extract from *Medical Gazette*, in *D.M.P.*, XVIII (1847), p. 283.
82. *Lancet*, ii (1847), p. 660.
83. Anon, 'In Memoriam. Sir Dominic John Corrigan', *D.J.M.S.*, LXIX (1882), pp. 268-72.
84. MacArthur, *History,* p. 298; Woodham-Smith, *Hunger,* p. 201; *Census 1851*. V. *passim.*
85. Cusack and Stokes, *D.J.M.S.*, V (1848), pp. 111-28 as corrected later (*Lancet*, i (1848), p. 645).
86. *D.M.P.*, XVIII (1847), p. 62.
87. Nicholls, *Irish Poor Law,* p. 326.

88. *Lancet*, i (1848), p. 645.

89. Letter from W.H. Hopper, secretary, Central Board of Health, to the clerk of the Union, Bailieborough, of 19 Sept. 1848 (*D.M.P.*, XX (1848), pp. 330-2.).

90. *Lancet*, ii (1847), p. 164.

91. MacArthur, *History*, pp. 263-315.

92. By end-1849, 114 fever hospitals supported by the rates and founded under the Fever Acts and 120 not under these Acts, were still open costing that year respectively some £50,000 and £32,000 (*Abstract of Returns of the Number of Temporary Fever Hospitals still kept in each Union in Ireland, under the Act 11 and 12 Vict. c.131 Etc.* (Brit. Parl. Papers, 1850 (442) LI), pp. 1-6. Also see *Abstract of Returns as to the Medical Charities in Ireland, County Hospitals or Infirmaries, Fever Hospitals, or any other Supported Wholly or in Part from County Funds* (Brit. Parl. Papers, 1850 (758) LI), pp. 1-7.

93. Cusack and Stokes, *D.J.M.S.*, IV (1847), pp. 134-45.

94. Cusack and Stokes, *D.J.M.S.*, V (1848), pp. 111-28.

95. *Lancet*, i, (1848), p. 645.

96. Figures from H.G. Croly, *The Irish Medical Directory*, (Dublin, 1843 & 1846), and *Census of 1841*, Table VI, p. 440.

97. 'Medical Benevolent Fund Society of Ireland', *D.M.P.*, XIX (1848), pp. 382-3. Carmichael was a prominent Dublin doctor, co-founder of the Richmond Hospital school of anatomy, medicine and surgery, and founder president of the Medical Association of Ireland, 1839-49. He was drowned in 1849, while riding on the shore from Dublin to his house at Sutton.

98. *D.J.M.S.*, V (1848), pp. 286-8.

99. 'Medical Benevolent Fund Society of Ireland', *D.M.P.*, XIX (1848), pp. 382-3.

100. Sir Henry Marsh (chairman), James William Cusack, Robert Graves, William Stokes, William Wilde, with Drs Croker and Benson (secretaries).

101. *D.J.M.S.*, V (1848), pp. 286-8.

102. 'Meical Benevolent Fund Society of Ireland', *D.M.P.*, XIX (1848), pp. 382-3.

103. W.R.W. Wilde, 'Memoir of Valentine Flood, MD, FRCSI', *D.J.M.S.*, V (1848), p. 282.

104. *D.M.P.*, XIX (1848), p. 127. The money was paid to Mrs Flood by Clarendon, the lord lieutenant, from his personal account to avoid delay (*D.M.P.*, XXI (1849), pp. 380-1). Carmichael's will gave a further £4,500 to the Society in 1849, nearly twice their existing funds (*Ibid*, p. 399).

105. Wilde, *D.J.M.S.*, VII (1849), pp. 64-126, 340-404; VIII (1849), pp. 1-86, 270-339.

106. MacArthur, *History*, pp. 290-1.

107. Anon (A. Jacob) 'Crowded State of our Profession', *D.M.P.*, XX (1848), p. 93.

108. Cited in MacArthur, *History*, p. 315.

7

THE POOR LAW DURING THE GREAT FAMINE: AN ADMINISTRATION IN CRISIS

Christine Kinealy

Early nineteenth century Ireland was a highly regionalised country about which it is difficult to make generalisations. In no area was this more true than in the history of the Irish Poor Law. Economic, social, political and geographical variations, combined with differences in the composition of the Boards of Guardians, produced Poor Law unions with their own individual character. These differences were no less pronounced during the Famine years of 1845-51, which generated a crisis in the administration of the Poor Law. Following the first appearance of blight in 1845, the Poor Law was by-passed in favour of other forms of relief, but after 1847, the Poor Law was declared the main agency for the relief of distress.

The impact of the Famine throughout the country was uneven. Initially the distress was localised and short-term measures were introduced to relieve it, but by 1847, the 'distress' had become a 'famine' as the whole country reeled under the impact not only of food shortages within Ireland, but also an international agricultural and commercial crisis. Following the 1848 harvest, the worst of the Famine was over in much of Ulster and following the 1849 harvest, the demarcation between the areas which were showing signs of recovery and those where conditions were deteriorating had become more marked. These differences had a major impact on the way in which the Poor Law functioned. To a large extent, the regional disparities within the economy contributed to regional variations in the provision of Poor Law relief. The government, however, by insisting that local resources should finance local poor relief, refused to acknowledge these differences. In this essay, I intend to show that the Poor Law played a major role in the relief of distress during the Famine, but that this role, especially in the southern and western unions, was controlled and restricted by a government which increasingly regarded the Poor Law as a vehicle for social change rather than just a medium for the provision of relief.

The 1838 Poor Law marked a new departure in Irish social history. Prior to its introduction, the poor were relieved almost totally by private charity, if at all. Following the end of the Napoleonic Wars, the question of legislative assistance to the poor had been increasingly discussed. This resulted in a Royal Commission being appointed in 1833 which carried out an extensive survey of Irish poverty over a period of three years. Although the Commissioners made various suggestions as to how the Irish poverty could be relieved, these were received unenthusiastically by the British government which regarded the proposals as inadequate, uneconomic, and generally not in accord with contemporary economic theories.[1] Significantly, at the time that the report was being compiled, a 'new' or amended Poor Law, based on the workhouse system, was being introduced into England. Although it had been hoped that the amended Poor Law would eliminate outdoor relief in England, this, in fact, proved to be impossible. Many of the supporters of the English Poor Law within the government, however, believed that a modified form could be extended to Ireland. Accordingly, George Nicholls, an English Poor Law Commissioner, was sent to Ireland to ascertain whether a workhouse system could be established there. Following two short visits to Ireland, Nicholls reported favourably on the suitability of the English system for Ireland and in 1838 an Irish Poor Law Bill, closely based on his recommendations, became Law.[2]

The Irish Poor Law was modelled on the new English Poor Law of 1834. Nicholls regarded the latter as the 'parent' of the Irish one and described their common object as being to relieve destitution without encouraging dependancy.[3] The two Poor Laws differed in three important respects: firstly, Irish relief could be administered only within the confines of the workhouse, no provision being made for outdoor relief; secondly, no right to relief existed in Ireland, so that if a workhouse became full, the Poor Law was not obliged to provide alternative relief; and thirdly, no Law of Settlement was included in the 1838 Act. The first two of these three features indicates that the Irish Poor Law was intended to be more stringent than its English counterpart, whilst the third reinforced the fact that Irish people, no matter how long their residence in an area, could not acquire a right to relief. The type of law introduced in 1838 was shaped by a reluctance, which at times bordered on obsession, to allow any form of outdoor relief in Ireland. The Irish Poor Law, therefore, was to be based on a total adherence to the workhouse test, that is, relief was available only within the confines of a strictly administered workhouse.

The introduction of the Poor Law was achieved by a division of the country into 130 new administrative units known as unions, each of which was to have its own workhouse. Each workhouse was administered by an elected Board of Guardians and financed by rates which were levied locally.

Unions, therefore, were to be financially self-supporting although a loan was provided for the building of the workhouses. The function of the workhouse was both to test and to relieve destitution and thus it was the foundation of the Poor Law. Relief could only be provided to whole family units within the confines of the workhouse. Destitution was the sole prerequisite for receiving relief and the absence of a Law of Settlement meant it could be obtained in any union. A stringent application of the Poor Law test was regarded as crucial, otherwise it was feared that Ireland would be unable to bear the cost of a poor relief system. A well-managed workhouse was one which deterred people from applying for relief, whilst those who did receive Poor Law relief, would not be encouraged to stay in the workhouse building for a protracted period.[4]

Because no provision was made for outdoor relief, the new Law was inoperative until the workhouses were ready to admit paupers. The speed with which the workhouses were built and opened was impressive. By 1845, 118 workhouses were open whilst rates had been struck in all of the unions. Within the space of just a few years, a Poor Law had been introduced into Ireland. Although certain aspects of the Law were unpopular, generally it was better received than its English counterpart and rates in Ireland were more readily paid than they had been in England.[5] Most importantly, the fear that the Poor Law would be swamped by large numbers of able-bodied men proved to be groundless. The workhouses were far from full and the inmates tended to be very young, old or infirm.[6] The Irish Poor Law, therefore, despite some teething problems, was firmly established in Ireland by 1845. The potato blight of this and subsequent years, however, was to stretch its resources to the limit and so, within ten years of its introduction, the workhouse system had become an administration in crisis.

Subsistence crises were not unusual in Ireland and consequently the potato blight of 1845 was not viewed with undue alarm. Since the end of the Napoleonic Wars there had been intermittent periods of distress in Ireland and even after the introduction of the Poor Law there had been localised hardship, notably in 1839 and 1842. The ability of the Poor Law to provide relief was limited by the fact that the workhouses could only accommodate 100,000 paupers. During these years, it was decided to introduce supplementary systems of relief which were to be kept totally separate from the Poor Law.[7] This established a precedent which the government followed in 1845 when it again decided that the introduction of temporary relief measures was preferable to an extension of the Poor Law. At this stage, it believed that it was applying a temporary remedy to a 'temporary, though widespread calamity'.[8] Accordingly, in 1845 a Relief Commission was established to co-ordinate the efforts of local relief committees and superinted the distribution of £100,000 worth of Indian corn. Also, the Board of Works was given a grant to implement relief works. The government saw its own role as supporting but not superseding the duties of the landlords.[9]

The first effect which the potato blight had on the Poor Law was in regard to the workhouse diet. As early as November 1845, some Guardians found it necessary to substitute other food for potatoes which had until then formed a substantial part of the inmates' diet. By May 1846, 69 unions had been forced to modify their diets.[10] Although there was an increase in the number of workhouse inmates at the beginning of 1846, the workhouses were by no means full. Because of this, neither the Commissioners nor the Guardians felt undue alarm about the Poor Law's ability to meet the increased distress.[11]

Although the government's relief operations were due to close in August 1846, by this time the potato blight had reappeared in all parts of Ireland, making a review of the temporary relief measures necessary. The blight of 1845 had been localised but in 1846 it was much more widespread thus forcing the British government again to intervene.[12] To prepare for the inevitable increase in distress, foreign grain was once more imported and public works were again sanctioned. This time, however, the system of relief introduced was deliberately intended to throw more of the responsibility for the distress onto the Irish themselves, most notably the local landlords.[13]

Although in 1846 and 1847 the Poor Law was intended to play a subsidiary role in the provision of relief, the Poor Law Commissioners were aware that a second failure of the potato crop would put a strain on their limited resources. Usually the annual peak of distress occurred in the summer months of the following year but as early as October in 1846 the number of inmates in workhouses throughout the country was abnormally high. A few weeks later, all of the workhouses were full and by February 1847, almost 100 workhouses contained more inmates than they were officially intended to accommodate.[14]

In 1847, the destitution was even more widespread than before and under this pressure some of the government's relief works collapsed. Consequently, crowds of people went to their local workhouses and demanded relief. This led to a system of outdoor relief being provided by many Boards of Guardians which contravened the provisions of the 1838 Act and directly opposed the instructions of the Commissioners. From September 1846 to April 1847 almost half of the country's unions were administering an *ad hoc* system of outdoor relief. When asked to stop, some Boards of Guardians refused outright whilst others promised to comply as soon as alternative relief was made available. Many of those who did stop recommenced within a few days as the pressure for relief in their unions continued. Thus outdoor relief on a wide scale, generally in the form of food rations, was being provided intermittently even before it was officially introduced in August 1847.[15]

The liberal provision of relief by the Guardians resulted in a change of policy by the Central Board of Poor Law Commissioners.[16] From December 1846, it allowed the Guardians to provide additional accommodation if their workhouses became full.[17] At the same time the Central Board impressed upon the Guardians that the government would not provide the necessary money.[18] Despite both the government's and the Commissioners' desire to keep both the Poor Law and the temporary relief systems separate, the demarcation between the two forms of relief was becoming less well defined.

By the end of 1846, the government realised that the measures introduced a few months earlier had failed. In January 1847, it announced that the public works were to close and be replaced by the Temporary Relief Acts. This legislation was popularly known as the Soup Kitchen Act because it provided for the distribution of free soup. It was to be financed by the local Poor Law rates and, therefore, marked a further step towards the local provision of relief. Simultaneously it was announced that there would be major changes made in the Poor Law which would enable it, following the harvest, to become the main provider of relief.[19] The Soup Kitchen Act thus was a temporary expedient, which was passed to facilitate the transfer of relief from the public works to the Poor Law.

Although there was little evidence of blight in the 1847 potato crop, a variety of factors combined to plunge the country into a third season of distress. Within Ireland, the amount of land cultivated was much less than in previous years. Also fever, which traditionally followed periods of distress, was rampant throughout the country. Internationally, grain harvests were below average. In Britain, there was an industrial and financial crisis which had repercussions on the linen trade in Ulster.[20] Consequently, the north-eastern part of Ireland was less resistant to the potato blight than it had been in the previous two years. Overall, the effect of a small harvest combined with a more general economic recession, made further widespread distress inevitable.

The 1847 Poor Law Extension Act marked a radical departure from the 1838 legislation. This Act acknowledged the right to relief of certain groups such as the old and infirm, either inside or outside the workhouse. The able-bodied, however, could receive outdoor relief only if the workhouse was full, and even then, only subject to certain conditions. The Commissioners, in an attempt to deny outdoor relief to the able-bodied as far as possible, recommended that the workhouses should be emptied of the old and infirm inmates who could be replaced by able-bodied paupers.[21]

The 1847 Act also extended the power of the Commissioners to dissolve a Board of Guardians and alter the size of a union. Both of these provisions were used to the full. Between 1847 and 1848, 39 Boards of Guardians were dissolved and the number of workhouses was increased to 163. The most controversial section of the Act was the Gregory, or Quarter-Acre Clause, which stated that any occupier of more than a quarter of an acre of land could not be deemed destitute and accordingly, was not eligible to receive relief.[22]

The introduction of the new Poor Law has been viewed as marking a reversal in the government's policy regarding Irish distress.[23] The Extension Act, however, consolidated certain strands already present in the relief operations rather than introducing any significant changes in the provision of relief. It did, however, separate labour from relief and it further extended the principle of local accountability.

Many of the Guardians were apprehensive about the transfer of distress relief to Poor Law and the strain which it would put on their stretched financial resources. Already in some unions, the rate-payers were unable to pay their rates and the Guardians were pessimistic that this would worsen. The Commissioners were uncompromising and informed the local Boards that rates should first be collected from the local gentry and the larger rate-payers. They also recommended that the Guardians publish the names of the ten highest defaulters in an effort to embarrass them into paying. Both the police and the military were put at the disposal of the Guardians for this purpose. If the Guardians still failed to collect what was considered to be a sufficient rate, they would be dissolved and the rates impounded.[24]

The new 1847 Extension Act placed the responsibility for providing relief almost exclusively on the Poor Law. In many of the southern and western unions shortly after the harvest, the demand for relief was even higher than in the previous year and showed no signs of abating. The seriousness of the situation was realised by the Commissioners who declared 22 unions along the western seaboard to be 'distressed', that is, it was officially recognised that those unions would require external financial asistance. As Map 1 shows, the 'distressed' unions were primarily situated in the areas which were traditionally dependant on the potato for subsistence.

Following an increase in the number of deaths from starvation at the beginning of 1848, Twistleton, the Chief Poor Law Commissioner, unofficially admitted that unless the Poor Law system of relief was extended, even more deaths from starvation could be expected. If the

MAP 1. POOR LAW UNIONS OF IRELAND 1838-49

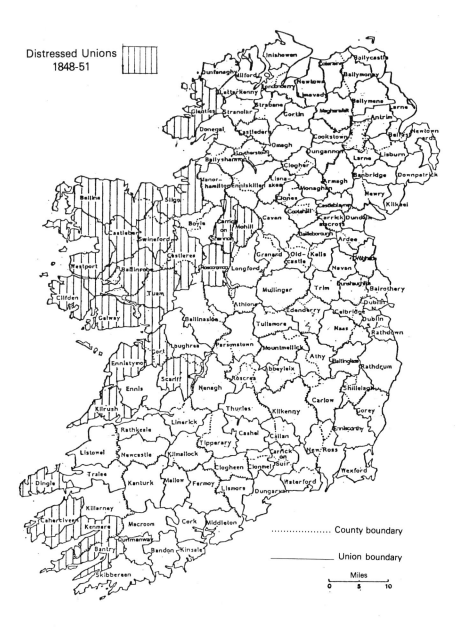

Distressed Unions
1848-51

.... County boundary

_____ Union boundary

Miles

0   5   10

Map outline courtesy of P. Ferguson

government wanted to avoid such deaths, he advised them to revive the Relief Acts of the previous year and give more money to the poorer unions. He predicted that if this happened, deaths from starvation would become unknown. Yet Twistleton was pessimistic that the government would continue to run the risk of more deaths from starvation because 'it seemed to be less evil to the Empire to encounter the risk than to continue the system of advances from the public purse'.[25]

The change-over to Poor Law relief was accompanied by hardship. Some landlords used the Poor Law, particularly the Quarter-Acre Clause, to justify evictions. The incentive for this was that the landlord was liable for the poor rate on holdings valued under £4 which meant that if rents were not being paid, the cost of the rates could exceed his income from rent.[26] Eviction threw a heavy burden on the poor rates and unless the poor could find alternative lodgings, they could not be offered outdoor relief.[27] But both the Commissioners and the government agreed that these evictions would bring long-term benefits to Ireland. The consolidation of property had been one of the aims of the Poor Law and so if poor people, or even impoverished landlords were allowed to hold onto unproductive land, they would be preventing somebody else from cultivating it more profitably.[28]

In spring 1848, the prospects for the approaching harvest seemed good but by July, blight had appeared along the western seaboard.[29] In the wake of this, even the Poor Law Commissioners were openly pessimistic about the financial ability of these unions to provide relief in the fourth consecutive year of distress.[30] The Treasury, however, who were increasingly taking control of the relief operations, declared that it still had faith in the ability of private resources to bring the country through this period.[31] It realised that as a consequence of its policies, there would be a great increase in the level of emigration, and although hopeful that this would include a large proportion of small tenants, it was apprehensive that if the more substantial farmers left the country, the collection of poor rates would become virtually impossible.[32]

The potato failure of 1848 was in many ways a watershed in the Famine. This was due to the uneven distribution of blight which resulted in an even greater contrast between the 'distressed' and 'non-distressed' unions. While in some parts of the country, most notably the north-east, the worst of the Famine was over, along the western seaboard, the effect of a fourth year of shortages was devastating. The improved situation in the north and some other parts of the country showed that in these areas, the potato failure was not a decisive factor in rural welfare. The distress in these areas, in fact, had been caused by a combination of a failure in both the potato and grain crops as well as a depression in the local linen trade. In contrast to this, in the areas where the potato was the mainstay of the subsistence economy, the population was left without resources. The Inspector of the Ballina union — one of the 'distressed' unions — summed up the situation when he said, 'the question must now be determined whether the experiment of making property support poverty is to be continued in the west of Ireland, and I have no doubt whatsoever, such a cruel experiment must ultimately fail and I therefore think it most cruel to persevere in it'.[33]

Apart from the failure of the potato crop in 1848, a number of factors combined in the west of Ireland to keep the level of destitution high. The yield from other crops was poor and fish catches were low. Although for a short period immediately following the harvest there was a glut of potatoes on the market in some areas, they were expensive. Because no employment was available, the poorest sections of the population did not have the financial resources to purchase this food. At the same time also, large-scale evictions were being carried out, most particularly in the 'distressed' unions. But of most significance was the fact that, after three years of shortage and famine, the resources of a large number of the population were totally exhausted. Twistleton described the reappearance of blight in 1848 as having reduced some of the Irish people to 'nearly the lowest point of squalor and want at which human beings can exist'.[34]

The control of the relief funds, however, lay in London, with the government and its agent, the Treasury. Their attitude was less sympathetic than that of the Poor Law Commissioners in Dublin. Both the government and the Treasury felt that the effect of the change-over to Poor Law relief was for the most part successful: it was preventing extreme destitution whilst at the same time forcing many small-holders in the poorest areas to give up their property. Sir Charles Trevelyan, who was in effect in charge of the disposal of Treasury funds, made no attempt to disguise the fact that he totally approved of the changes which were being brought about in Ireland. He likened the 'distressed' unions to a prodigal son who, while he could not be sent away, at the same time was not to be given a fatted calf; instead, the workhouse was to be offered and 1 lb. meal per day. He disliked the fact that the 'distressed' unions still needed to receive so much external financial assistance and desired to put an end to their dependence on the government.[35]

The financial resources of many unions were put under further strain in the spring of 1849 because of an outbreak of cholera in many parts of Ireland. The epidemic was particularly virulent in the western and north-western unions, especially those close to a seaport. The treatment of the disease depended largely on the individual unions' financial resources.[36] The Commissioners, for their part, wanted some of the government's advances to be used to treat the cholera but initially, the Treasury refused to sanction this.[37] When it became clear that the loss of many lives would ensue without this money, the Treasury relented but told the Commissioners that government aid and involvement was more limited than the Commissioners seemed to realise.[38] The cholera epidemic and its impact on the Irish workhouses was short-term, as it had mostly disappeared by June, but as a result of it, during the early part of 1849, in many unions outside of Ulster, the mortality rate was its highest since 1847.[39]

At this stage, a division between how the Famine was viewed by both the English and Irish administrators, was becoming obvious. When giving evidence before a Parliamentary Committee on the Poor Law in 1849, Twistleton was repeatedly very critical of the policies being enforced by the British government in response to Irish distress. He informed the Committee that in the 32 poorest unions the sum required to meet their debts and expenses for the half-year ending September 1849 was £700,000, which he described as 'very trifling indeed'. He further stated, 'I wish to remark that it is wholly unnecessary that there should be a single death from starvation this year in the distressed unions in Ireland. The machinery for the administration of relief is now tolerably complete and all that is requisite is that the necessary funds should be furnished to those who are entrusted with the administration of relief'.[40] Twistleton was emphatic about the relatively small amount of money needed in Ireland and returned to the point saying,

> the comparatively trifling sum with which it is possible for this country to spare itself the deep disgrace of permitting any of our miserable fellow subjects in the Distressed Unions to die of starvation. I wish to leave distinctly on record that, from want of sufficient food, many persons in these unions are at present dying or wasting away; and at the same time it is quite possible for this country to prevent the occurrence there of any death from starvation by the advance of a few hundred pounds'.[41]

By this time there was a noticeable change in the attitude of the government to the Commissioners. Despite protests from Ireland, the government now proposed to advance to Ireland a further £100,000 to be charged to a new national rate to be known as the Rate-in-Aid.[42] A Bill which was introduced in May 1849, made it possible for the government to provide relief to the 'distressed' unions whilst at the same time severing financial dependance on the Treasury. This was to be achieved by levying a rate on the more prosperous unions which was then to be distributed under the directions of the Treasury. The Rate-in-Aid was accompanied by a grant of £50,000 for the immediate use of the 'distressed' unions, but the government was hopeful that this would be the last grant they would have to give to these unions.[43] The introduction of this Bill marks an important change of policy by the British government in relieving Irish distress; the responsibility for relief was now to become a national rather than a local charge, but definitely not an imperial one.

Within Ireland the response to this Bill was generally unfavourable, especially in the wealthier northern unions which would be enforced to bear most of the burden of this rate.[44] But the most vociferous opponent of the Rate-in-Aid was Edward Twistleton. He believed that rates within Ireland had been generally well paid and that this Bill would not only anger ratepayers, but might deter farmers from investing capital in their land. Twistleton recommended that aid should continue to come from the state. Because he felt unable to implement this legislation 'with honour', he resigned in protest at its introduction.[45] George Nicholls, who had been responsible for establishing the Poor Law in Ireland, also objected to the Rate-in-Aid Bill. He argued that as the potato blight had been designated an imperial calamity, it warranted special treatment. Irish distress was so widespread and so severe that it required a continuation of outside aid rather than an attempt being made by the government to make Irish property alone responsible for the relief of Irish poverty. Nicholls felt that the government was ignoring the fact that 'where the land has ceased to be reproductive, the necessary means of relief cannot be obtained from it, and a Poor Law will no longer be operative, or at least not operative to the extent adequate to meet such an emergency as then existed in Ireland'.[46]

Both the government and the Treasury, however, remained intransigent. They were determined to make local landlords and the neighbours of the 'distressed' unions responsible for providing relief, believing that they would be in the best position to detect fraud and resist any unnecessary applications for aid. Trevelyan believed that by doing this, a great principle of the Poor Law would be realised, that is, 'to make the burden as near local as possible in order that it may be locally scrutinised and locally checked'.[47] The Imperial Treasury had contributed almost £10,000,000 to Irish distress and it was now determined to end Ireland's dependance on external aid. This new policy was partly determined by the fact that Britain herself was undergoing an economic recession, but more importantly it was thought that this extra tax, would loosen the dependance of many Irish people on the potato and this would facilitate a transition from small or subsistence farming to large-scale production in Ireland.[48]

Although the number of people receiving Poor Law relief increased in 1849 compared with the previous year, certain changes had occurred which the Poor Law Commissioners regarded as favourable. In 1849, a shift from outdoor to indoor relief was evident: 1,210,482 people received outdoor relief in 1849 compared with 1,433,042 people in 1848, whilst the total number receiving indoor relief was 932,284 compared with 610,463 in the previous year. Also, the living conditions within the workhouses had improved and this contributed to an overall decline in the Irish mortality rate.[49] Both of these factors resulted from an extension in the amount of workhouse accommodation available. It had increased by 70,000 places in 1849 and the Boundary Commission which had been appointed in the spring of 1848, recommended that 32 additional unions should be formed.[50] The Commissioners were optimistic that following the building of new, permanent workhouses, the granting of outdoor relief, at least to the able-bodied, would no longer be necessary.[51]

The harvest of 1849 marked the first of a series of good harvests in many parts of the country, the potato blight appearing only in some areas of the west. As a result, the Commissioners believed that abundant employment would be available in the following year to the labouring classes and this would lead to a 'stabilisation' in the administration of the Poor Law.[52] In recognition of this, all except five of the 39 Boards of Guardians which had been dissolved were reinstated in November 1849.[53] In 1849, the blight was more localised than in any year since 1845, tending to be confined to some of the unions which had already been designated 'distressed'. In their Annual Report of 1850, the Commissioners optimistically referred to an 'abundant harvest in 1849, which suffered less from blight than in previous years', but they did not mention the implications for those areas where blight had reappeared.[54] Consequently, following the harvest of 1849, it was necessary to provide 23 unions with external financial assistance, whilst a number of other unions required aid intermittently throughout the early months of 1850.[55]

Towards the end of 1849, there was a marked contrast between areas in which the Famine could be said to be 'over', and where the union was again almost able to manage its own resources, and those where the consequences of the blight were still having a devastating effect on the local population. In Ulster, the area which had suffered least during the Famine, the local Poor Law Inspector observed that he had never before seen such an abundant harvest, the potato crop being especially luxuriant. In Mayo also, an area where there had been much distress since 1845, the resident Inspector reported favourably on the prospects of the local unions. He described a new spirit of activity in the region, resulting in a reinvestment of capital in the land. This optimism was well-founded because, by the end of the year, plenty of food and fuel were available for the first time in four years. In contrast, in counties Clare, Kerry, Limerick and Tipperary, blight was widespread and it was feared that if the potato crop was not immediately consumed, it would be useless.[56]

Although by the end of 1849, a reduction in Poor Law expenditure was apparent, the impact was uneven and the poorest unions still remained in debt.[57] The Treasury viewed this partial amelioration in conditions as an opportunity to enforce the repayment of debts to the government. In the past, the amount of repayments to be made by the Irish unions had frequently caused conflict between the Commissioners and the Treasury, but Alfred Power, who replaced Twistleton, was more acquiescent than his predecessor and he promised to enforce these payments.[58] But even in the unions unaffected by blight, the financial prospects of the Poor Law were less promising than the Treasury chose to believe, and these new demands caused alarm amongst the local Guardians. Thus, the payments made were much smaller than the Treasury had estimated.[59]

At the beginning of 1850, in some of the poorer unions lack of funds for ordinary relief purposes resulted in the local administrators complaining of an increased number of deaths from starvation. In the Ennistymon union, for example, a man and his family who had been in receipt of 24½ lbs. of meal per week, for a short peiod was given only 12¼ lbs. because the local rate collecton had been so low. He died shortly afterwards. A similar case occurred in the Scariff union. There was considerable irregularity in the supply of meal to the union and this resulted in the death of a man who had received only 3½ lbs. of meal instead of the usual 21 lbs.[60] The situation within the Scariff workhouse also reflected the union's lack of funds. In January, only one-third of the meal required had been delivered to the workhouse and there had been no milk in the house for six weeks. Although the workhouse was full, pressure for admittance was increasing which resulted in overcrowding and meant that the paupers could not be provided with a change of clothing. Consequently, fever and other infectious diseases were prevalent in the house. At the beginning of February, the supplies being delivered to the union were seized by sheriff to pay off some of the unions' debts to the contractors. He then took possession of the workhouse and threatened to sell the goods within it. The meal contractor also refused to deliver any further supplies to the workhouse until he received some money. As a result, deaths from starvation were occurring daily. Although the Guardians repeatedly appealed to both the Lord Lieutenant and the Commissioners for financial help, all that the latter could do was send them small sums of money — usualy £50 to £100 — and promises to make representations on their behalf to the Treasury.[61] But in this and other similar cases of emergency, the Treasury refused to relinquish its control over the government funds, Trevelyan making it very clear that he would decide in what manner they were to be distributed.[62]

The necessity of providing the most distressed unions with financial aid forced the government again to come to the rescue of the Irish Poor Law. But although it agreed to put more money at the disposal of the Treasury, it was also determined to force the unions to repay their accumulated debts. This was to be achieved by the Consolidated Annuity Act of May 1850 which rescheduled the debts of each union and provided for their repayment in the form of annuities.[63] But genuine inability to pay this money combined with the continuing distress in some unions forced the government to relax the provisions of this Act and modify the scale of payments.[64]

Although following the 1850 harvest there was a further improvement in the condition of the poor and destitute in Ireland, again this did not apply to all unions. In parts of the west, most notably Clare, the level of destitution actually increased. In the Kilrush, Scariff and Ennistymon unions, the Poor Law Commissioners reported that there existed 'a degree of desitutuion which has no parallel in other parts of Ireland at the present time'.[65] In the county of Clare as a whole, nearly 30,000 people were in receipt of outdoor relief, almost twice the number of people who were being relieved in the whole of Connaught at that time.[66] In 1851, although the amount of poor relief being provided in the country dropped further, this improvement again did not include County Clare. In the Ennistymon union, for example, the situation was no better than it had been in 1848 — because of lack of funds the Guardians were unable to provide outdoor relief and were again dissolved.[67]

Of all the unions in Clare, it was in Kilrush where distress was most severe and prolonged. In 1848, the union had achieved notoriety because of the high number of evictions which were taking place there daily. In April of that year, the local Inspector reported that as many as 300 people were being evicted in the union each day and that these people were then becoming dependant on the Poor Law for relief.[68] The motive was the burden of poor rates on holdings valued under £4. These fell exclusively on the landlords who were using the distress and the high poor rates as an excuse to clear their land of small occupiers.[69]

The continuation of a high rate of evictions and distress in Kilrush resulted in various Parliamentary Reports about the union and in 1850 and 1851 Select Committees were appointed to enquire into the local administration of poor relief. The resulting reports were scathing about the local Poor Law and the role played by the local landlords. One of the Committees described the suffering in the union which had been 'intense to a degree almost beyond conception'. It estimated that there had been a decrease in the local population of between 25-50%, even though there had been little emigration from the area. The Select Committee also accused many of the local landlords of being inactive and, on occasion, of evicting their tenants in the hope of being subsidised by the government. Overall, it felt that the Poor Law had not provided sufficient relief to save the lives of the local destitute.[70]

The Select Committee recognised that the high level of distress in Kilrush and the other 'distressed' unions, had made the Guardians totally dependant on external financial aid from the Poor Law Commissioners who, themselves, depended on the Treasury for funds. The Treasury, in turn, was reluctant to give money to any Irish union unless the alternative was clearly starvation. Despite this, the Select Committee was convinced that neither the public nor parliament would have allowed the situation in Kilrush and other unions to continue if they had been aware of it. It acknowledged, however, that there had been a neglect of public duty which it doubted would ever have been allowed to exist in England. The problem was that Kilrush and the other 'distressed' unions were not in England, and what occurred was an extreme example of a government trying to force local resources to support local distress without realising that in some parts of Ireland the land was not capable of any form of production.[71] The recommendations of this committee were made too late to have any impact on the Kilrush union or to affect the policies of the government. This can be judged by the fact that in May 1851, there were 3,319 people in receipt of outdoor relief and 4,903 people receiving indoor relief in Kilrush, all of whom the Guardians described as being in 'low physical condition'.[72]

Although Kilrush was the most distressed union in Ireland at this time, other unions were still greatly impoverished. In the Tipperary and Limerick unions, for example, blight had reappeared in 1849 ruining most of the potato crop and leaving the unions dependant on external aid.[73] In 1850, both the Galway and the Listowel Boards of Guardians needed the aid of the police and the military to collect the rates. Following the harvest of 1850, the finances of the Ballina union were so bad that the local sheriff took possession of the workhouse and then sold the workhouse clothes.[74] The Kenmare Guardians also were unable to obtain credit from their contractors and the chairman had to use his personal credit in order to purchase supplies.[75] In December 1850, even though the harvest had been good in many parts of Ireland, the continuation of distress in some localities resulted in a second Rate-in-Aid being introduced.[76]

The harvest of 1851 was virtually free from potato blight. By 1852, the Famine could be said to be over in Ireland, although the levels of disease, mortality and emigration were still much higher than they had been prior to 1845. The Poor Law therefore, had survived this period of unprecedented distress although radical changes had been necessary. In 1838, George

Nicholls had pointed out that it was beyond the capabilities of the Poor Law to deal with a period of prolonged distress or famine.[77] After 1846, it was obvious that the distress in Ireland could no longer be viewed as just another localised subsistence crisis. Despite this, in an effort to force changes within Ireland, the British government increasingly used the Poor Law as the main agency for relief, choosing to ignore the fact that when the land had ceased to be productive, the necessary means for providing relief could not be obtained from it.[78]

As well as the general appearance of potato blight after 1846, depression and recession in other sectors of the economy, combined temporarily to leave Ireland without the resources to compensate for such a widespread deficit. The larger and more buoyant economic unit, the United Kingdom, and ultimately, the British Empire, chose not to use its resources beyond a certain point to relieve this distress, preferring instead to use the Famine as an opportunity to rationalise the Irish system of land-holding. The Treasury, which was the distributor of the government's funds, often showed more concern with balancing the Imperial books rather than with financing the local poor-rates, welcoming the changes it hoped would be brought about in Ireland. The sympathy which was frequently evident amongst the local providers of poor relief never penetrated to London where ultimately the real financial control lay. Within Ireland itself, large-scale evictions, mass emigration, deaths from starvation and large tracts of land being left waste because the country could no longer bear the burden of poor rates, were part of the price to be paid for these changes. But the Ireland envisaged — on where landless labourers would be employed on large farms owned by men of energy and capital — never emerged. The Poor Law during the Famine, therefore, was an example of social legislation being subjected to economic theory, even though the economic theory was itself imperfect.

References

1. *Remarks on the Third Report of the Irish Poor Commissioners* by G.C. Lewis, Brit. Parl. Papers, 1837[91]LI, pp. 10-31. Lord John Russell, quoted in Royal Commission on the Poor Laws and the relief of distress — report on Ireland, (hereafter *Royal Commission*, 1909), p. 8, Brit, Parl. Papers, 1909(4630)XXXVII, 1.

2. *Report by G. Nicholls to his Majesty's Secretary of State for the Home Department,* on Poor Laws, Ireland, pp. 1-2, Brit.Parl.Papers. 1837[69]LI. 201; 1 & 2 Vic. c.56. An Act for the more effectual Relief of the Destitute Poor in Ireland (31 July 1838).

3. Nicholls, George, *A History of the Irish Poor Law* (London, 1856), p. 250.

4. Evidence of Alfred Power, *Reports of the Select Committee of the House of Lords, appointed to enquire into the operation of the Irish Poor Law and the expediency of making any amendment in its enactments,* (hereafter *Select Committee,* 1849), pp. 91-92, H.L. 1849 (192) xvi, 1.

5. *Seventh Annual Report of the Poor Law Commissioners* (he* A.R., P.L. Coms.), 1841, p. 65.*

6. *Eleventh A.R., P.L. Coms.,* 1845, *passim.*

7. Minute of P.L. Coms. quoted in *Report of the Royal Commission, 1909,* p. 13; see, Kinealy, C. The Administration of the Poor Law in Ireland, 1838-62, (unpublished Ph.D. thesis Trinity College, Dublin), 1984.

8. Sir James Graham to Lord Lieutenant (L.L.), (P.R.O.), H.O.45, 1080, Box 1, May 1846.

9. R. Routh to Trevelyan, *Correspondence explanatory of the Measures adopted by Her Majesty's Government for the Relief of Distress arising from the Failure of the Potato Crop in Ireland* (hereafter *Correspondence Explanatory*), Brit. Parl. Papers, 1846 [735] XXXVII, p. 76, 23 March 1846; *ibid.,* Trevelyan to Routh, p. 14, 26 Jan. 1846.

10. *Twelfth A.R., P.L. Coms.,* 1846, p. 51.

11. *Ibid.,* pp. 37-41.

12. Redington to Trevelyan, *Correspondence Explanatory,* p. 102, 28 July 1846; *ibid.,* Routh to Trevelyan, p. 208, 14 July 1846.

13. *Ibid.,* Treasury Minute, p. 330, 26 June 1846.

14. P.L. Coms. to L.L., State Paper Office (S.P.O.), Chief Secretary's Office Registered Papers (C.S.O. R.P.), 1846 O. 18344, 17 October 1846.

15. There is real evidence that at least 25 per cent of unions were providing outdoor relief, see, Kinealy, Irish Poor Law.

16. The Irish section of the Poor Law Commission was headed by Edward Twistleton. In November 1845 he had been appointed Poor Law Commissioner for Ireland. At this stage, however, he was part of the English Poor Law Board and it was not until August 1847 that the different interests of the two countries were established and a separate Irish Commission created.

17. P.L. Coms. to L.L. S.P.O., C.S.O.R.P., 1846 O.23630, 18 Dec. 1846.

18. *Ibid.,* P.L. Coms. to L.L., 19 Dec. 1846.

19. G. Grey to L.L., printed in *Kerry Evening Post,* 10 Feb. 1847; *Royal Commission,* 1090, p. 117.

20. E. Senior Assistant (P.L. Coms.) to P.L. Coms., S.P.O., C.S.O.R.P., 1847 07584, 26 June 1847: *Armagh Guardian,* 17 Aug. 1847; J.D. Chambers, *The Workshop of the World. British Economic History from 1820-1880,* (London, 1961). pp. 101-15.

21. General orders of the P.L. Coms. for regulating outdoor relief. *Papers relating to the Proceedings for the Relief of the Distress and State of the Unions and Workhouses in Ireland,* (fourth series) (hereafter, *Relief of Distress*) pp. 18-19, Brit. Parl. Papers, 1847-48[896]LIV, 1 July 1847.

22. 10 & 11 Vic. c.31, sections 4-18.

23. Cecil Woodham-Smith, *The Great Hunger: Ireland 1845-49,* (London, 1962), pp. 106-7.

24. Circular to Boards of Guardians, *Relief of Distress,* p. 6, 1 July 1947: *ibid.,* Circular as to collection of poor rates, p. 25, 26 Oct. 1847.

25. Twistleton to Trevelyan, P.R.O., T.64. 367.A 24 Oct. 1847; *ibid.*, H.O.45 2472, 9 Feb. 1848.

26. *Dublin Evening Post*, 15 Jan. 1848, 10 Feb. 1848; *Armagh Guardian*, 4 May 1847.

27. Twistleton to Trevelyan P.R.O., T.64.367 c/1, 3 Jan. 1848; *ibid.*, 12 Jan. 1848.

28. P.L. Coms. to Chief Secretary (C.S.) S.P.O., C.S.O.R.P., 1848 O.28, Dec. 1847; *ibid.*, 1848 O.6588, 8 July 1848.

29. Reports to Trevelyan on state of potato crop in Ireland, P.R.O., T.64. 367 B/2, 15 July 1848.

30. *Ibid.*, Twistleton to Trevelyan, 10 Aug. 1848.

31. Treasury to P.L. Coms. N.L.I., microfilm, T.14.31., 17258, 8 Aug. 1848.

32. Twistleton to Trevelyan P.R.O., T. 64. 366A, 9 Sept. 1848; *ibid.*, J. Russell to Trevelyan, 11 Sept. 1848.

33. Poor Law Inspector P.L.I., Ballina to P.L. Coms. S.P.O., C.S.O.R.P., 1848 O.11984, 5 Dec. 1848.

34. P.L. Coms. to Grey, *Papers relating to the Aid afforded to the Distressed Unions in the West of Ireland* (hereafter *Distressed Union*), p. 26. Brit. Parl. Papers, 1849[1010] XLVIII, p. 26.

35. Report by Trevelyan P.R.O., T64. 366 A. Undated, (probably March 1849).

36. *Second Annual Report of the Commissioners for Administering the Laws for Relief of the Poor in Ireland* (hereafter *A.R. Coms. R.P.Ir*), 1849 p. 11.

37. Coms. to Treasury S.P.O., C.S.O.R.P. 1849 O.8338, 11 April 1849; *ibid.*, 11 Aug. 1849.

38. *Ibid.*, Treasury to Coms., 14 April 1849, 21 July 1849.

39. S.M. Cousens, 'The Regional Variation in Mortality during the Great Irish Famine', *Proceedings of the Royal Irish Academy*, lxiii (section C), no. 3, (1963).

40. Evidence of Twistleton, *Select Committee on Irish Poor Law*, 1848, p. 47.

41. *Ibid.*, p. 717.

42. 12 & 13 Vic. c. 24.

43. Treasury Minute, *Distressed Unions*, 111, p. 19, 17 May 1849.

44. *The Northern Whig*, 22 Feb. 1849, 1 March 1849, 3 March 1849.

45. Evidence of Twistleton, *Select Committee on Irish Poor Law*, 1849, pp. 699-714.; Twistleton to Trevelyan, P.R.O. T. 64. 366 A. 24 March 1849.

46. Nicholls, *Irish Poor Law*, pp. 309, 357.

47. Report of Trevelyan P.R.O., T. 64. 366 A. Undated, probably March 1849.

48. *Ibid.*

49. *Third A.R. Coms.R.P.Ir.*, 1850, pp. 5-7.

50. A Workhouse at Dingle was opened in 1848.

51. Coms. to Trevelyan, *Distressed Unions III*, p. 30. 26 May 1849.

52. Coms. to all Vice-Guardians P.R.O., Letter Books. 21 Aug. 1849.

53. *Third A.R. Coms.R.P.Ir.*, 1850, *passim*.

54. *Ibid.*, p. 5.

55. Coms. to Home Office S.P.O., C.S.O.R.P. 1849 O.5256, 2 July 1949; Fourth A.R. 1851.

56. *Ibid.*, Lynch to Coms. 1849, O.7488 19 Aug. 1849.

57. *Third A.R. Coms.R.P.Ir.*, 1850, pp. 5-8.

58. A. Power to Trevelyan P.R.O., T. 64 366 A. 13 July 1849; *ibid.*, Trevelyan to Wood, T. 64 370 A. File 2, 19 Oct. 1847.

59. *Third A.R. Coms.R.P.Ir.*, 1850, pp. 5-8; Trevelyan to Wood (P.R.O.), T. 64 370 A; File 2, 19 Oct. 1849; *ibid.* note to Trevelyan T. 64 366 A. 13 July 1849.

60. Coms. to C.S. S.P.O., C.S.O.R.P. 1850 O.1385, 28 Feb. 1850; *ibid.*, Scariff Guardians to L.L. and reply, 1850 O.1282, 12 Feb. 1850.

61. *Ibid.*

62. Trevelyan to Coms. P.R.O., H.O.45 2521 A, 7 Nov. 1849.

63. 13 & 14 Vic. c. 14.

64. Treasury Minute, P.R.O. T. 64 368 A, 21 Oct. 1851.

65. *Third A.R. Coms.R.P.Ir.*, 1850, p. 57; *Fourth A.R.* 1851, pp. 4-8; Cousens, *Regional Variations in Mortality,* p. 127.

66. *Third A.R. Coms.R.P.Ir.*, 1850, p. 8.

67. *Ibid.*, p. 7; *Fourth A.R. Coms.R.P.Ir.*, 1851, p. 7; Cousens, *Regional Variations in Mortality, passim.*

68. *Report of the Select Committee appointed to enquire into the administration of the Poor Law in the Kilrush Union since 19 September 1848,* Brit. Parl. Papers, 1850(613)XI, p. 529.

69. *Ibid.*, Report of Committee, p. xii; *ibid.*, p. viii.

70. *Ibid.*, p. xi.

71. *Ibid.*, p. xiii.

72. *Third A.R. Coms.R.P.Ir.*, 1850, p. 7; *Fourth A.R. Coms.R.P.Ir.*, 1851, p. 6.

73. Poor Law Inspector P.L.I. Tipperary to Limerick Unions S.P.O., C.S.O.R.P., 1849 O.7488, 19 Aug. 1849.

74. *Copy of Report made to the Board of Guardians of the Castlebar Union on 20 April 1850 by Dr Ronayne, Medical Superintendent of the Union, relative to the State of the Workhouse,* Brit. Parl. Papers, 1850(382)L, 79.

75. Minute Book, Kenmare Union, (Kerry County Library), BG100/A/7, 1 Nov. 1850; *ibid.*, BG100/A/8, 15 Nov. 1850.

76. Coms. to J. Burke P.R.O., Letter Books, 8 Jan. 181.

77. Nicholls to Russell, *Report by G. Nicholls,* p. 9.

78. Nicholls, *Irish Poor Law,* pp. 309, 357.

8

THE FOOD CRISIS OF THE 1890s

T.P. O'Neill

There has been a revived interest in the study of poverty in Ireland in the past decade as the effects of the oil crisis reminded Ireland as well as the rest of the western world of the vulnerability of its economic base.[1] Famine in Africa brought a new dimension to this interest and new problems brought a questioning of long held assumptions concerning welfare at home and famine abroad. While greater concern is shown for famine there is a hardening of attitudes to domestic poverty in western societies. In America just as books like *The Other America* began a national debate on poverty in 1963 which led to the great society programmes, so *Losing Ground* sets the intellectual stage for reducing those efforts.[2] This trend is reflected in other countries, including Ireland, in recent years.

Surprisingly this is happening at a time when a better understanding of the nature of poverty is emerging. The old definitions of poverty have been refined and the Macawber-style approach of Seebohm Rowntree of earnings insufficient to obtain the minimum necessities for the maintenance of physical efficiency is gone in favour of a more relative, culturally determined test applied by each society. So economic distress is a subjective concept and its definition varies in place and time.[3] Similarly the roots of poverty have been closely analysed and two models are presented, the 'case model' and the 'generic model'. The case model holds that poverty is the product of individual characteristics such as intelligence, education, skills, handicaps, health, age, marital status, sex, religion, family size or region of residence. This model is sometimes subdivided by separating the existence of regional pockets of poverty. The generic model holds that poverty results from more general, economy-wide economic problems, mainly inadequate employment opportunities, rather than individual characteristics. In this model some will be poor as long as social policies do not spread the consequences of generic poverty over the entire population. Both models agree that the poor are still most likely to be those who have characteristic handicaps. Depending upon which is perceived as the most likely cause of poverty then attitudes to relief will differ. In the late nineteenth century, though ideas of poverty were less codified, these central issues were equally well understood.[4]

Historically the last of the Irish famines occurred in the 1890s. On three occasions during that decade in 1890-1, 1894-5 and 1897-8, the spectre of starvation loomed on the Irish landscape. In each of these periods the situation in restricted areas of a small number of counties became so serious that widespread relief measures became necessary and there was general acceptance of the need for relief. People in the distressed areas, in Ireland generally, in England, and wider afield accepted that the west of Ireland was in economic distress in relation to current living standards. As those standards were low, distress was serious in absolute terms.

Reports of distress began in the summer of 1890 when bad weather once again threatened the potato crop[5] as 20.8 inches of rain fell in the first nine months.[6] Police and resident magistrates were asked to report on the state of the potato crop and as bad weather continued Arthur J. Balfour, the Chief Secretary, directed the Irish Land Commissioners to send agents to investigate.[7] As reports of distress continued the inspectors of the Local Government Board were also asked to inquire into the conditions. The result of these investigations was that while the general harvest was satisfactory, in the case of the potato, failure was very general in the west. The worst effects of this were manifested along the seaboard from Donegal to Cork. By the Autumn the Lord Lieutenant had before him quarter inch administrative maps with every district electoral division where distress was anticipated coloured either pink, brown or blue to indicate either acute, severe or slight anticipated distress. Acute distress was predicted in the west generally, more particularly in the following divisions:

Knockboy, Skarrine, Crumpaun and Silkerna in Co. Galway;
Ballintober, Annoghmore and Bellacare E. in Co. Roscommon;
Roosky, Oughteragh and Carrick-on-Shannon in Co. Leitrim; and also Drumreilly S. in Co. Cavan.[8]

In these districts the potato crop was estimated to be one half to one third of the average yield, while in some of the Congested Districts the crop was hardly one quarter of the average and of this a considerable proportion was unfit for human food.[9] The main problem was blight.

By the 8th November 1890 the *West Cork Eagle* reported alarming distress in Schull and Goleen and declared that the situation was no less deadly than that of black '47. Optimistic as always, the report commented that:

the English public who will give without a murmer many millions of money to raise defences for our shores, would not grumble if a very few millions were spent in raising a defence against the ravages of a foe more deadly than any invader — the worst of all human foes — Famine.[10]

In September Balfour had decided to organise relief projects and called in Colonel Fraser R.E., who had worked on famine relief works in Ireland in 1886. Fraser was to examine conditions and advise on works.[11] The principles to apply were Balfour's. Relief measures were to be kept as secret as possible to avoid excessive demands; and kept out of the hands of Local Authorities; they should be real works and not simply an excuse for gratuitous relief, and of permanent utility. Furthermore, no distressed district was to be without work either on a new railway or a relief project.[12] Having carried out some preliminary planning Fraser resigned and was replaced by Major Peacocke also of the Royal Engineers.[13] Plans were completed by the 2nd December when a meeting of all department heads involved was held in Dublin Castle.[14] The police were to act as time keepers and gangers. Mr Micks of the Local Government Board organised works in Donegal. The County surveyors co-operated in the selection of roads and the Local Government Board appointed seven extra inspectors to supervise the west. The District Inspectors of the constabulary were made responsible for accounting generally while police sergeants were to act as paymasters. To get relief underway quickly the government negotiated with the railway companies to bring work forward by anticipating formal contracts and even in one case guaranteeing the company against the loss.[15] Dublin Castle at the end of the distress estimated that this arrangement provided work for seven or eight thousand persons at a wage of 12 shillings per week for men.[16] These light railways were ideally located to provide relief in some of the distressed districts.

Where railways were not planned Peacocke visited those distressed districts and by the 8th December 1890 the first relief works were begun in the Crumpaun Electoral District in Oughterard, Co. Galway. Between then and 31st July 1891, when most works finished, 161 separate schemes were undertaken. The numbers thus employed grew steadily as distress worsened and peaked for the week ended 6th June 1891 when 16,192 persons were at work.[17] A number of smaller experimental schemes were tried. The state purchased 914 acres at Knockboy near Carna, Co. Galway and seventy distressed labourers were employed draining, fencing and planting trees.[18] For eleven western islands and Letterass near Westport, Co. Mayo, a seed potato scheme was introduced. Potatoes were distributed and the recipients later paid for the seed by work in relief schemes. One hundred and sixty-one tons of potatoes were distributed to 889 persons in this way.[19]

Since the early nineteenth century government relief had always been seen as a support for private charity. As in other years of distress many local committees were established but the major charitable committee in 1891 was launched by the Lord Lieutenant and Mr Balfour by a letter to the *Times* on 5th January 1891. Contributions to the *'Irish Distress Fund'* were invited for the benefit of persons affected by the loss of the potato crop and for whom neither Poor Laws nor the government relief measures would afford relief.[20] £50,287 0s. 7d. was collected and the fund's headquarters were in the Under-Secretary's House in Dublin Castle.[21] The private secretary of the Lord Lieutenant, Mr Mulhall, was appointed secretary to the fund. The constabulary provided lists of worthy candidates for relief and three inspectors were appointed to supervise distribution in different districts in the west. While distress lasted 50,641 persons were given one stone of Indian meal weekly, or its flour or oatmeal equivalent. The fund also provided school meals in 933 national primary schools and clothing too was distributed through school managers.[22]

In all periods of distress in nineteenth century Ireland the western islands were a cause of great concern. In 1891 emergency food depots were opened in the islands of Inishmurry, Clare, Inishturk and Iniskea and the government chartered two steamships the *Hawk* and the *Falcon* for much of the distress period. These vessels were used extensively for the conveyance of seed potatoes and also for officials sent to investigate conditions. With government aid the *'Citie of the Tribes'* steamship undertook regular communication with the Aran Islands and Connemara. This service was later supported by the new Congested Districts Board when distress passed.[23]

It was generally believed that the quality of seed potatoes available in Ireland was a major problem. 'Champions' a variety of potato introduced in 1880 accounted for 78.6% of the total acreage under potatoes, and in the ten counties most affected by crop failure in 1890 the percentage of Champions grown was 84% of the total potato crop.[24] The Reports on Agricultural Statistics showed that the rate of produce per acre of Champions had more than halved between 1881 and 1890.[25] On the 9th December 1890 a Seed Potatoes Supply Act was passed.[26] This Act made provision for the Board of Works to make advances through the Board of Guardians for the purchase of seed potatoes in any area where the Local Government Board was satisfied that the occupiers of land were unable, by reason of poverty and the failure of the potato crop, to purchase an adequate supply of seed. In 1891, 110 out of a total of 160 unions adopted its provisions and loans of over £¼ million were advanced. This measure was regarded as being of major importance in improving the quality of seed in the poorer districts and thereby preventing future failure.[27]

In the early years of this present century there was a widespread belief that enormous amounts had been spent on relief in Ireland and the Royal Commission on Congestion in Ireland made valiant attempts to quantify the amounts. A memorandum was prepared by Walter Callan dated 12th August 1907 which showed that the total for 1879-80 was £2,562,476 which included £267,000 donated by private charities. For the period from 1880 to 1905 Callan produced the following figures (see Table 1):[28]

Table 1. *Amounts of Free Grants and Loans made in connection with the Relief of Distress in Ireland from 1880 to 1905, distinguishing Irish from Imperial Sources*

	FREE GRANTS		LOANS	
	From Irish Funds	From Imperial Sources	From Irish Funds	From Imperial Sources
Period	£	£	£	£
1880-2	41,067	57,596	1,228,239	841,414
1882-3	923,923	—	27,010	—
1885-6	40,000	—	—	—
1890-1	17,564	238,597	—	272,854
1894-5	3,738	80,025	—	62,034
1897-8	4,769	43,833	—	77,763
1904-5	9,500	14,635	—	70,018
TOTAL	1,040,561	434,686	1,255,249	1,324,083
	1,475,247		2,579,332	
		4,054,579		

This table though backed up by impressive detail in the public record was not published as too many difficutlies presented. One of the main problems was that of drawing a line of demarcation between money spent on relief for distress purposes, meaning the immediate alleviation of exceptional and acute distress, and money spent to ameliorate chronic poverty. Callan estimated that all the free grants and half the loans were applied in Relief of Distress properly so called. A further difficulty which arose was that of estimating the amount of money applied out of the local rates for relief as their accounting procedure did not allow for such estimates to be made. Finally there was the difficulty of compiling accurate accounts of charitable contributions many of which were sent directly to distressed districts.[29] The final relief figures arrived at for 1890-1 were £238,597 grants from Imperial funds, £17,564 grants from Irish funds and £272,854 loans from Imperial funds for the purpose of the seed potato supply. The loans for seed potatoes were recovered from the persons to whom seed was supplied or became a charge on the local rates and the repayment of a mere £766 was subsequently remitted and must therefore be seen as a free grant.[30] The grants from Irish funds were used to pay for discounts on cash sales, interest and similar charges and were drawn from the Irish Church Fund. To this government expenditure must be added the £50,287 contributed by the public to the Irish Distress Fund. The final cost of non-recoverable relief was as follows:

		£
1.	Irish Church Fund	17,564
2.	Imperial Grants	238,597
3.	'Irish Distress Fund'	50,287
4.	Seed Potato Grants	766
	TOTAL	307,214

This total excludes all smaller private charities. When this expenditure is related to limited areas of distress and the small number of recipients already listed it constituted a major injection of capital into the distressed districts and showed a remarkable response to Irish distress. If this response of 1890-1 is compared to relief offered in 1822, when distress in the west was severe and relief generous, it appears as more than adequate even allowing for changes in prices and the value of money. In 1822 government relief amounted to £221,437, private charity in Ireland was estimated at £44,585, the London Tavern Committee spent £232,573 on relief, and the Dublin Mansion House spent £18,340.[31] This gives a total of £516,935 at a time when government officials estimated that one million people — 50 per cent of the population — were distressed, in Mayo, Galway, Sligo, Leitrim, Roscommon, Clare, Limerick, Kerry, Cork and Tipperary and needed relief.[32] Later, in 1890-1 £307,214 was used to provide relief for a maximum of 100,000 persons in very restricted areas.[33]

Distress in 1890-1 attracted little attention from Irish members of parliament. Many were preoccupied by the events surrounding Captain O'Shea's divorce suit which was made public on 17th November 1890. William O'Brien, John Dillon, T. O'Sulivan, T.P. O'Connor, T.P. Gill and T.C. Harrington were all on a delegation to America in the autumn of 1890 when distress threatened.[34] This group contained the most likely political agitators for relief and by the time of their return the Parnellite split and the relief measures already begun discouraged them from taking up the cause of Irish tenants. It was not until the political climate had recovered from the trauma of the Parnell split that O'Brien was able to use distress as a unifying cause to unite the opposing factions.[35]

Before that however, another crisis occurred in 1894-5. Again, failure of the potato crop precipitated a crisis in the western parts of Galway, Mayo and Donegal. From Mayo by the spring of 1895 reports of distress were commonplace. In parts of the county the potato crop was a mere one-eighth of its usual yield and a depression in cattle, cereal and butter prices aggravated the situation.[36] Relief was organised on similar lines to 1890-1 under the supervision of Major C.R. Condor of the Royal Engineers with the, by now, usual support of County Surveyors, Constabulary and Local Government Board Inspectors.[37] A further Seed Supply Act was passed under which £62,034 was advanced of which £3,738 was finally written off as 'a free grant'.[38] The bulk of the expenditure on this occasion was on road works in the four counties — the fourth county being Cavan where 190 relief workers were employed to construct a 'cart road' at Carlough to enable communication between Callinamore, Co. Leitrim and Swanlinbar in Cavan. This road cost £1,500 between March and September 1895.[39] It was the traditionally distressed areas like Erris, Co. Mayo which again attracted the major relief effort. Typical of the type of work was that on the Jubilee Road between Belmullet and Geesala near Glencastle where 105 workers were regularly employed rebuilding the line of an old ruined road and building a small bridge, 10 feet span with masonry abutments and steel girders.[40] The cost of grants for this period of distress amounted to £80,025 from Imperial funds and £3,738 from Irish funds some of which was handed over to the Congested Districts Board for distribution.[41]

The final period of severe distress in the 1890s was in 1897 and reached its climax in the following year. Though it was not as serious as the distress of 1890-1 it attracted considerable comment at the time because of the attention given to the crisis by Irish politicians. It was almost as if Irish politicians and public figures suddenly rediscovered the starving peasantry and impassioned speeches, reminiscent of those made by Archbishop MacHale or Michael Davitt, during earlier famines were again heard.[42] Davitt indeed again reappeared along with W. O'Brien, John Dillon, T.M. Healy and J. Redmond, all attacking government policies and there was general dissatisfaction with the pace of government action.[43] Maud Gonne's Mayo famine speeches are memorable.[44] The political outcome was the establishment of the United Irish League and the coming together of Irish political factions.

In truth the condition of the people in certain isolated areas was always on the borderline. In 1896 a wet autumn made harvesting difficult and reports of distress in Mayo and Galway were common.[45] Low agricultural prices made the situation difficult as graziers unable to sell their mature stock were unwilling to buy young stock from their poorer neighbours.[46] Spring of 1897 brought reports of great distress in the traditionally poor areas and outdoor relief in Belmullet union trebled in February.[47] Balfour, the Chief Secretary, reluctant to be drawn into emergency relief, denied the reports.[48] A wet spring, with people already eating their seed potatoes, led many people to anticipate severe distress.[49] Typhus was reported on the Iniskea Islands and the *Irish Times* predicted calamity there.[50] This epidemic was to grow and later spread to the neighbouring mainland.[51] Blight again affected the potato crop and the crop generally was down. By October 1897 the *Connaught Telegraph* reported widespread distress in the Poor Law unions of Killala, Ballina, Ballinrobe, Castlebar, Ballyhaunis, Claremorris, Swinford, Oughterard, Galway and Clifden.[52] Daniel Tallon, Lord Mayor of Dublin and Colonel Speight, a Local Government Board Inspector, both experienced observers, warned in the press of a crisis similar to 1847.[53] To add to the potato and prices problems, turf had been difficult to save and typhus spread to new areas in Mayo. Colonel Speight warned of distress in many western counties and Professor James Long and the Bishop of Achonry added their warnings.[54] A Roman Catholic curate, Fr. Lavelle, warned both the press and Dublin Castle that on the islands of Gorumna, Lettermullen, Farnish and Inishark many families were dependent on Indian meal purchased on credit, which was becoming difficult to obtain.[55] Calls on the government to intervene were made at meetings in Westport, Carna and Louisburgh and a detailed account of the situation in Connemara by William O'Malley M.P. appeared in the *Galway Express.*[56]

By January 1898 famine was widely reported in Mayo, Galway, Donegal and in parts of Clare, West Cork and in South-West Kerry. Reports of distress in Donegal became common early in the year.[57] On Tory Island the seed potatoes were eaten and a wet spring made matters worse. The Poor Law unions increased their efforts both through the workhouses and outdoor relief but many unions like Belmullet were bankrupt.[58] People demanding work were a feature of society in Mayo and Galway and the government response was to allow the Board of Guardians to begin relief works with a guarantee that central government would meet 75% of the cost as well as the costs of supervision.[59] Six shillings per week was to be the maximum wages offered to keep pay below the commercial rate which would have been only slightly higher in those districts. The County Surveyors had again to approve and supervise the works.[60] Protesting their inability to meet even the 25% cost, Boards of Guardians began relief works in January of 1898 commencing in Belmullet,[61] followed by Swinford, Westport, Killala, Oughterard, Clifden and Galway.[62] In all, eleven unions eventually came into the scheme as the following Table 2 shows.[63]

Why did the government abandon its well tried and tested relief schemes used in the two earlier crises? This was a means of forcing local contribution, of avoiding total reliance on central government and prevented the recurring prospect of central government works being relied upon by the distressed areas. Most administrators believed that people

G

Table 2. Money Expended in Relief of Distress in Ireland in 1897-1898
(Supplied by the Local Government Board)

Unions	No. of Electoral Divisions in which relief works were opened Congested	Non-Congested	Amount recouped by Government, *i.e.* 75 per cent. of approved expenditure upon relief works £ s. d.	Additional Grants in aid of Rates £	Free Grants of Seed £ s. d.	Total of Government Grants £ s. d.
Ballinrobe	4	—	747 19 6	—	194 14 4	942 13 10
Bawnboy	1	2	255 7 11	—	—	255 7 11
Belmullet	All	—	4,626 15 11	1,675	624 12 9	6,926 8 8
Caherciveen	1	—	41 9 9	—	—	41 9 9
Clifden	14	—	2,379 11 3	500	389 15 7	3,269 6 10
Dunfanaghy	1	—	50 4 6	—	—	50 4 6
Galway	3	—	708 5 9	—	102 11 7	810 17 4
Killala	2	2	1,392 7 4	—	203 10 0	1,505 17 4
Oughterard	10	—	4,024 4 9	500	651 5 6	5,175 10 3
Swinford	19	2	5,177 16 9	1,319	1,109 13 5	7,606 10 2
Westport	9	—	2,868 14 7	—	591 11 10	3,460 6 5
Totals	—	—	22,182 18 0	3,994	3,867 15 0	35,044 13 0

accustomed to a particular relief scheme were able to meet the requirements of relief administrators from experience rather than want. Regular changes in the administration of relief in an attempt to get greater economy, efficiency and force local contributions, had led to the introduction of new relief machinery in 1839 under Captain Chads.[64] Similarly in 1898 this was an attempt to find a better and more economical way.

The scheme had the advantage that once the limit was reached under the Poor Law Rating Act of 1876 for indoor relief in any of the electoral divisions, further sums were levied off the entire union.[65] The Local Government Board expected the unions to be able to bear the 25% burden but also promised to consider special problems encountered by poorer unions.[66] Four unions, as the table above shows, were eventually supported by additional grants to aid the rates. Besides works the government introduced another Seed Potatoes Supply Act in 1898 which allowed Boards of Guardians to apply for seed. Ninety-nine unions applied stating that there were electoral divisions in their areas in which a seed supply was required.[67] Seventy-five of these unions decided to apply for loans and by 1907 the total cost of the 1898 scheme was calculated by Walter Callan as £4,769 18s. 8d. which meant that some seed given on loans was later regarded as a free grant.[68] In the distressed districts 550 tons of Scottish seed potatoes were distributed free to every labourer each receiving 2 cwt.[69] From those purchasing seed potatoes there were complaints about the price which was fixed by the Guardians at 10¼d. per stone.[70] The price of potatoes in the poorer districts varied considerably. In April 1891 at the height of distress, prices per stone ranged from 6d. in Scarriff, 8d. in Clonakilty to 9d. in Castletownbere having risen 1d. or 2d. on average from the previous December.[71] The average price in 1889 was 4.03d. per stone so there was a considerable price increase in the distressed districts from December 1890 to July 1891.[72] Daniel Tallon, a tireless relief worker as Chairman of the Mansion House Relief Committee in Dublin, advised that seed should be distributed at low cost to avoid keeping the people of the west in 'perennial poverty'.[73] As with most relief there were complaints about abuses. The unworthy rich were benefiting and the poor were eating the seed, thereby rendering the planned relief ineffective.[74] Such complaints however, were isolated and few.

There was also a number of other government relief measures. In March, 1898, unions were authorised to purchase potato spraying machines using interest-free loans from the Board of Works. These machines were to be hired out or purchased by occupiers of land where rateable valuation was below £15.[75] Loans were also made available for spraying compounds.[76] Voluntary relief committees supported this work and the Congested Districts Board employed demonstrators and supplied the copper sulphate and lime free.[77] Blight which had threatened was greatly reduced and education showed people how to contain blight even using besoms and white wash brushes.[78]

Looking at government's response, the total spent in 1897-8 was much lower than in 1890-1. There were two reasons for this. Firstly, distress was more limited than in 1890-1 and secondly, the government relief was not as generous and was administered to tighter guidelines and controls. Gerald Balfour, Chief Secretary of Ireland, delayed relief as long as possible and his principle of intervention was that of absolute necessity.

> The duty of government was to see no starvation occurred. It would be a mistake for the government to try to do what properly belonged to the province of private charity. To pay people for doing work on their own farms would be the equivalent of paying them for doing nothing at all.[79]

Translated by a political opponent who viewed relief from a different perspective another assessment of the government response was given by Daniel Tallon.

> When at length the government tardily acknowledged that real distress existed it adopted a scheme most scientifically calculated to do least good and afford a minimum of relief.[80]

One reason why Balfour could be penurious in 1898 was because private charity was well marshalled in that year. Two major relief committees were established, one in Manchester and one in Dublin at the Mansion House where the Lord Mayor, following a long charitable tradition, called for aid for the starving west.[81] The Manchester committee collected in excess of £20,000 while the Dublin committee raised £11,155 2s. 10d.[82] This aid made it possible for Balfour to delay and hold back particularly as it also conformed to his belief that charity as a matter of principle should come from private individuals. The Manchester fund was inspired by letters to the *Manchester Guardian* by Professor James Long.[83] Long, a protestant unionist, came to Ireland in 1897 'steeped in prejudice against the Irish and believing that the popular cries of distress were greatly exaggerated and hardly worth consideration.'[84] He became the great advocate of the need for relief and at a public meeting in the Town Hall in Manchester on December 30th, 1897 a fund was established. A local administrative Board was set up in Dublin under James Talbot Power, D.L. which distributed aid to eleven Poor Law districts in Galway and Mayo with the main support going to Foxford, Barna, Belmullet and Carrigaholt. Funds were distributed for the following purposes:[85]

	£	*s.*	*d.*
Food, Meal, Clothing and Flannel	2,262	6	4
Works, Tools, and Grants for fishing and other industries	4,917	1	5
Potato Seed	4,944	2	11
Spraying Potatoes	3,032	15	0
Oats, Rye and Grass Seed	2,344	6	5

Other funds had already been expended before the Dublin administrative board was set up. The large proportion of funds spent on seed potatoes, spraying and cereal seed was perceived by the committee as essential to prevent 'distress in 1898 [becoming] famine in 1899.'[86] The other unusual feature of relief was the large amount of clothing sent for distribution.

Following the example of Manchester, the Lord Mayor of Dublin's Mansion House Fund was launched at a meeting in Dublin on 24th February 1898. This fund raised £11,155 for relief and while it passed £1,192 10s. 0d. to the Manchester Fund for supplying seed potatoes it distributed the balance as follows:

1. food in pressing cases including a school meals scheme,
2. seed potatoes and seed oats,
3. work on recipients own lands of a useful nature, and
4. public works under supervision of county surveyors.

Tallon's comprehensive report shows how widespread support was for Irish relief even if the amounts were modest.[87] Besides these two funds a variety of smaller funds existed.

The distress of 1898 was the last of the crises which had been a feature of the century. Six years later a similar crisis of much more restricted nature occurred,[88] but even in the 1930s emergency relief was still a feature of Irish administrative practice.[89] In 1924 there were reports that conditions in Connemara were at their worst since 1879.[90] When the 1954 Commission on Emigration wanted a specific county to examine it chose Mayo and concluded that by 1954 two fundamental causes of emigration could be seen at work in the area: firstly, the absence of opportunities for making an adequate livelihood; and secondly a growing desire for higher standards of living on the part of the community, in particular, the rural community.[91] The tradition of western poverty, if not distress or famine, was a lingering if declining feature of Irish rural society.

In looking at the causes of distress in the areas mentioned a wide variety of explanations can be offered. Basically the areas affected were congested, in remote locations, with low valuations where pre-1845 conditions lingered longer than elsewhere.[92] When E. Keogh, Secretary of the Manchester Relief Fund visited Gorumna Island off the coast of Connemara in June 1898 he reported universal poverty with the population all at an equally miserable level with practically no distinction or question of degree in the economic condition of the inhabitants.[93] The inhabitants never had enough money to save and all their necessities of life were of the poorest kind. Their cabins were built of loose stones thatched with straw or sedge and the doors in many were large straw mats. Keogh went on to comment on subdivision of holdings and houses and the difficulty of assessing poverty in a society which was so poor that the only question to be asked concerned the adequacy of the food supply. There was an absence of savings and employment. Kelp which had once been profitable was no longer so and fishing and migration seemed to him to offer the only hope of improvement on an island where even in 1898 he reported 'the population of these districts is so dense, owing to large families the result of early marriages, that it will be necessary to thin it out.' The problems of the poorer areas were well understood. A.H. Synge in 1890 wrote of Donegal that the absence of employment for males especially in the unions of Dunfanaghy and Glenties was a major problem, overcrowding on small holdings of poor land made matters worse and the population was apparently unable to make the best uses of the resources they possessed.[94]

In his study of the early 1860s Donnelly used the agricultural statistics to indicate the extent of distress but a similar approach for this period, while it indicates years of crop failure, gives no indication of the severity of the consequences of those failures in the distressed districts.[95] Potatoes had declined in importance in the country generally[96] but they still constituted 50-60% of the tilled acreage in the west[97] where the consumption was still 1 ton per annum on some holdings.[98] Yet the dependence was less even in the distressed areas than in the 1840s and pigs and hens were more common.[99] Despite this the potato was still of crucial importance in some local economies. Illiteracy and a general lack of educational opportunities must also have contributed to poverty in the distressed areas. In the general election of 1892 the illiterate vote as a percentage of the total vote was 48.9% in Mayo North, 38.4% in Mayo East, 46.9% in Galway North and 56.1% in Galway (Connemara). Such percentages were exceptionally high when compared with a national average of 26.6%.[100] It is possible that these figures are exaggerated by the survival of Irish in these areas and by the peculiar practice of pretending to be illiterate at election time.

Furthermore, the shifts in ownership had enormous consequences. As the expansion of graziers' holdings continued the holdings of the poor were limited by the acquisitiveness of the graziers.[101] For many survival depended on seasonal migration which was heaviest from the western counties. From the Dillon estate in Mayo it was estimated that half the labouring tenants emigrated annually in the 1890s. Conditions in west Donegal were not as bad as west Galway and Mayo because of seasonal migration. In the early 1890s about a thousand Gaoth Dobhair people annually moved eastwards to the Lagan and beyond. Seasonal migration increased in 1890 and 1898-1900[102] and even in 1915 the Poor Law unions with the highest percentage migration were still in the distressed areas.[103] The basic problem as the Congested Districts Board, *Baseline Reports* stated was that holdings were too small and it was only in the 1880s and 1890s that emigration rates increased and marriage rates decreased to produce some improvement generally in the west. But in spite of this when the weather caused problems with crops especially with the potato, these areas slid beneath even the harsh contemporary concept of poverty.

There has been a lively debate on the influence of shopkeepers, the availability of credit and the gombeenism of this period.[104] Keogh reported that on Gorumna;

> before income arrives at its destination it is long ago fixed; on receipt of cash it is carried off to the local shopkeeper, with whom every man in the island has a standing account. I use the word 'standing' advisedly as opposed to running, as it more aptly fits the case.[105]

This is not necessarily condemning shopkeepers who provided a needed service in remote areas and even if one examines the actual interest charged as long credit and short credit by Durkins — the only business records extant for a distressed district — the level of interest was not excessive.[106] It is possible to find many individual complaints about shopkeepers and their influence on relief but, in general,[107] they do not feature among contemporary accounts as exacerbating the general level of poverty. Hugh Alexander Law, who was elected M.P. for Donegal West in 1902, submitted a long memorandum on 'Gombeening' to the Royal Commission on Congestion in which he claimed that in many districts in the west and north west a minority of shopkeepers or little 'rings' of shopkeepers were 'in possession of a monopoly' and condemned the 'irresponsible power which monopoly brings. This they were able to do because of lack of transit facilities, the ignorance and apathy of the bulk of the people themselves [and] above all the choking entanglement of old debts.'[108] He explained the gombeen man's operations under four headings:

1. Money lending at usurious rates of interst.
2. Goods sold and entered into books at exorbitant price, and interest added at pleasure.
3. Goods purchased from people but not paid for in cash but vaguely taken in exchange for tea or groceries or 'on account' of existing debt.
4. Trust auctions.

Law believed these practices were confined to the north and north west. He maintained that in at least one parish in Donegal shopkeepers brought suits 'in sheaves' for possession of land for money owed every year, though this was unknown in Gweedore. There was concern that small holders should not lose their land and Dillon and other Irish members agreed at a National Convention in 1903 to attempt to introduce a Homestead provision on the lines already exisiting in some Canadian provinces which would have prevented small farms with rateable valuations of under £20 from being so seized. The proposal had its opponents, O'Doherty, another Donegal M.P., said it was a 'no debt manifesto' and he maintained that there were very few gombeenmen in Donegal and that 'the people largely depended upon shopkeepers to make both ends meet.' The Homestead provision he maintained struck at small farmers and fishermen.[109] The Homestead provision was withdrawn. The great suspicion of shopkeepers which existed is evidence of some abuse and the shopkeeper undoubtedly had enormous influence. The line of credit which they extended was seen by many contemporaries like O'Doherty as a life line for the poor while for others it brought the poor into a cycle of poverty. Judgment of their narrow role in the economic sphere is a political one. Certainly co-operative stores, co-operative credit societies and statutory provisions against alienation and excessive interest would all have improved the lot of the poor[110], but by 1910 the main thrust of Irish politics was not interested in such matters and the shopkeepers who abused their influence were largely unchecked if not unnoticed. No specific measures to remedy the Irish situation were introduced but after the Usury Law Repeal Act of 1854 lenders were free to charge such interest as they could get, the Moneylenders Act of 1900 began to introduce some controls for both Britain and Ireland.[111]

Views of the effectiveness of relief in the 1890s varied enormously. The United Irish League members in 1898 were unimpressed by government measures,[112] yet the overall expenditure in the decade was high both in terms of grants and loans. As with the pre-Famine crises, when famine deaths were few, in the 1890s no-one claimed people died of starvation.[113] The drive was always to keep people alive. Sir Robert Peel had bowed to necessity in 1817, 1822, 1826 and in the 1840s.[114] Graham had written to Stanley in 1831 that no government could 'allow its people to starve, according to the most approved rules of political economy.'[115] Interestingly the idea of necessity remains at the core of Irish welfare legislation. The Social Welfare Act of 1981[116] guarantees people their basic needs including fuel but, like their nineteenth century predecessors, administrators are usually concerned with limiting expenditure and so in recent times it has taken High Court and Supreme Court actions to implement the wishes of the legislators.[117] In the 1890s government relief for rural distress was effective. It prevented deaths, provided employment, improved the seed supply and while it added to the rates burden in certain areas it also poured substantial amounts into these same areas as free grants. Indeed there was a bias in favour of the rural poor by comparison with the urban poor. Dublin, though a city with an enormous number and variety of charities, rarely received any comparable aid.[118] It is no surprise to a student of nineteenth century poverty that while rural poverty has been virtually eliminated, urban poverty persisted and still persists in Ireland.

The relief offered for the immediate crises of the 1890s must also be viewed against the background of the wider reform movement. The setting up of the Congested Districts Board began a search for social reforms which eventually led to state involvement in a wide range of areas.[119] The Recess Committee Report of 1895 was a reaction to the social conditions of the time and legislative and other developments for the permanent improvement of the poor were a feature of the age.[120] The major Public Health Act was passed in 1878 but amendments and additions in 1889

1896, 1898 and 1900 continued the process.[121] The Local Government Act in 1898 brought a new era in local administration. In 1890 the Housing of the Working Classes Act continued the process of state built housing for the poor.[122] By 1901, 15,000 cottages had been built in Ireland.[123] The building of light railways attempted to improve the infrastructure aided by the Tramways Act. Balfour's land legislation attempted to create a new peasant proprietorship[124] and the Registration of Title Act facilitated the transfer of small holdings.[125] Though the Wyndham Land Act came in the new century it was the culmination of a long process of reform.[126] The great years of change in social policy came in the years of Liberal Government from 1906 to 1914.[127] Direct welfare legislation attempted to provide relief for the old, the unemployed and other specific groups.[128] These reforms were to be of great importance in Ireland but the generic problem of poverty remained even if not at famine proportions.

Conditions improved in the west gradually. Emigrants' remittances, improved agricultural practices, population changes, improved markets and even new products all facilitated improvement.[129] Almquist has drawn attention to the significance of the egg market in Mayo — the traditionally most distressed county. He compares poultry rearing there in the late nineteenth century to domestic spinning of the late eighteenth century.[130] Both were of great economic significance to the poor inhabitants. The contribution of public and private relief also aided the process. Distress in restricted, remote areas attracted great sums of relief and caused serious attempts to be made at removing fundamental problems. In the process of change the expenditure of £4 million in loans and grants helped to break the cycle of poverty. The 1890s stand not just as the end of a century but also the end of an era of famine, disease and suffering in the remote areas. In the new century while the problems remained, change and movement broke the static nature of those isolated communities.

References

1. Stanislaus Kennedy, R.S.C. ed., *One Million Poor?* (Dublin, 1981); Lorraine Joyce and A. McCashin (Compilers), *Poverty and Social Policy* (Dublin, 1981); *Report of the Commission on Social Welfare* (Dublin, 1986).

2. Michael Harrington, *The Other America* (New York, 1962); Charles Murray, *Losing Ground, American Social Policy, 1950-1980* (New York, 1984); Keith Griffin, *Land Concentration and Rural Poverty* (Oxford, 1981).

3. Raymond Crotty, *Irish Agricultural Production; Its Volume and Structure* (Cork, 1966), p.94.

4. A. Dale Tussing, 'Poverty Research and Political Analysis in the United States: Implications for Ireland', *Economic and Social Review,* 5, no.1, (1973), pp.75-98.

5. Report on Relief of Distress, Ireland, 1890-1891, S.P.O.I. Box 5, Room VIII, 4; *Agricultural Statistics Report for 1890,* p. 89; *Annual Register,* 1890, p. 275.

6. *Agricultural Statistics Report for 1893,* p. 15.

7. Report on Relief of Distress, Ireland, 1890-1891, pp. 3-4 S.P.O.I. Box 5, Room VIII, 4.

8. Maps of Distressed Districts; Relief of Distress Papers, 1890-1891, S.P.O.I. IX/4/38.

9. Relief of Distress Papers, 1890-1891, Leitrim, Clarke, Corke, Donegal, Galway, Kerry, Mayo, Roscommon and Sligo, S.P.O.I. IX/4/1-19; Report on Distress, 20 November 1890, S.P.O.I. IX/4/28.

10. Miscellaneous Registered Papers; Relief of Distress Papers, 1890-1891, S.P.O.I. IX/1/28.

11. Report on Relief of Distress, Ireland, 1890-1891, p. 8, S.P.O.I. Box 5, Room VIII, 4; Colonel Frazer to West Ridgeway, 5 November 1890, S.P.O.I. IX/1/28.

12. A.J. Balfour to Colonel Frazer, 2 December 1890, S.P.O.I. IX/1/39.

13. Relief Papers, 26 November 1890, S.P.O.I. IX/1/39.

14. Relief Papers, 2 December 1890, S.P.O.I. IX/1/39.

15. Report on Relief of Distress, Ireland, 1890-1891, pp. 9-10 S.P.O.I. Box 5, Room VIII, 4.

16. *Ibid.,* pp. 72-5

17. *Ibid.,* pp. 10-13 and Appendix A, pp. 3-25

18. *Ibid.,* p. 15.

19. *Ibid.,* pp. 20-3.

20. Relief of Distress Papers, Ireland, 1890-1891, S.P.O.I. IX/4/40.

21. Report on Relief of Distress, Ireland, 1890-1891, pp. 17-20, S.P.O.I. Box 5, Room VIII, 4. £3,000 remained unexpended.

22. *Ibid.,* p. 18.

23. *Ibid.,* pp. 20-1.

24. Report on Relief of Distress, Ireland, 1890-1891, pp. 3-5, S.P.O.I. Box 5, Room VIII, 4.

25. *Ibid.; Agricultural Statistics 1880-1890.*

26. Report on Relief of Distress, Ireland, 1890-1891, pp. 22, 83-7, S.P.O.I. IX/4/40; *Reports on Potato Failure,* Brit. Parl. Papers, 1890-91(131)LXIII: *Reports on Distress,* Brit. Parl. Papers, 1892 (85-session I)LXIC.

27. Walter Callan, Secretary, 'Memorandum on the Financial Aspect of the Relief of Distress in Ireland' S.P.O.I. Royal Commission on Congestion Papers, 1980, Box 5. Hereafter cited as 'Memorandum'.

28. *Ibid.,* p. 3.

29. *Ibid.,* pp. 1-3.

30. *Ibid.,* p. 2.

31. Timothy P. O'Neill, 'The State, Poverty and Distress in Ireland, 1815-'45'. Unpublished Ph.D. thesis N.U.I. 1971, pp. 309-10. See also 'Report of the Commissioners for the Relief of the Poor in Ireland' in *Eleventh Report of the Commissioners for Auditing the Public Accounts of Ireland for 1822,* Brit. Parl.

Papers, 1823(199)X, pp.114-130.
32. Final Report of Commissioners for the Employment of the Poor in Ireland, 31 August 1822, S.P.O.I. Reg. Papers 1822, 1960.
33. 'Memorandum', p. 6.
34. J.V. O'Brien, *William O'Brien and the Course of Irish Politics 1881-1918* (Los Angeles, 1976), p.79; *Annual Register, 1890,* p. 275.
35. O'Brien, *William O'Brien,* chapter five.
36. Dillon Papers, T.C.D. Mss. 6803, ff. 16-58.
37. Relief Works, 1895; *General Report,* pp.3-5, S.P.O.I. IX/4/42.
38. Memorandum, pp. 2 and 6.
39. *Relief Works, 1895,: detailed report on works,* p. 55, S.P.O.I. IX/4/42.
40. *Ibid.,* p. 32.
41. *Ibid.,* p. 61; Memorandum, pp. 2 and 6.
42. T.P. O'Neill, 'Seán Mac Héil agus Bochtaineacht an Iarthair' in A. Ni Cheannain, Eag., *Leon on Iarthair* (Baile Atha Cliath, 1983), pp. 25-37.
43. Gerald Balfour letter dated 23 March 1898, S.P.O.I. C.S.O. Reg. Papers, 1898, 14369.
44. M. Gonne, *Servant of the Queen* (Dublin, 1925), pp. 229-235; *The Western People,* 12 March, 1898.
45. Dillon Papers T.C.D. Mss. 6803, ff. 58.
46. *Freeman's Journal,* 23 February 1897.
47. *Ibid.*
48. *The Galway Express,* 30 January 1897.
49. *Freeman's Journal,* 25 September, 1897.
50. *Irish Times,* 6 February 1897.
51. *Connaught Telegraph,* 10, 14 July 1897.
52. *Ibid.,* 2, 9, 16 October 1897.
53. D. Tallon, *Relief of Distress in the West and South of Ireland. Report of the Mansion House Committee* (Dublin, 1898), p. 12; *Freeman's Journal,* 25 April, 1898.
54. *Freeman's Journal,* 1 March 1898.
55. Lavelle to Balfour, 23 November 1897, S.P.O.I. C.S.O. Reg. Papers 1897, 19667; *Freeman's Journal,* 29 September 1897.
56. *The Galway Express,* 2 October 1897.
57. *Donegal Independent,* 21 March 1898.
58. Gonne, *Servant of the Queen,* p. 230.
59. Charles Stevenson, 'West of Ireland Distress 1898', *The New Ireland Review,* X, December 1898, pp. 193-6.
60. *Ibid.,* p. 196.
61. Memorandum, pp. 3 and 6.
62. Tallon, *Relief of Distress in the West and South of Ireland, Report of the Mansion House Committee.* p. 44; Stevenson, 'West of Ireland Distress 1898', p. 196.
63. Memorandum, p. 6.
64. O'Neill, 'The State, Poverty and Distress in Ireland, 1815-45' pp. 40-2, 140-3.
65. C.S.O. Reg. Papers, 1898, 136312, S.P.O.I.
66. C.S.O. Reg. Papers, 1898, 14370, S.P.O.I.
67. *Report of the Local Government Board for Ireland, 1897* Brit. Parl. Papers, 1898 [c.8958] XLI, pp. 18-9; *Report of the Local Government Board for Ireland, 1898,* Brit. Parl. Papers, 1899 [c.9480] XXXIX, pp. 1-22.

68. Memorandum, pp. 3 and 6.

69. *Report of the Local Government Board, 1897,* Brit. Parl. Papers, 1898[c.8958]XLI, p. 18.

70. *Freeman's Journal,* 12 March 1898.

71. Police Reports on Prices, 22 December 1890 and 18 April 1891, Relief Papers 1890-1, S.P.O.I. IX/1/27.

72. *Agricultural Statistics for the Year 1890,* p. 21.

73. Tallon, *Relief of Distress in the West and South of Ireland, Report of the Mansion House Committee,* p. 9.

74. C.S.O. Reg. Papers, 1898, 14369 and 7572, S.P.O.I.; Thomas Kelly, (Constable/Timekeeper) to A.H. Crozier, R.E., 25 June 1895. (Sapper Shark's envelope, Relief Papers, IX/4/43).

75. *Freeman's Journal,* 14, 18 and 28 March 1898.

76. *Report of the Local Government Board, 1897,* Brit. Parl. Papers, 1898[8958]XLI, p. 19; C.S.O. Reg. Papers, 1898, 14366, S.P.O.I.; *The Western People,* 28 May 1898.

77. *Report of the Local Government Board, 1898,* Brit. Parl. Papers, 1899[c.9480]XXXIX p. 21; *The Western People,* 25 June 1898.

78. *The Western People,* 9 July 1898.

79. C.S.O. Reg. Papers, 1898, 14369, S.P.O.I., G. Balfour, 'Memorandum', 2 November 1897 (P.R.O.I. Cabinet Minutes, 1899, 37/45, no. 41).

80. Tallon, *Relief of Distress in the West and South of Ireland, Report of the Mansion House Committee,* p. 8.

81. In almost every year of minor famine in nineteenth century Ireland a relief committee was established at the Mansion House. Most committees published an account of their activities but the full record of such a committee survives for only one year. The records of the 1879 committee are in the city archives in City Hall. Tallon, *Relief of Distress in the West and South of Ireland, Report of the Mansion House Committee, passim.*

82. Stevenson, 'West of Ireland Distress 1898', p. 155; Memorandum, p. 3.

83. Stevenson, 'West of Ireland Distress 1898', p. 193.

84. *Ibid.,* p. 193.

85. *Ibid.,* p. 195. The Manchester fund was supported by donations from twenty-six cities and towns in the north of England and by a collection made in Belfast.

86. *Ibid.,* p. 197.

87. Tallon, *Relief of Distress in the West and South of Ireland, Report of the Mansion House Committee, passim.*

88. Memorandum, p. 3.

89. *Dáil Debates,* November 1930, V 43.

90. *Irish Independent,* 1 January 1925; 3 February 1925.

91. *Report of the Commission on Emigration and other Population Problems* (Dublin, 1954) pp. 84, 272.

92. See: *Baseline Reports of the Inspectors of the Congested Districts Board 1892-98* (Dublin, 1898).

93. E. Keogh, 'In Gorumna Island', *The New Ireland Review,* June 1898, IX, pp. 194-9; L.M. Cullen, 'Man, Landscape and Roads: the Changing Eighteenth Century' in W. Nolan, *The Shaping of Ireland: the Geographical Perspective* (Dublin, 1986), p. 125.

94. A.H. Synge, *A plan for developing the resources of north-west Donegal* (Dublin, 1890), *passim.*

95. J.S. Donnelly, Jr., 'The agricultural depression of 1859-64', *Irish Economic and Social History*, III (1976) pp. 33-54;
The following table shows the fluctuations in the produce per acre of potatoes:

Years	Tons	Years	Tons	Years	Tons
1882	2.4	1889	3.6	1896	3.8
1883	4.3	1890	2.3	1897	2.2
1884	3.8	1891	4.0	1898	4.4
1885	4.0	1892	3.5	1899	4.2
1886	3.3	1893	4.2	1900	2.8
1887	4.5	1894	2.6	1901	5.3
1888	3.1	1895	4.9	Mean	3.7

'Statistical Survey of Irish Agriculture' in *Ireland Industrial and Agricultural* (Department of Agriculture and Technical Instruction for Ireland, Dublin, 1902), p. 311.

96. R. Crotty, 'Modernisation and Land Reform: Real or Cosmetic? The Irish case.' *The Journal of Peasant Studies*, XI, no.1, October (1983), pp. 110-1.

97. L.M. Cullen, *The Emergence of Modern Ireland* (London, 1972), p. 135.

98. C. Ó Gráda, 'Seasonal Migration and Post Famine Adjustment in the West of Ireland' *Studia Hibernica*, no. 13 (1973), p. 14.

99. E.L. Almquist, Mayo and Beyond, Land, Domestic Industry, and Rural Transformation in the Irish West (Ph.D. thesis Boston University, 1977), chapter 7.

100. C.J. Woods, 'The general election of 1892: the catholic clergy and the defeat of the Parnellites' in F.S.L. Lyons and R.A.J. Hawkins eds., *Ireland under the Union: Varieties of Tension: essays in honour of T.W. Moody* (Oxford, 1980), p. 309; Charles R. Browne, 'Ethnography of Ballcroy, Co. Mayo', *Proceedings of the Royal Irish Academy*, XX (1896-8), p. 92.

101. R. Crotty, *Irish Agricultural Production*, pp. 110-1; David S. Jones, 'The cleavage between graziers and peasants in the land struggle, 1890-1910' in S. Clark and J.S. Donnelly, Jr. eds., *Irish Peasants: Violence and Political Unrest 1780-1914* (Madison, 1983), pp. 374-419.

102. C. Ó Gráda, 'Seasonal Migration', pp. 62-72.

103. *Report of the Interdepartmental Committee on Seasonal Migration to Great Britain, 1937-1938* (Dublin, 1938).

104. Peter Gribbon and M.D. Higgins, 'Patronage, Traditional and Moderisation: the case of the Irish 'Gombeenman', *Economic and Social Review*, VI, no. 1 (1974), pp. 27-44; Peter Gribbon and M.D. Higgins, 'The Irish 'Gombeenman': Reincarnation or Rehabilitation?', *Economic and Social Review*, VIII, no.4 (1977), pp. 313-20; Liam Kennedy, 'Traders in the Irish Rural Economy, 1880-1914', *Economic History Review*, 2nd series, XXXII (1979), pp.201-10; L. Kennedy, 'Farmers, Traders and Agricultural Politics' in S. Clark and J.S. Donnelly eds., *Irish Peasants*, pp. 339-373.

105. E. Keogh, 'In Gorumna Island', p.194.

106. Business Records, Mayo 5/10. Durkins, P.R.O.I.

107. Michael Flannery, Coocastle, Mayo to Under-Secretary 5 June 1891, Relief Papers IX/1/28 (S.P.O.I.); Capt. Francis Welch, R.N. 'Report', 11/3/1891, Relief Papers IX/1/27, S.P.O.I., Thomas Kelly (Constable/Timekeeper) to A.H. Crozier R.E. 25 June 1895, Relief Papers IX/4/43, S.P.O.I.

108. H.L. (Hugh Alexander Law), Gombeening. (Royal Commission on Congestion Papers, Carton 7, S.P.O.I.). I want to thank Miss Neary for locating this typescript for me.

109. Hansard, 1903, 124, col. 1444.

110. *Ibid.*, col. 1443-1446.

111. A Moneylenders Act, 63/4 Vict., C.51; See also: Sale of Goods Act, 1893, 56/7 Vict., C.71; Nevill v. Snelling (1880), 15 ch. D. 679.

112. Hansard, 19 February 1898 M. Davitt, John Dillon, T.M. Healy.

113. Gonne, *Servant of the Queen*, p. 230.

114. O'Neill, 'The State, Property and Distress in Ireland, 1815-45', pp. 186-201.

115. Graham to Stanley, 6 June 1831 (Graham Papers, Netherby).

116. '. . . the amount of supplementary welfare allowance to which a person is entitled shall be the amount by which his means fall short of his needs' S.207, Social Welfare (Consolidation) Act 1981.

117. State (Kershaw) v Eastern Health Board in *Irish Law Reports Monthly*, 5 (1985), pp. 235-9; State (McLoughlin) v Eastern Health Board, unreported, Supreme Court, 288/86.

118. F.S.L. Lyons, *Ireland since the Famine* (London, 1971), pp. 277-8; M.E. Daly, *Dublin: the Deposed Capital, a Social and Economic History, 1860-1914* (Cork, 1984), pp. 77-116.

119. M.L. Micks, *History of the Congested Districts Board* (Dublin, 1925). Micks as a Local Government Board inspector organised relief in Donegal in 1891 before the C.D.B. was established. A prolific writer his reports were often humourous. M.L. Hicks to C. Davies, 6 May 1891 Relief Papers, IX/1/28., S.P.O.I.

120. *Report of the Recess Committee on the Establishment of a Department of Agriculture and Industries for Ireland* (Dublin, 1892).

121. Sir C. Cameron, 'Report on Public Health' in *Dublin Journal of Medical Science*, 1909; 'Report on poor-law medical system in Ireland' in *British Medical Journal*, 1904; J. Vanston, *Law of Public Health in Ireland* (London, 1913); *Report on Irish Public Health and Medical Services*, Brit. Parl. Papers, 1920 [Cmd.761] XVII.

122. 53-54, Vict. c.70.

123. *Public Subvention to Housing in Ireland* (An Foras Forbartha, Dublin, 1984); John W. Boyle, 'A Marginal Figure: the Irish Rural Labourer' in S. Clark and J. Donnelly eds., *Irish Peasants*, p. 332.

124. 54-55 Vict. c.48; The Act was named after Arthur James Balfour, who was Chief Secretary of Ireland in 1891.

125. J.C. Wylie, *Irish Land Law* (London, 1975), pp. 35-6.

126. *Ibid.*, p. 38.

127. A. Briggs, 'The Welfare State in Historical Perspective' in *Archives Europeenes de Sociologie*, 2 (1961), *passim.*

128. *Report of the Commission on Social Welfare* (Dublin, 1986), chapter 1.
129. L.M. Cullen, *Economic History of Ireland since 1660* (London, 1972).
130. E.L. Almquist, *Mayo and Beyond,* p. 255.

9

SUBSISTENCE CRISES AND FAMINES IN IRELAND: A NUTRITIONIST'S VIEWS

E. Margaret Crawford

Although famine has been an intermittent threat to man's existence throughout history, the nature of the threat is complex and much still remains unexplained. Nevertheless our understanding of the interaction between starvation and disease is advancing. Nutritional studies in particular have made a major contribution in this field. Famine diseases, dietary deficiency diseases, and the relationship between starvation and infections have all been the subject of intensive research in recent years. Famine has been banished from Ireland, but many underdeveloped regions are still vulnerable and, when stricken, nutritional disorders, once familiar to our ancestors, occur. Advances in nutritional science, therefore, not only benefit countries still suffering the ravages of famine, but also provide insight into the experience of dietary deprivation suffered by our forefathers. How then, would the nutritionist view famine years in Ireland's history?

I

Famine Diseases

As the essays in this volume show Ireland experienced several very severe famines as well as numerous lesser scarcities. Indeed in 1845-9 it had the doubtful distintion of staging the last great Western European famine not associated with war. Newspapers and television reports today leave us in no doubt to the appearance of famine victims. A careful reading of famine accounts in Ireland, particularly in 1845-9, reveal symptoms of starvation remarkably similar to the stark images from Ethiopia and elsewhere that haunt our television screens.

Thy physiological manifestations of starvation emerge gradually. The first and most noticeable sign of dietary deprivation in individuals is depletion of fat deposits. Abdominal and thoracic organs degenerate, and the intestinal mucosa becomes thin and smooth and loses some of its absorptive ability. The heart acquires the brownish hue and atrophy characteristic of starvation, and blood pressure falls significantly. In time 'famine oedema' (retention of fluid) occurs. Still further stigmata appear. Hair becomes dull, eyes gaunt, and in children abnormal 'lanugo' hair grows on the forearms and back. The skin acquires a paper-like quality, is dull, inelastic, and grey in hue with brown blotches sometimes appearing which are irreversible. Body weight falls, basal metabolic rate decreases and activity is reduced. 'How far there is any adjustment of the internal work done by the body . . . is not known'.[1] Meyer has suggested that an 'adaptation' or precarious 'equilibrium' to starvation can be established, which may be sustained for weeks or even several months.[2] The terminal events of starvation are usually intractable diarrhoea because of a non-functioning gut and cardiovascular collapse.

Widespread and prolonged famine leads to very high levels of mortality. In historical accounts precise details of the age groups most affected by starvation are generally not available. However, recent evidence clearly shows that both the biological and psychological brunt of starvation falls first and most severely on young children because of their exacting dietary requirements. Consequently the six month to 5 year olds are selectively erased from the population.

Among famine victims children nutritional marasmus and kwashiorkor, collectively referred to as protein-energy malnutrition (PEM),[3] are the most commonly encountered clinical disorders. The differences between nutritional marasmus and kwashiorkor are well defined. A marasmic child exhibits low body weight as growth stops, fat stores are depleted and muscles waste away. The child becomes wizened and shrunken and acquires the appearance of an old man or woman. Irritability, fretfulness and apathy can be observed, and in the final stages, diarrhoea, which is clearly the same condition as famine diarrhoea.[4] Kwashiorkor is characterised by oedema, usually concentrated in the abdomen and lower limbs.[5] In addition, body weight is low in relation to age, muscles waste away, skin pigmentation and lesions appear, hair discolouration occurs, along with diarrhoea. Kwashiorkor was once thought to be the result of severe protein deficiency, while nutritional marasmus was attributed to generalised nutritional deficiency. Some authorities now believe that both deficiencies are simultaneously involved. Why some victims contract kwashiorkor and others marasmus, while experiencing common dietary deprivation, is still not established.[6]

Irish medical and administrative reports contain graphic descriptions of these symptoms. William Harty writing about disease and distress in 1817, a year of serious food shortage, noted the prevalence of dropsy (oedema) among the poor. In the same year Dr Francis Rogan, physician to the Strabane Dispensary described how, 'in some [patients] who were not brought to the hospital till the disease was far advanced, the belly was found tense, swollen and very painful on pressure'.[7] Rogan treated 222 cases of anasarca (oedema). Such observations were not confined to one location. In the next year a physician in Waterford, Dr Bracken noted that many children under the age of ten years 'died in the hospital, not so much of fever as other disorders which supervened: [such as] atrophy or marasmus.'[8] Famine oedema was very marked during the Great Famine. William Bennett, who was involved with the Society of Friends Central Relief Committee, observed during his travels through County Mayo in 1847 that 'in many [cases] the husbands or sons were prostrate under the horrid disease, — the result of long-continued famine and low living — in which first the limbs, and then the body, swell most frightfully . . .'[9] Bennett continued 'we entered upwards of fifty . . . tenements. The scene was invariably the same . . .'[10] The nutritionist, W.R. Aykroyd has suggested that 'famine oedema' experienced during the 1845-9 crisis may have been exacerbated by the relief measures.[11] Bowlfuls of watery soup containing oxheads, maize, and a few vegetables, were doled out which provided some calories, but added further fluid to already water-logged consumers.

Marasmic children made an indelible image on Joseph Crosfield, another aid worker for the Society of Friends. In 1846 he reported a 'heart-rending scene [of] poor wretches in the last stages of famine imploring to be received into the [work]house; . . . Some of [the] children were worn to skeletons, their features sharpened with hunger, and their limbs wasted almost to the bone.'[12] On the island of North Arran, where families were subsisting on sea-weed and limpets the people had the 'same gaunt looks in the men, and the peculiar worn-out expression of premature old age in the countenances of the women and children.'[13] William Forster also noted in Carrick-on-Shannon that 'the children exhibit the effects of famine in a remarkable degree, their faces looking wan and haggard with hunger, and seeming like old men and women.'[14]

Among victims of starvation, the skin not only becomes wrinkled and dry but also assumes an abnormal brown pigmentation deeper than a good sun tan. 'Our skin was black like an oven because of the terrible famine', lamented Old Testament Jeremiah.[15] More prosaically Dr Daniel Donovan, a medical doctor in Skibbereen described the starving masses in 1848:

> In a short time the face and limbs become frightfully emaciated; the eyes acquire
> a most peculiar stare; the skin exhaled a peculiar and offensive foetor, and was

covered with a brownish filthy-looking coating, almost as indelible as varnish. This I was at first inclined to regard as encrusted filth, but further experience has convinced me that it is a secretion poured out from the exhalants on the surface of the body.[16]

Yet another feature of famine — lanugo hair — was observed on the faces of starving Irish children during the mid 1840s. Richard D. Webb, also a Friends' worker, noted a growth of fine downy hair on the faces of children.[17] W. Curran described the feature in a medical article of 1880 and stated that he was informed by the Rev Canon Bourke 'that . . . hundreds of such cases [were witnessed] in Ireland' in the 1845-9 famine.[18]

Starvation death is protracted and agonising. In the final stages the ability of the body to absorb food diminishes as the intestinal lining becomes thin and smooth, causing diarrhoea. Post mortem examinations carried out by Dr Donovan during the 1845-9 crisis revealed the severity of the famine conditions. He observed:

a particularly thin condition of the small intestines, which (in such cases) were so transparent that if the deceased had taken any food immediately before death the contents could be seen through the coats of the bowel; and on one occasion I was able to recognise a portion of raw green cabbage in the duodenum of a man who died of want. This condition of the intestines I look upon as the strongest proof of starvation.[19]

All Ireland's major famines occurred before compulsory registration of deaths. Mortality levels from starvation diseases can only be guessed at. For the Great Famine we do have some good modern estimates of total famine mortality.[20] There are also data of questionable quality contained in the 1851 census, which recorded the numbers of deaths from various causes in the previous ten years as returned by householders.[21] These statistics are flawed on two counts. They were filled in by unqualified people, unskilled in diagnosing causes of death; and they are based on the memory of what happened in earlier years.

Table 1 reveals that between 1845 and 1850 over 100,000 (104,638) people died of marasmus, dropsy and starvation. Thus almost 10 per cent of famine deaths as calculated by Mokyr[22] can be attributed directly to hunger. Bearing in mind that during famines fever is a bigger killer than starvation this total represents a horrifying harvest of suffering.

In addition to young children aged between one and five years the most vulnerable famine victims are old people, pregnant and lactating women. Adolescents and adult women tend to survive better than men. Details of the age groups most affected are frequently absent in historical accounts of

Table 1: Deaths from Famine Diseases in Ireland 1841-51

	Marasmus	Dropsy	Starvation
1841		2143	60
1842	3583	1502	187
1843	3587	1603	211
1844	3871	1700	268
1845	4341	2078	516
1846	6360	2774	2041
1847	11711	5246	6058
1848	10551	4027	4678
1849	11823	4407	4717
1850	8721	3852	2392
1851	5160	2358	827

SOURCE: *Census of Ireland 1841, 1851 & 1861*

famines. We are fortunate, therefore, to have age data for 1845-9. Boyle and Ó Gráda have calculated that 29 per cent of excess deaths occurred in the 0-4 age group although this group represented only 13.5 per cent of the population.[23] Over the ten year period 1841-51 75% of deaths from marasmus were of children aged 0-4, although this age cohort constituted only 14 per cent of the population. The Rev Dr Traill Hall's description of the distress in the parish of Schull, County Cork makes the point vividly: 'frightful and fearful is the havoc around me . . . the aged, who, with the young — are almost without exception swollen and ripening for the grave.'[24]

In addition to physical deterioration, starvation produces dramatic psychological changes. Although the intellect remains clear, the personality of victims is altered in various ways. The earliest changes to appear are apathy, depression, and mental restlessness; food becomes an obsession. Victims become self-centred and indifferent to others, even to their own kin, producing a total breakdown of family ties. Donovan, once again wrote vividly about these harrowing events:

> Another symptom of starvation, and one which accounts for the horrible scenes that famine usually exhibits, is the total insensibility of the sufferers to every other feeling except that of supplying their own wants. I have seen mothers snatch food from the hands of their starving children; known a son to engage in a fatal struggle with his father for a potato; and have seen parents look on the putrid bodies of their offspring without evincing a sympton of sorrow.[25]

Death released many from hunger, but many survived with the long-term scars of prolonged food deprivation. There is now a considerable literature on the effects of malnutrition on physical and intellectual development. During a period of dietary deprivation, particularly protein deficiency, children fail to grow or put on weight. However, Ashworth has shown that even in the most extreme cases of PEM 'catch-up' growth can be achieved relatively quickly at about 4-6 weeks with the benefit of supplementary feeding.[26] Correction of height deficit takes longer, since skeletal growth occurs at a much slower pace. Whether the full deficit is ever restored depends on age at time of food crisis, and the duration of dietary deprivation. To quote a nutritionist, Martorell, 'the possibilities for catch-up growth are very limited once [a] child reaches 3 to 5 years of age. If the child is already stunted at those ages, he will in all probability remain small throughout the growing years, eventually becoming a small adult.'[27]

This information is useful to our understanding of the major Irish famines. Relief programmes were primitive. Maize rations and inferior soup were the only supplies provided on a large scale. The need for particular nutrients, especially during the growing phase of life, was not understood. For those who survived until food supplies returned to normal the rehabilitation phase would have taken considerably longer than for those treated for malnutrition today. Historical evidence is lacking but modern research leads us to conclude that Irish children of between the ages of 0 and 5 years who survived prolonged food crises probably failed to achieve their full potential stature.

Turning to intellectual development, here too extreme malnutrition in child survivors causes impairment. Eighty per cent of brain growth takes place by the age of three, for which protein foods are most important. Hence a deficiency in protein intake at the crucial phase of brain growth would be expected to hinder intellectual development. Testing the hypothesis is difficult.[28] 'Learning and behavioural deficiencies, in relation to malnutrition, are areas of great disagreement.'[29] Certain scientists have suggested a direct correlation between low protein intakes in childhood and retarded intellectual development. Indeed recent research 'has shown that survivors of early severe malnutrition differ from well nourished children in a great variety of functional aspects.'[30] Even children who have suffered malnutrition before the age of six months have shown behavioural deficiencies.[31] Cravioto *et.al.* examined language development as an index of intelligence and discovered that, compared with the well nourished children, those suffering from malnutrition lagged in this skill. Furthermore, the deficit continued even after clinical recovery had taken place.[32] From this and other similar experimental work stems the belief that a strong association exists between malnutrition early in life and intellectual impairment. In the light of such findings we may wonder whether the hungry cohort of Irish children 0 to 5 year olds who survived the famine of 1845-9 failed to fulfill their full intellectual prowess.

II

Infections

There is no doubt that starvation diseases increase morbidity and mortality at times of famine, but they are far outnumbered by epidemic diseases.[33] Yet a simple link cannot be established between famine and infection; instead a more complex set of connections appears to operate.

Many historical records reveal a trail of disease accompanying or following periods of subsistence crisis and famine. Understandably, therefore, contemporaries thought famine was responsible for increased incidence of disease; hence the belief 'first famine then fever'. Several historians have re-examined the evidence and challenged the conclusion. Meuvret, drawing on French evidence, for example concluded that famine *favours* rather than *causes* epidemics. He pointed to the mass migration of rural populations into towns at times of famine, resulting in worsening sanitation, which spread the contagion,[34] though concedes that epidemic diseases were propagated and even engendered by undernourishment.[35]

More recent work by Post and Carmichael is also sceptical about linking undernutrition directly with increased incidence and virulence of infection. Post even questions whether it is possible to argue from present experience to the historical past, contending that 'it is possible to discover significant environmental, behavioural, and cultural differences between present-day underdeveloped societies and pre-industrial European societies, and they may affect any interpretation of the relationship of famine and disease.'[36] In his study of the 1740s European food crisis, Post summarises his position thus:'on the basis of medical findings in regard to the influence of nutritional status on . . . specific infections, the probable conclusion is that the western Europe epidemics of 1740-42 did not originate primarily in the biological effects of undernutrition or malnutrition.'[37]

Carmichael's attack on a simple link running from famine to fever challenges the whole notion of a synergistic action between undernutrition and infection.[38] Put simply, synergism implies that acute infectious diseases adversely affect nutritional status in several ways. Firstly, malnourished persons are more susceptible to the development of infectious diseases; secondly, these diseases tend to be more severe in the malnourished; and finally, when malnutrition and infection occur simultaneously, the consequences are more serious than the occurrence of each independently, creating a synergistic interaction.[39] However, Carmichael finds the theory unacceptable arguing that micro-organisms require many of the same nutrients necessary for maintaining good health. Thus, 'a malnourished host may even have a slight advantage in forestalling clinical infection.'[40] Nevertheless, Carmichael does concede that the immune system will fail at the starvation stage,[41] and it is at this level that we are interested in examining the Irish experience.

This reluctance of some historians to accept a direct relationship between undernutrition and vulnerability to disease is not shared by nutritionists who generally subscribe to the synergistic theory. For instance, protein, vitamin A, C, and B- complex deficiencies have all been shown to produce synergistic effects.[42] Severe protein depletion, in particular lowers antibody activity, and thus children with kwashiorkor have a reduced capacity to produce specific antibodies. Nevertheless, research demonstrates that we are not looking at a simple connection, but at a complex set of relationships. Foege explains thus:

The problem of infectious diseases in times of famine involves two definable mechanisms. One, there are indications that malnutrition often results in a more severe clinical infection. Second, the social disruption, crowding, and decrease in sanitation often fostered by famine enhance the transmissibility of many infectious diseases.[43]

Not all infections are influenced to the same degree by nutritional status. Lethal diseases such as plague, influenza, and smallpox are so virulent that their activity is independent of nutrition, while other diseases, for example, typhoid, malaria and typhus are influenced only to a minimal degree by nutrition. Measles, diarrhoeal diseases, tuberculosis, most respiratory infections, pertussis, many intestinal parasites, and cholera are, however, strongly conditioned by nutritional status.[44]

Measles, for example, imposes unusually severe nutritional stress, and is particularly virulent among PEM children; it will even precipitate PEM in the subclinically malnourished.[45] Among poorly nourished children mortality rates rise higher in a measles epidemic compared with the well nourished who have a significantly lower mortality rate.[46] Hendrickes has summarised the opinion of many when he writes, 'it must be concluded that interaction between malnourishment and measles is strongly synergistic.'[47] Turning to Ireland, during the Great Famine we know from the annual reports of the dispensaries that infectious diseases were on the increase. Dr John Colvan the Doctor to the Armagh Dispensary recorded in 1846 that 'measles, quinsy and whooping cough, [were] very rife amongst the children.'[48] Over Ireland as a whole, recorded deaths from measles in the years 1845-9 were 67 per cent higher than the average of the previous decade, and almost three times greater than in the next decade (See Table 2).

Table 2: Number of Deaths recorded from Measles in Ireland 1842-53

1842	1589	1846	2544	1850	2512
1843	1715	1847	5416	1851	1561
1844	1745	1848	5343	1852	1548
1845	1890	1849	5358	1853	1250

SOURCE: *Census of Ireland 1851 and 1861*

Tuberculosis too increases in frequency in times of famine, progressing more quickly in malnourished victims, leading to high mortality.[49] Adolescents in particular are vulnerable to tuberculosis. In Ireland the years 1847, 1848 and 1849 saw an upsurge in the number of deaths attributed to tuberculosis of the lung; the published 1847 figure was more than double that of 1844, and over the five years 1845-9 65 per cent higher than the previous 5 years.

Table 3: Number of Deaths recorded from Consumption in Ireland 1841-50

1842	9896	1846	15792	1850	19755
1843	9988	1847	22664	1851	11299
1844	11109	1848	21293	1852	11721
1845	12682	1849	21968	1853	12898

SOURCE: *Census of Ireland 1841 and 1851*

Diarrhoeal diseases were common in Ireland, and during food crises they were particularly virulent. Although infective organisms are rare in famine diarrhoea, social dislocation with insanitary and overcrowded conditions created an ideal environment for the spread of infectious diarrhoeal diseases and added to the cases of non-infective diarrhoea. Once again our statistical data are flimsy. Nevertheless the censuses record a rise in deaths attributed to dysentery and diarrhoea between 1842 and 1850.

Table 4: Number Deaths recorded from Dysentery & Diarrhoea in Ireland 1843-50

	Dysentery	Diarrhoea		Dysentery	Diarrhoea
1843	1033	780	1847	25757	10717
1844	1249	849	1848	18430	7264
1845	1940	1251	1849	20667	8779
1846	5492	3595	1850	13675	5549

SOURCE: *Census of Ireland 1851*

III

Vitamin Deficiency Diseases

Vitamin deficiency diseases are not usually major features of famine despite grossly deficient diets. The vitamin requirements of famine victims are reduced because of their low level of general and basal metabolism. Nevertheless, these diseases do occur, their prevalence depending to a greater or lesser degree on the customary diet. Some diets will provide greater physiological reserves than others of storable vitamins. Specific vitamin deficiency diseases have been observed in Ireland during and after famine crises. Some were the consequence of the sudden withdrawal of the main food staple, others were induced by ill-conceived relief programmes. Symptoms of scurvy, pellagra, and xerophthalmia all appear in Ireland's historical records, though only scurvy was recognised as such at the time.

(a) Scurvy

Scurvy was not common in Ireland during the decades before 1845 and, therefore, not always instantly recognisable to all in the medical profession.[50] Some doctors, however, did identify the disease. One was Dr J.O. Curran, whose very comprehensive account of its presence was published in 1847. His research failed to turn up any evidence of scurvy during the food crisis of 1740-1, though he refers to comments of Dr O'Connell who noted that 'epistaxis (nose bleeding) was then exceedingly common, whilst intense rheumatic pains, and large ecchymoses (bruising), seem to have been tolerably frequent in fever.'[51] Curran wisely concluded: 'whether any of these were really symptoms of scurvy it is now impossible to say.'[52] William Wilde in 1851 referred to the presence of scurvy in 1757. The document he cited, in the Medico-Philosophical Memoirs is missing, and so we cannot evaluate his interpretation.[53] More revealing are the medical reports of 1817-19. Several references to scorbutic symptoms occur in the writings of a few physicians who tended the sick, particularly the poor. Dr Francis Rogan observed small haemorrhagic spots (petechiae) of the skin, very dark and well defined, and blood oozing from the gums, though never mentioned scurvy. Most remarkable was his effective treatment. 'In cases of this kind', wrote Rogan, 'the remedies on which the greatest reliance was placed were *fresh lemon juice,* yeast and mineral acids. When lemons could be procured an ounce of the juice was given every two hours . . . ' Rogan's brother was a naval surgeon which may explain his remedy.[54]

The presence of scurvy during the Great Famine is well documented. The first recorded signs were in the final months of 1845, when Dr J.D. O'Brien, doctor to the Ballymore Eustace Dispensary, Naas, County Kildare saw several patients who, among their numerous symptoms complained of 'rose-coloured patches . . . swollen state of the muscles of the neck, shoulders, and arms, with pain so acute that the patients [winced] on the slightest pressure . . . [also] pains in the bones.'[55] O'Brien diagnosed an ailment of a 'gastro-enterite' nature, caused in his opinion by eating diseased potatoes.[56] The link between the described symptoms and scurvy was made by a Dr M.J. McCormack of Buncrana, County Donegal. Replying to O'Brien, he confidently pronounced that, 'those [cases] which have been recorded . . . by Dr O'Brien of Naas, as a peculiar form of gastro enterite are in fact cases of land scurvy.'[57]

Scurvy soon became widespread. Dispensary records abound with references to the symptoms of scurvy and doctors from all over the country commented on the prevalence of the disease. Reports poured into the editors of Irish medical journals on the ever increasing incidence of scurvy. The extent of the disease prompted Curran to write, 'scurvy, which formerly was the very rarest of diseases in Ireland, has within the last two years been making its appearance in various towns and rural districts, and has latterly become exceedingly prevalent in all parts of the kingdom.'[58]

Scurvy is caused by a lack of vitamin C in the diet. Initially the scorbutic patient complains of tiredness, breathlessness, and mental depression. Later cutaneous haemorrhages, from bleeding under the surface of the skin, produce purple blotches (purpuric spots) which usually appear first on the limbs, and then on other parts of the body. Joints become swollen and painful from haemorrhaging into the joints and muscles. The gums are red, soft, spongy, swollen and easily bleed. Eventually teeth loosen and fall out. Scurvy unrestrained is a killer disease, death being the result of haemorrhages into the heart muscle or brain.

The Irish case histories display all these classical symptoms. To quote one of many physicians, Dr Long of Arthurstown, County Wexford in 1847 wrote:

> the lower extremities were marked with large patches of *purpura;* they were also the seat of intense pain, so as to render the slightest movement intolerable. The gums were spongy, covering the teeth, and breath was foetid; the breathing short and oppressive; debility extreme.[59]

All doctors pointed to diet as the cause of the disease. Some blamed the eating of diseased potatoes, others, the lack of food. Dr Bellingham of Dublin noted the strong comparison between the scorbutic symptoms seen in Ireland and those observed among sailors by Lind.[60] On questioning his patients Bellingham discovered that all had eaten no vegetables for a considerable time.[61] From evidence such as this Bellingham identified the lack of potatoes rather than the eating of diseased potatoes as the problem. 'This disease prevails only among that class of the population whose diet consisted formerly, in a great measure, of the potato,' stated Bellingham, 'and who, as long as they had this vegetable in abundance, enjoyed a perfect immunity from it.'[62]

Bellingham had indeed made the right connection. The potato, while not noted as a rich source of vitamin C, did provide the population with more than an adequate amount by virtue of the colossal quantities eaten daily. Potato consumption by a labouring man reached a level of between 8 and 15 lbs daily in the years immediately prior to the Famine.[63] Although vitamin C is a very unstable substance, being soluble in water, and destroyed by storage and heat, nevertheless the large potato intake provided levels far in excess of daily requirement (30-60 mg), and placed the Irish labourers' diet in the mega-dose league.[64]

If the vitamin C content of the Irish diet was so good when food supplies were adequate why did scurvy appear so quickly? The most obvious reason is that man is unable to manufacture vitamin C endogenously consequently dietary supplies are the sole source.[65] More important, the exceptionally high levels of vitamin C in the potato diet operated to the disadvantage of the Irish in times of potato shortages. Research has demonstrated that people accustomed to saturated levels of vitamin C become depleted of the vitamin more quickly than those used to a low intake.[66] The explanation is based on the thesis that 'the body may have become conditioned to the 'deluxe' treatment, [and] sudden withdrawal of the treatment does not allow the physiology of the individual to accommodate immediately to a lower intake.'[67] The Irish fell into this trap. Had their usual intake of vitamin C been at a lower level before the Famine — say between 20 and 30 mg daily — deficiency symptoms would have appeared more slowly.

Scurvy vanished as quickly as it appeared once the potato was again available to supply the population with vitamin C. Dr J. Pratt, physician to the Churchill Dispensary, County Donegal, observed, 'as soon as the potato came to maturity, and begun to be generally used among the poor, the disease disappeared.'[68] Despite its lethal potential, mortality from scurvy during the Famine can never be measured. The census figure of 167 deaths between 1841 and 1851 simply cannot be believed. Sir William Wilde at the time felt this figure to be a gross underestimation, if only because so many scurvy victims died from some other ailment before scurvy claimed them.

(c) Xerophthalmia

Another vitamin deficiency disease witnessed at the end of the Great Famine, though not at the time identified, was xerophthalmia. Xerophthalmia is an eye disease caused by a prolonged lack of the fat soluble vitamin A in the diet. Reference to William Wilde's historical survey of diseases in Ireland reveals that an eye disease which contemporaries called opthalmia was endemic in Ireland.[69] Several severe outbreaks either coincided or immediately followed periods of food shortage, for example, in 1701, 1740, 1758, 1801, 1825, 1840 and 1849-50. We do not have sufficient dietary material of a quantative nature bearing on those earlier episodes, but it is certain that the problem in 1849-50 was not so much opthalmia (an infectious eye disease) but xerophthalmia.

Xerophthalmia damages the iris, conjunctivae and cornea of the eye, and ultimately causes blindness. Dietary sources of vitamin A are fish liver oils, such as cod-liver oil, and red palm oil. Liver, butter, cream, cheese, whole milk, and egg yolk are good sources. Because the Irish diet traditionally included milk and its derivatives this disease was not present while supplies were good. Furthermore vitamin A is a storable vitamin, reserves being located in the liver. However, when famine was both severe and prolonged, as in 1845-9 the chances of xerophthalmia occurring increased, especially among children whose stores of vitamin A were small.

Conclusive evidence for the presence of xerophthalmia in Ireland during the late 1840s comes from the Poor Law medical records.[70] In 1849 the Irish Poor Law Commissioners were greatly alarmed by an epidemic of what was commonly called ophthalmia, in the overcrowded and insanitary workhouses. It was particularly rife in workhouses in the south and west of the country and was especially common among children. Table 5 shows the marked increase in the number of cases of so-called ophthalmia in the Irish workhouses between 1849 and 1852.

Table 5: Number of Ophthalmia Cases treated in Irish Workhouses

	1849	1850	1851	1852
Total No. of cases in workhouses	13812	27200	45947	31876
Cases arising in workhouse	11368	24882	42067	28765
Cases admitted to workhouse with ophthalmia	532	758	963	1360

SOURCE: *Annual Reports of the Poor Law Commissions 1850-3*

Two eminent physicians of the day, Professor Arthur Jacob and Sir William Wilde, were invited to investigate the disease. Comparison of the clinical manifestations of xerophthalmia with the symptoms described in Wilde's report is illuminating. The highest incidence of xerophthalmia is found among children who are particularly vulnerable because of their small reserves of vitamin A, and the greater demands rapid growth places on their stores, particularly when meagre. Adults usually have sufficient supplies to meet requirements for many months or even years.[71] In the Tipperary workhouse Wilde found 340 cases of so-called opthalmia in the workhouse hospital; 326 or almost ninety-six per cent of these were children; their ages ranged from 4 to 14 years. Only 14 patients were adults.[72]

The earliest symptom of xerophthalmia is night blindness, frequently followed by Bitot's spots[73] and dryness (xerosis) of conjunctiva. None of these symptoms were reported by Wilde. However, they are rather subtle indicators and may have been overlooked or not thought worthy of note. The next stage of xerophthalmia is irreversible damage to the eye caused by ulceration leading in advanced cases to complete perforation of the cornea and iris prolapse. Wilde reported from the Tipperary Union that in the eyes of some patients 'several . . . [ulcers] were nearly transparent, as if a piece had been clipped out of the cornea'.[74] Wilde continued by describing corneal changes which produced 'either staphyloma or extensive leucoma with adhesion of the [iris] to the cornea.'[75] These are classic clinical symptoms of xerophthalmia.

Untreated xerophthalmia ultimately results in blindness. Frequently, blindness occurs in one eye only. Here again, this pattern corresponds to that found by Wilde. Of the 340 cases he examined, sixteen had irrecoverably lost the sight of both eyes and thirty-two had lost vision in one eye. A further thirty-three had one eye blemished so as to impair vision though not altogether to destroy sight.[76] This feature is also reflected in the statistics on blindness for all the workhouses in Ireland at this time (See Table 6).

Table 6: Statistics of Blindness in Irish Workhouses 1849-51

	1849	*1850*	*1851*
One eye lost	114	202	656
Both eyes lost	37	80	263

SOURCE: *Annual Reports of the P.L.C. 1851 and 1852*

The explanation for xerophthalmia in the Irish workhouses is not hard to find. The diets served there during the famine period consisted of Indian meal, oatmeal, rice, bread, gruel, with whole milk, skimmed milk or buttermilk. The best source of vitamin A in such a menu was whole milk, and so long as whole milk was drunk in sufficient quantities for at least part of the year, enough vitamin A to meet body requirements was acquired.[77] When, however, whole milk was replaced by buttermilk or skimmed milk children were very vulnerable to the effects of vitamin A deficiency in time, because buttermilk and skimmed milk contain merely a trace of the vitamin.[78] Such was the case in 1848-9 when the Irish potato famine was at its height. In such circumstances children's small stores of vitamin A quickly depleted. The example of the Tipperaray Union highlights the problem. Nutritional analysis of workhouse diets laid down for children aged 5-9 year olds reveals that the vitamin A content was only around 130 μg retinol equivalent (RE) when whole milk was served, and but a trace when the beverage was buttermilk or skimmed milk. Both regimes were below the quantity needed to meet a child's requirement (4-14 year olds) of 300 μg to 725 μg RE.[79]

The temptation to substitute whole milk with skimmed milk or buttermilk was great, as the price of buttermilk and skimmed milk was about half that of whole milk, and indeed the Tipperaray Union was not the only workhouse who succumbed.[80] Dr John Forbes observed during his tour of Irish workhouses that: 'milk mentioned in the Irish dietaries is almost always buttermilk, sometimes it is ordinary skimmed milk, but I think, never (or very rarely) fresh or new milk containing the cream'.[81] Not only was buttermilk and skimmed milk cheap but also plentiful. As a by-product of butter production, large supplies of buttermilk were available particularly in those regions where dairying was a major industry. Tipperaray was just such a region.[82]

The Tipperaray Assistant Physician, Dr Reardon, made a significant remark:

> the class of patients attacked were debilitated, starved, female children, generally those *recently admitted,* worn out by previous want and privation of every kind — many having refused to come into the house in consequence of its crowded state, until they were exhausted to the last degree.[83]

Sir William Wilde's treatment for the eye disease provides final proof that he was dealing with xerophthalmia. Three times in his report he recommended the use of cod-liver oil for the treatment of certain patients, advising:

> where the patient is much broken down in health, and . . . the disease is in a chronic stage, I beg to suggest the plentiful use of cod-liver oil, of which medicine a large supply should at once be procured, and a tablespoonful given to each child, two or three times a day. I saw I am sure fifty cases among those under your care which would be greatly benefited by the use of this remedy.[84]

Incidentally, Wilde's recommendation predated by 60 years the recognition that cod-liver oil was effective treatment for vitamin A deficiency.

(b) Pellagra

Another vitamin deficiency disease to make brief visitations to Ireland was pellagra. An exotic visitor to the island, pellagra was more usually found in warmer climates where maize (Indian meal) was the staple food, notably in Spain, Italy, south-west France, Romania, the Turkish Empire and southern states of America. Unlike these countries Ireland did not grow maize, but from the turn of the nineteenth century it was imported as a relief food in times of crop failures, and during the second half of the century became a staple in the daily diet.

Pellagra is caused by a lack of the B vitamin, niacin (nicotinic acid) in the diet. In general, cereals are a moderate source of niacin, but maize differs from other cereals in important nutritional respects. In maize meal, i.e. Indian meal, the greater part of the niacin is unavilable for utilisation by man.[85] Fortunately man is not entirely dependent on dietary sources of niacin; it may be synthesised from tryptophan, a protein constitutent. The tryptophan content of maize is, however, small. This defect is most important in the relationship between maize and pellagra. A diet may contain a low level of niacin, but if the diet includes enough foods with sufficient tryptophan pellagra will not occur.[86]

The relevance of this discussion to Ireland is that in good seasons when the diet contained oatmeal, potatoes, milk, as well as Indian meal, pellagra was not pleasant. In bad years when only Indian meal was available to eat the likelihood increased. During the height of the 1845-9 crisis the labouring classes had little else but Indian meal. However, it is difficult to identify pellagra in the period because the population was in such a debilitated state and their physical condition displayed marks of so many deficiencies, that symptoms of pellagra were obscured.

The picture is much clearer during the crisis of 1879-80 when a regional famine affected the west and the south-west of the country. In that season the potato crop was a complete disaster, as also was the grain harvest. Furthermore, during the previous three years the produce of both potato and grain crops was very low.[87] Consequently the poorer sections of the population were totally dependent on Indian meal. To make matters worse milk was also scarce. Cows in the region had to be sold or where dry because grass was in short supply. The population was ripe for pellagra.

The medical and dietary evidence demonstrating the case for the prevalence of disease in Ireland has been discussed in detail elsewhere.[88] It will suffice here to quote from Dr Sigerson's medical report to the Dublin Mansion House Relief Commitee:

> Many of those . . . found stricken with fever and other diseases had been compelled to subsist for four, five or six months on Indian meal, generally insufficiently boiled: as adjuncts, they had very rarely any milk; in one or two districts, weak coffee; in some sweetened water; and not a few cases, water only.[89]

Considering that the American physician Goldberger, in the early years of the twentieth century, experimentally induced pellagra with a diet containing more niacin than that present in the Irish relief rations, and furthermore, within a shorter time span,[90] the presence of pellagra in Ireland in 1879-80 is readily understood.

There is a possible further unexpected consequence stemming from the continued use of Indian meal long after the Great Famine had passed. One of the concerns of both medical and government officers in the late nineteenth century was the dramatic increase in the level of insanity in Ireland.[91] Many explanations were given, including an excess of tea drinking. A nutritional study points to a different dietary cause. From research in other countries we know that a diet of Indian meal, not supplemented by foods containing sufficient niacin or tryptophan, causes pellagra. We also know that one symptom of this disease can be dementia.[92] Does a cause of the rise in insanity lie here? In 1859 the Poor Law Commissioners ordered a dietary survey to be taken among the labouring classes covering over 1021 people.[93] Nutritional analysis reveals that 63 per cent of the diets failed to meet the Recommended Dietary Intake (RDI) of 18 mg,[94] and 52 per cent were at or below the level of niacin used by Goldberger to produce the disease. An explanation for the increase in Irish insanity, therefore, may partly be the result not of an excess of tea drinking but of surfeit of Indian meal.

Conclusion

This paper has reviewed some of the nutritional consequences of famine in Ireland, necessarily concentrating on the nineteenth century crises. What can be learned from these well-known events by looking at them through the nutritionists's eye?

The science of nutrition illuminates the complexity of the relationship between famine, starvation, and the human condition. At the level of society famine may be caused by a fracturing of food supplies, by pestilence, war, or weather, or by a breakdown in the system of distribution. At the level of the individual the essential needs of the human body for protein, fat and carbohydrates *in the correct proportions* are only now becoming fully understood. Even more recent are the discoveries of the imporant roles of vitamins, minerals and trace elements in the maintenance of health. The inter-relationship of one nutrient with another, and the variations in chemical changes given different biological environments add even further complexities. Once one, or more than one, of these substances are withdrawn from the diet, evidence of deficiencies appears sooner or later. Hence in earlier times symptomatic descriptions of, for example, pot-bellied children now give us an indication of the severity of dietary deprivation.

The techniques of nutritional science have greatly aided the uncovering of the presence of diseases in the past unheard of by our ancestors, and in explaining their causes. For example, as we have seen, nutritional analysis enabled us to correctly identify the 1849-50 epidemic of 'opthalmia' recorded in the Tipperaray workhouse as xerophthalmia. This conclusion is arrived at because nutritional analysis pinpoints vitamin A deficiency in the diet, thus making it possible to arrive at a positive identification of xerophthalmia. Our forefathers observed the changes in their state of health, but knew only that it was due to poor diet. With the advent of the nutritional sciences many unexplained events are now illuminated.

References

1. K. Blaxter, 'Energy Intake and Expenditure', in K. Blaxter and J.C. Waterlow, eds., *Nutritional Adaptation in Man* (London, 1985), p. 93.

2. Jean Mayer, 'Famine', *World Nutrition: A U.S. View,* eds., Jean Mayer and Dorothy Campbell (Washington, 1978), p. 27.

3. PEM is not exclusive to childhood, it can occur in adolescents and adults.

4. W.R. Aykroyd, 'Definition of Different Degrees of Starvation' (hereafter 'Definition') in ed., G. Blix, *Famine: A Symposium dealing with Nutrition and Relief Operations in Times of Disaster,* Symposia of the Swedish Nutrition Foundation, 9 (1971) (hereafter *Famine*) p. 18.

5. Kwashiorkor is not specifically a famine disease, it is common in children aged 1-3 years, particularly the penultimate child, in regions of the world where the weaning foods is inadequate to meet protein and energy requirements.

6. C. Gopalan, 'Kwashiorkor and Marasmus: evolution and distinguishing features' in R.A. McCance & E.M. Widdowson, eds., *Calorie Deficiencies and Protein Deficiencies* (London, 1968), p. 49. Gopalan suggests that kwashiorkor is not specifically the outcome of protein deficiency, but a failure of the body to adapt to protein deprivation.

H

7. Francis Rogan, *Observations on the Condition of the Middle and Lower Classes in the North of Ireland . . . with History and Treatment of the late Epidemical Disorder* (London, 1819), p. 25.

8. F. Barker and J. Cheyne, *An Account of the Rise, Progress, and Decline of the Fever lately Epidemical in Ireland* (Dublin, 1821), I, p. 207.

9. William Bennett's Account of his Journey in Ireland in *Transactions of the Central Relief Committee of the Society of Friends during the Famine in Ireland in 1846 and 1847* (Dublin, 1852), p. 163.

10. *Ibid.*

11. Aykroyd, 'Definition', p. 18.

12. Extracts of Joseph Crosfield's Report . . . to the London Relief Committee of the Society of Friends, in *Transactions of the Central Relief Committee of the Society of Friends during the Famine in Ireland in 1846 and 1847* (Dublin, 1852), pp. 145-6.

13. William Bennett, 'Accounts of his Journey', p. 167.

14. William Forster's Observations in the Report of Joseph Crosfield, *Transactions*, p. 146.

15. Lamentations, Chapter 5, verse 10.

16. D. Donovan, 'Observations on the Peculiar Diseases to which the famine of the last year gave origin and on the morbid effects of insufficient nourishment' (hereafter 'Observations') *Dublin Medical Press* (hereafter *D.P.M.*) XIX (1848), p. 67.

17. C. Woodham-Smith, *The Great Hunger* (London, 1962), 6th Edition, p. 196.

18. Quoted in Ancel Keys, J. Brozek, A. Hanschel, O. Michelsen & H.L. Taylor, *The Biology of Human Starvation* (Minneapolis, 1950), I, p. 241.

19. D. Donovan, 'Observations', pp. 67-8.

20. J. Mokyr, *Why Ireland Starved: A Quantitative and Analytical History of the Irish Economy 1800-1851* (London, 1983), pp. 265-6.

21. *Census of Ireland for the year 1851*, Brit.Parl.Papers, 1856[2087-I]XXIX.

22. J. Mokyr, *Why Ireland Starved*, pp. 265-6.

23. P.P. Boyle and C. Ó Gráda, 'Fertility Trends, Excess Mortality and the Great Famine', *Demography*, 23, 4 (1986), p. 555.

24. W.P. MacArthur, 'Medical History of the Famine', in R.D. Edwards and T.D. Williams eds., *The Great Famine: Studies in Irish History 1845-1852* (Dublin, 1956), p. 289.

25. D. Donovan, 'Observations', p. 67.

26. A. Ashworth, 'Progress in the treatment of Protein-Energy Malnutrition', *Proceedings of the Nutrition Society*, 38, 1, (1979), p. 89.

27. R. Martorell, 'Child Growth Retardation: a discussion of its causes and its relationship to health', in K. Blaxter and J.C. Waterlow, eds., *Nutritional Adaptation*, p. 20.

28. A problem in assessing nutritional status against intellectual development is separating the specific roles played by deficient diets from the contribution of poverty, sanitation, family size, etc. See M.E. Hertzig, H.G. Birch, S.A. Richardson & J. Tizard, 'Intellectual Levels of School Children Severely Malnourished during the First Two Years of Life, *Pediatrics*, 49 (1972), pp. 814-24; R.J.C. Stewart, 'Long Continued Marginal Protein-Energy Deficiency', in G. Serban ed., *Nutrition and Mental Functions*, Advances in Behavioural Biology (New York, 1975), p. 29.

29. R.J.C. Stewart, 'Long Continued Marginal Protein-Energy Deficiency', p. 28.

30. J. Cravioto and E. Delicardie, 'Language Development in Severely Malnourished Children', in G. Serban ed., *Nutrition and Mental Function*, p. 144.

31. L.M. Brockman and H.N. Ricciuti, 'Severe protein-calorie malnutrition and cognitive development in infancy and early childhood', *Development Psychology*, 4 (1971), pp. 312-19.

32. J. Cravioto *et.al.*, 'Language Development', p. 179.

33. S. Davidson, R. Passmore, J.F. Brock and A.S. Truswell, *Human Nutrition and Dietetics* (7th ed. Edinburgh, 1979), p. 502.

34. J. Meuvret, 'Demographic Crisis in France from the Sixteenth to the Eighteenth Century' in D.V. Glass and D.E.C. Eversley, eds., *Population in History: Essays in Historical Demography* (London, 1965), p. 511.

35. *Ibid.*, p. 518.

36. John D. Post, *Food Shortage, Climatic Variability, and Epidemic Disease in Pre-industrial Europe: The Mortality Peaks in the early 1740s* (Ithaca & London, 1985), p. 274.

37. *Ibid.*, p. 273.

38. Ann G. Carmichael, 'Infection, Hidden Hunger, and History', in Robert I. Rotberg and Theodore K. Rabb eds., *Hunger and History: The Impact of Changing Food Production and Consumption Patterns on Society* (Cambridge, 1985), pp. 51-2.

39. N.S. Scrimshaw, C.E. Taylor and J.E. Gordon, *Interaction of Nutrition and Infection* (Geneva, 1968), pp. 11-14. In some circumstances malnutrition can discourage infectious agents, known as antagonism. See Scrimshaw, p. 16.

40. Ann G. Carmichael, 'Infection', p. 53. Carmichael cites the example of competing host and microbes for iron, concluding that a severely malnourished individual will be unable to provide sufficient iron-binding protein to sustain the microbes' existence. Recent research, however, has demonstrated that iron deficiency can adversely effect immune responsiveness and resistance to infection. J.H. Brock and T. Mainou-Fowler, 'Iron and Immunity', *Proceedings of the Nutrition Society*, 45 (1986), p. 311.

41. Ann G. Carmichael, 'Infection', pp. 52-3.

42. N.S. Scrimshaw, *et.al.*, *Interaction*, p. 263.

43. W.H. Foege, 'Famine, Infection, and Epidemics' in G. Blix ed., *Famine*, p. 64.

44. See 'The Relationship of Nutrition, Disease and Social Conditions: A Graphical Presentation', in Rotberg and Rabb eds., *Hunger and History*, p. 308.

45. N.S. Scrimshaw, *et.al.*, *Interaction*, p. 30.

46. W.H. Foege, in G. Blix ed., *Famine*, p. 65.

47. Cited in *Ibid.*

48. J. Colvan, 'Report of the Armagh Dispensary for 1846', *D.M.P.*, XVII (1847), p. 223.

49. A. Keys, *et.al.*, *The Biology of Human Starvation*, 2, p. 1015.

50. P. Froggatt, 'The Response of the Medical Profession to the Great Famine', p. 135, above.

51. J.O. Curran, 'Observations on Scurvy as it has lately appeared throughout Ireland, . . .', *Dublin Quarterly Journal of Medical Science*, IV, 7 (1847), p. 111. (hereafter 'On Scurvy').

52. *Ibid.*

53. *The Census of Ireland, 1851*, Part V, 1, p. 139.

54. F. Rogan, Observations, p. 42.

55. J.D. O'Brien, 'Symptoms Produced by Eating Diseased Potatoes', *Dublin Hospital Gazette*, 15 January 1846, p. 166.

56. J.D. O'Brien, 'Cases of a Peculiar Form of Gastro-Enterite Resulting from the use of Diseased Potatoes', *Dublin Hospital Gazette*, 1 February 1846, p. 184.

57. M.J. McCormack, 'A Case of Land Scurvy produced by eating Diseased Potatoes', *Dublin Hospital Gazette*, 15 April 1846, p. 263.

58. J.O. Curran, 'On Scurvy', p. 84.

59. R. Long, 'Medical Report of the Arthurstown Dispensary and Fever Hospital for the year 1847', *D.M.P.*, XIX (1848), p. 69.

60. O'B. Bellingham, 'Cases of Scurvy: with Observations', *D.M.P.*, XVIII (1847), p. 37.

61. *Ibid.*, p. 35.

62. *Ibid.*, p. 37.

63. K.H. Connell, *The Population of Ireland 1750-1845*, (Reprint Westport, Connecticut, 1975), p. 150 f/n; P.M.B. Bourke, 'The Potato Blight, Weather and Irish Famine' (unpublished Ph.D. thesis, N.U.I. 1965), p. 95; *Appendix to the Sixth Annual Report of the Poor Law Commissioners* Brit.Parl.Paper, 1840(245)XVII, p. 244; *Report of Commissioners for Inquiring into the Poorer Classes in Ireland, (Poor Inquiry (Ireland))*, Brit. Parl. Papers, 1836(37)XXXII, pp. 10, 13, 17 & 19.

64. For the vitamin C requirement debate see: T.K. Basu and C.J. Schorah, *Vitamin C in Health and Disease* (London, 1982), p. 81; Silvia Nobile and Joan Mary Woodhill, *Vitamin C, The Mysterious Redox-System — A Trigger of Life?* (Lancaster, 1981), p. 69; *Recommended Intakes of Nutrients for the United Kingdom*, (Report on Public Health and Medical Subjects, DHSS No. 120, 1969), London, H.M.S.O.; Food and Agriculture Organisation of the United Nations (FAO/WHO) 1970, *Requirements of Ascorbic Acid* . . . A report of A Joint FAO/WHO Expert Group, FAO No. 47 and WHO No. 452, Rome; M.I. Irwin and B.K. Hutchins, 'A Conspectus of Research on Vitamin C Requirements of Man', *Journal of Nutrition*, 106 (1976), pp. 821-79.

65. Primates, guinea-pigs and the Indian fruit bat are among those animals which cannot synthesise vitamin C from glucose via the enzyme L-gulonolactone. See Silvia Nobile *et.al.*, p. 69.

66. R. Elwyn Hughes, *Vitamin C: Some Current Problems* (London, 1981), p. 51; T.K. Basu *et.al.*, p. 121. See also G.N. Schrauzer & W.J. Rhead, 'Ascorbic Acid abuse: effects of long term investigation of excessive amounts on blood levels and urinary excretion', *International Journal of Vitamin and Nutritional Research*, 43 (1973), pp. 201-11. For a more detailed account of scurvy in Ireland see E. Margaret Crawford, 'Scurvy in Ireland during the Great Famine' *Social History of Medicine*, vol 1, 3 (1988), 1-20.

67. Silvia Nobile *et.al.*, p. 129.

68. J. Pratt, 'Medical Report of the Churchill Dispensary', *D.M.P.*, XIX (1848), p. 69.

69. *Census of Ireland, 1851*, p. 117.

70. *Fourth Annual Report of the Commissioners for Administering the Laws for Relief of the Poor in Ireland*, 1851, pp. 130-151 (hereafter *Fourth Annual Report P.L.C.*); *Fifth Annual Report of the Commissioners for Administering the Laws for Relief of the Poor in Ireland*, 1852, p. 14; W.R. Wilde, *Observations on the Epidemic*

Opthalmia which had prevailed in the Workhouses and Schools of the Tipperaray and Athlone Unions (Dublin, 1851).

71. S. Davidson, *et.al., Human Nutrition*, p. 119; H.A.P.C. Oomen, 'Xerophthlmia' in G.H. Beaton and J.M. Bengoa eds., *Nutrition in Preventive Medicine*, WHO Monograph (Geneva, 1976), p. 94.

72. *Fourth Annual Report P.L.C.*, p. 137.

73. Bitôts spots are grey or whitish areas, cheese-like or foamy, on either side of the cornea.

74. *Fourth Annual Report P.L.C.*, p. 146.

75. *Ibid.*, p. 145.

76. *Ibid.*, p. 140.

77. See E. Margaret Crawford, 'Dearth, Diet, and Disease in Ireland 1850: A Case Study of Nutritional Deficiency', *Medical History*, 28 (1984), p. 159.

78. *Ibid.*

79. *Recommended Daily Amounts of Food Energy and Nutrients for Groups of People in the United Kingdom*, Report on Health and Social Subjects No. 15 D.H.S.S. (London, 1979), pp. 6-7.

80. Minute Book of the Tipperaray Union, BG152/A/11.

81. J. Forbes, *Memorandums of a Tour in Ireland* (London, 1853), 2, p. 232.

82. Captain Hayes, the Tipperaray Temporary Poor Law Inspector, in a letter to the Poor Law Commissioners commented on the extensive butter trade Tipperaray had with England, Brit. Parl. Papers, 1847-8(955)LVI, p. 162.

83. *Fourth Annual Report P.L.C.*, p. 136.

84. *Ibid.*, p. 145.

85. In many cereals, especially maize, and perhaps also potatoes nicotinic acid is in a bound form, and so unavailable for absorption.

86. E. Margaret Crawford, 'Indian Meal and Pellagra in Nineteenth Century Ireland', in J.M. Goldstrom and L.A. Clarkson, eds., *Irish Population, Economy, and Society: Essays in Honour of K.H. Connell* (Oxford, 1981), p. 126.

87. G. Sigerson, 'Final Report on Destitution Diseases in the West', in *The Irish Crisis of 1879-80, Proceedings of the Dublin Mansion House Relief Committee*, 1880 (Dublin, 1881), p. 162. Sigerson's Report was originally published, in August 1880 as *Report of the Medical Commission of the Mansion House Committee* (Dublin, 1880). The latter version was without footnotes, which were added later.

88. E. Margaret Crawford, 'Indian Meal and Pellagra . . .'

89. G. Sigerson, 'Final Report', p. 166.

90. J. Goldberger and G.A. Wheeler, 'The Experimental Production of Pellagra in Human Subjects by Means of Diet' in M. Terris, ed., *Goldberger on Pellagra* (Baton Rouge, 1964), p. 54.

91. 'Alleged Increasing Prevalence of Insanity in Ireland', *Special Report from the Inspectors of Lunatics to the Chief Secretary 1894*, Brit. Parl. Papers, 1894[c7331]XLIII.

92. S. Davidson, *et.al., Human Nutrition*, p. 454.

93. *Thirteenth Annual Report of the Commissioners for Administering the Relief of the Poor in Ireland*, Brit. Parl. Papers, 1860 [2654]XXXVII, pp. 31-81; *Sixth Report of the Medical Officer of the Privy Council*, Appendix No. 6, 'Food of the Lowest-fed Classes', Brit. Parl. Papers 1864 [3416] XXVIII, pp. 220-333.

94. *Recommended Daily amounts of Food Energy and Nutrients for Groups of People in the United Kingdom*, Report on Health and Social Subjects No. 15 DHSS.

10

CONCLUSION: FAMINE AND IRISH HISTORY

L. A. Clarkson

The Malthusian spectre hangs heavily over popular perceptions of Irish history. Among the cultural legacies of the Great Famine of 1845-49 (forever enshrined in capital letters) are scarecrow images wracked by hunger slipping unceasingly into the mists of time. In the words of George O'Brien, 'the country lived in a chronic state approaching famine, and . . . the particular years which are mentioned by historians as famine years were simply the years in which the chronic symptoms became acute'.[1] By a peculiarly Irish inversion of Whig historiography, the Great Famine has become the climax of centuries of actual or potential starvation.

Yet, as Cormac Ó Gráda has pointed out, scholarly work on famine in Ireland is thin and there is a contrast between the emotive approaches of popular writers and political polemicists and the restrained and sanitised treatment by professional historians.[2] Studies of famines and subsistence crises before the Great Famine are particularly few. This volume has been an attempt to fill the gap. Until we know more about the history of famines in Ireland it is difficult to put the Great Famine into context.

Four themes emerge from the essays in this volume. The first is the frequency or otherwise of famines and their causes, the second the responses of society to periods of dearth, the third the effects — demographic and economic — of failures in the food supply, and the fourth the uniqueness of the Great Famine, thus bringing us back to our starting point.

I

The identification of famines and subsistence crises in the past is not easy. The reason is partly conceptual. What is the distinction between a famine and a subsistence crisis? The latter may be thought of as an episode of hunger afflicting a society, or a substantial section of society, but which falls short of outright famine; the distinction is one of degree. More important is

220

the difference between a famine or subsistence crisis on the one hand and starvation on the other. A useful rule of thumb is that famines or crises are what happen to societies, and starvation to individuals. Starvation always occurs during famines, but the former can be present without the latter.[3] It is not difficult to find instances in the past of individuals, even many thousands of individuals, going hungry, but it is more difficult — except in the most extreme cases — to know when hunger extended into starvation and when starvation became generalised into famine.

A more serious problem is evidential. Evidence of famines and crises of subsistence include the direct observation of contemporaries, data relating to food supplies and climate — crop yields, rainfall records and the like — food prices, and demographic information, particularly concerning mortality. For Ireland there is plenty of the first, although uneven in quality and chronological extent, and not nearly enough of the other three.

For the period 900-1500 Dr Lyons has exploited the Gaelic and Anglo-Irish annals. As a source for identifying subsistence crises and famines they require subtlety and imagination. Their coverage is best for the thirteenth, fourteenth and fifteenth centuries and even then there are many gaps. They become very patchy during the sixteenth century and virtually cease by 1600. For the sixteenth century we are almost entirely dependent on William Wilde's Table of Irish Famines compiled from contemporary chronicles of extremely variable quality. We have also to use Wilde for the seventeenth and eighteenth centuries, although scholars such as Gillespie, Dickson, Drake, and Post are beginning to explore this territory with evidence of other kinds.[4] By contrast, in the nineteenth century there is no lack of official accounts and eye witness reports of the Great Famine and other crises.

With the exception of the dendrochronological data used by Dr Lyons, information about famine and subsistence crises before 1600 comes from contemporary and near contemporary descriptions. For the early seventeenth century, though, Dr Gillespie employs general economic indicators about the state of the harvests, the balance of payments, food prices, and some extremely fragmentary mortality data.[5] But only for the eighteenth century are price and mortality data available in reasonable quantities. David Dickson's essay demonstrates how frail such information is. It is a measure of the weakness of much of the historical record about famine in Ireland that until recently the scale of mortality has been uncertain even for the disaster of 1845-9.[6]

Given the evidential problems it is unwise to be dogmatic, but it does not seem that Irish history is a chronicle of ever-recurring famine. Dr Lyons's findings are especially intriguing. During the tenth, eleventh, twelfth and thirteenth centuries, up to the 1270s, she sees little evidence even of mild subsistence crises. But for seventy years after 1270 there was a series of crises caused by bad weather and crop failure. The most serious were the great famine of 1294-6, the three-year famine of 1308-10, and Ireland's share in the north European famine of 1315-18. The 1320s and '30s witnessed nothing so dramatic but there were regional crop failures in several years during these decades.

Dr Lyons interprets these events within a Malthusian mode, with population growth from the tenth century to the mid-thirteenth putting pressure on food supplies and encouraging the spread of tillage into unsuitable areas. According to this analysis the Black Death and subsequent outbreaks of plague reduced the demographic pressure and reversed the spread of corn cultivation. Consequently the fifteenth century was relatively free of crises of subsistence. The analysis is plausible although it would be useful to have it supported by reliable population figures. One straw in the wind is that the population of Dublin — a commuity whose feeding was particularly susceptible to the state of the grain harvest — has been variously estimated at between 10,000 and 20,000 on the eve of the Black Death, but at 8,000 or below in the early sixteenth century.[7]

In 1500 Ireland was very lightly populated and there is no evidence of any sustained increase in population during the sixteenth century. This is at least consistent with the near absence of famines indicated by William Wilde. In 1505 excessive rains at harvest time caused famine in the winter of that year; and there was severe famine again in 1523-4 arising from the same cause. Wilde also reported scarcities in 1520, 1545 and 1552 which did not climax in famine and starvation. He does not mention apparent harvest failures in 1557, 1561 and 1574, possibly because they were too insignificant to attract the attention of contemporary chroniclers.[8] By contrast famine conditions, noted by Wilde, were severe during the Desmond rebellion in the late 1580s because of the destruction of crops. However the misery was confined to Munster. If Wilde is to be believed sixteenth-century Ireland stands largely acquitted of famines and susbsistence crises.

In essence the story for the seventeenth century is the same apart from a few scattered years of severe difficulty. The century opened with widespread famine brought on by bad weather and exacerbated during the Nine-years War by military campaigning. The effect of the latter was explained in 1600 by Sir George Carew:

> in the summer season . . . [the Irish live] on the milk and butter of their kine
> grazing on the mountains and in fastness, which holds this rebellion on foot

longer than otherwise it would. But of their harvest, wherein their chief hope remaineth to live in winter, I propose, God willing, to frustrate their expectations in burning and consuming the same.[9]

With the coming of peace there followed 'an unbroken period of eighteen years almost uniformly good harvests', which ended with the harvest failures of 1621-3. The economic dislocations of these years are described by Dr Gillespie above, although he can uncover no evidence of starvation. However, since people are known to have starved to death in North-west England where climatic conditions were broadly similar it is likely that the Irish evidence is simply inadequate.[10] Recovery was rapid but cut short by harvest failures in 1627-9 which culminated in what Professor Cullen has described as 'devastating famine'.[11]

The 1627-9 famine does not appear in Wilde's table, but he picks up the population losses of the 1640s and '50s caused by bad weather, destruction of crops by marauding armies, and epidemic disease. There were serious difficulties with food suplies in 1642-3 and 1648 and wholesale famine in 1652-3.[12]

According to Professor Cullen, 'between 1652 and 1725 Ireland was dramatically free of major food shortage or famine'.[13] This judgment may need modification by future research. Cullen himself acknowledges a possible famine in 1674; and Wilde and other sources have noted difficulties in 1689-90 arising from military activity. In general, though, agricultural production was little disturbed by the Williamite wars. Ireland was also mysteriously unaffected by the bad weather that brought harvest failure to many parts of south-west Scotland and north-west England in the later 1690s; the influx of Scots into Ireland seeking escape from famine at home testifies to the generally good conditions then prevailing in Ireland.[14]

The years of plenty came to an end in the later 1720s. Unchecked population growth between 1650 and 1725 had possibly made Ireland susceptible to harvest crises. But in absolute terms the increase in population was no more than about 700,000 — from 1.5 million to 2.2 million — equivalent to an annual growth rate of only 0.6 per cent.[15] The problem was more complicated than simple population pressure. From the Restoration the grain-producing capacity of Ireland had expanded and a considerable export trade in corn developed in the first two decades of the eighteenth century. But, as Dr Dickson shows above, cereal prices were sluggish and by 1720s there was already a drift away from tillage towards fatstock and dairying in the old granary districts of Dublin. Bad weather and consequent harvest failures in the later part of the decade also coincided with a more general trade depression which depressed incomes.[16]

The sources cited by Wilde show that scarcities of grain first emerged in 1726 and became severe by 1727-9, compelling the poor to live on potatoes to a greater extent than was then usual. If the evidence of just one parish be accepted 1728 was the worst year for deaths.[17] Unfortunately our knowledge of this episode is sparse, but sharply rising wheat prices in Dublin, and reports of distress and mortality throughout England and Scotland, suggest that Ireland shared in a famine of widespread proportions.[18]

By contrast the events of 1740-1 are comparatively well known. Not only did they produce the worst demographic disaster since the early 1650s and unmatched again before the Great Famine, but mortality in Ireland probably rose more sharply than in Britain and continental Europe.[19] Severe weather in the winter of 1739-40 damaged both the cereal and the potato crops and a poor summer and autumn extended the shortages into 1741. Imports of corn to ease the scarcity were unavailable because of a general European shortage.

The unprecedented growth of population between 1750 and 1845 led Professor Connell to identify 'a gap in famines' between 1741 and 1822. Dr Dickson offers good reasons for rejecting the hypothesis. Perhaps the most cogent is that it implies that famine was the norm and that there was something exceptional about the decades after 1741. Yet our survey suggests that it was the early 1650s, the late 1720s, and the early 1740s that were exceptional. Near famines of a localised kind rumbled on in the later eighteenth century, notably in 1755-6, 1766 and 1782-3, their effects muted by a more developed economy and better organised methods of poor relief. In the nineteenth century there were threatening crises in 1800-01, 1816-8, 1822 and 1831.[20] But there was nothing to prepare the country for the fate awaiting it in 1845-9.

The essay by Solar brings out the enormity of the Great Famine. In 1845 and again in 1848 a third of the potato crop was destroyed by blight, losses at the very extremes of previous European experience. Even more disastrously, three-quarters of the crop failed in 1846. Not only were these failures massive, but there was nothing in earlier experiences that could have led anybody to predict such a sequence of failures. In terms of mortality, 1845-6 escaped lightly, but 1846-7 and 1847-8 were 'murderously' bad years and mortality levels were still excessively high as late as 1850-1. In all, one million died of famine-related diseases.[21]

The Great Famine was not quite the last subsistence crisis to afflict Ireland. A succession of bad seasons between 1859 and 1864 caused crop failures and in the West raised fears of a return of famine, but cheap food imports — especially Indian meal — and efficient marketing systems kept the threat at bay.[22] Indian meal also assisted Mayo and other counties in the West to surive the potato failures of 1879-80. Men and women went hungry but did not starve.[23] Finally, as Dr O'Neill's essay shows, there were three localised subsistence crises in 1890-1, 1894-5 and 1897-8, bringing with them 'the spectre of starvation'. However, the spectre remained remote both in a geographical and a statistical sense. The modernising forces of trade were finally banishing even minor crises to the lumber room of history.

Figure 1 and Table 1 summarise the chronology of dearth over six centuries. The data earlier than the 1290s are too fragmentary to be useful and for later centuries a few subsistence crises may have been overlooked. The absolute heights of the bars in Figure 1 have no significance. They have been drawn purely to distinguish famines from subsistence crises.

Table 1: Subsistence Crises and Famines 1290-1900

Years	Crises	Famines	Total
1290-1300	0	3	3
1301-1350	6	9	15
1351-1400	1	1	2
1401-1450	3	0	3
1451-1500	4	0	4
1501-1550	2	3	5
1551-1600	5	1	6
1601-1650	8	3	11
1651-1700	3	2	5
1701-1750	2	4	6
1751-1800	6	0	6
1801-1850	8	3	11
1851-1900	8	0	8
1290-1900	56	29	85

Over a period of six centuries, 85 years — one in seven — emerge as years in which a crisis or famine took place. Only 29 years — fewer than five per cent — can be identified as years of major famine and these are clustered in a few discrete periods. As for the 'gap in famines' there were four rather than one, the longest running for over a century and a half and the shortest for three-quarters of a century. Table 1 shows that the most hazardous decades, taking subsistence crises and famines together, were in the first half of the fourteenth century, the first half of the seventeenth century and the first half of the nineteenth century. The first came at the end of a long period of population growth and may reflect pressure on food supplies. The second also occurred in an era of population growth but owes something to

226 *Famine — The Irish Experience*

Figure 1
Subsistence crises and famines 1290 - 1900

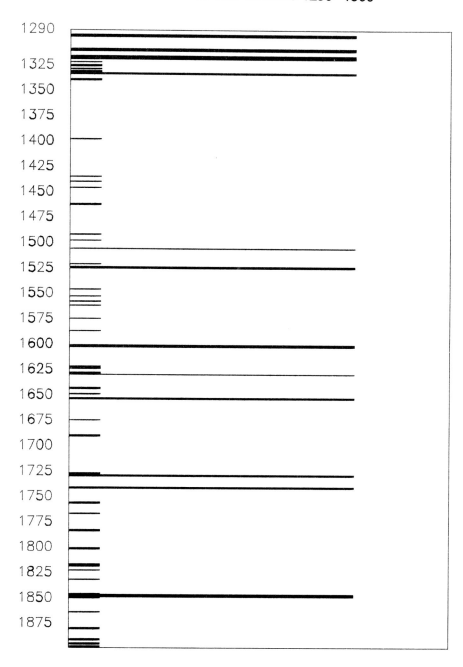

war-time destruction of crops. The third is partly a reflection of better evidence of regional food crises; but the early nineteenth century was also a period of rapid population growth and included the Great Famine. Malthus would not have been surprised by the message of Table 1.

II

One bad year in seven has a certain Biblical ring to it and was enough to encourage society to develop and refine communal reactions to times of dearth. These responses were of several kinds. The oldest was the moral, based on traditional Christian concepts of the just price and enshrined in the medieval assizes of bread and beer, which persisted in Dublin and elsewhere untl the nineteenth century. They were reinforced, as in the 1620s, by public fasting and prayer, and pulpit exhortations against engrossers and forestallers of corn.

Such attitudes underpinned more practical approaches by municipal and national authorities. The latter imposed restrictions on the stock-piling of grain, prohibitions on corn exports in times of shortage, encouraged the importation of corn, and banned bullion movements except to buy grain. They also restricted the use of grain by brewers and distillers. Dr Dickson describes the temporary prohibition of distilling in 1757 as a novelty but it had happened much earlier. More novel in 1758 was the introduction of a bounty, or subsidy, payable on the transport of corn overland to Dublin, an innovation described by Arthur Young as 'one of the most singular measures that have anywhere been adopted'.[24]

The concern with the grain trade highlights a feature of Irish subsistence crises worthy of comment. Most of the evidence relates to difficulties caused by failures of the grain harvests even though up to the end of the sixteenth century — and beyond — meat and dairy produce were the main components of Gaelic-Irish diets and were also eaten in large amounts by the Old-English and New-English settlers. How is the paradox to be resolved? One way is to play down the importance of pastoral products in Irish diets, an approach hinted at by Gillespie. Another is to argue that population growth stimulated arable farming, creating a greater dependence on grain as a basic food. This carried with it two dangers. First, corn growing spread to marginal areas particularly vulnerable to bad weather, leading to a second difficulty noted by Dr Gillespie. Grain yields were lower in Ireland than they were in England. Therefore any further reduction in yields in poor seasons was disproportionately serious, carrying over into subsequent years through a sharp reduction in the quantity of seed available for sowing.

Whether these explanations sufficiently dispose of the paradox is a matter for conjecture. The native Irish used grain as a winter food, supplementing the meat and milk of summer; its loss, as Sir George Carew knew well, could make all the difference between living and dying. During the seventeenth century grain became increasingly important and any dislocation of supply consequently more critical. The problems caused by harvest failure were eventually ameliorated by improvements in markets and communications; Dr Dickson explains the diminishing severity of subsistence crises after 1741 principally in this way. Finally not all food crises were grain crises. Diseases of cattle and sheep figure in the annalistic accounts; and bad weather caused losses among livestock in the seventeenth century, thus imperilling supplies of meat and milk. In 1740-41 it was the failure of the potato as well as the grain harvest that made that famine so severe. And in 1845-9 the Great Famine was caused by a diseased potato crop although aggravated by a shortfall in the grain harvest.

A third communal approach to subsistence crises was to tackle the destitution they caused by a mixture of public and private charity. Dickson suggests that these activities became more effective in relieving distress after 1740.[25] By the beginning of the nineteenth century quite elaborate public relief measures had evolved, including the importation at government expense of rice and maize in times of shortage and culminating in 1817 and 1822 in public work schemes financed by the Dublin administration. A model for action two decades later had been established.[26]

As is well known Ireland lacked a national system of poor relief before 1838, unlike England where the great Elizabethan poor law had been codified at the end of the sixteenth century in the wake of a disastrous sequence of harvest failures. But in 1838 a centrally administered poor law, erected on the English altar of the Dismal Science, was imported with breath-taking speed into Ireland and was well established by the time of the Great Famine. Nevertheless, it was not at this shrine of social engineering that the suffering were relieved. The purpose of the Irish Poor Law, as Dr Kinealy tells us, was not to alleviate poverty so much as to abolish it by a combination of harsh regimes for the paupers and heavy financial burdens for the rate payers. Instead the Dublin administration distributed modest amounts of Indian corn through local relief committees and financed a rather more generous programme of public works. Inevitably, though, as the tide of distress engulfed these temporary expedients, workhouse guardians, grounded in the principles of indoor relief, were sucked into dispensing outdoor relief to the starving. It was only at the beginning of 1847 that the Poor Law Commissioners formally sanctioned the exercise of famine relief through the workhouses, and then at local expense.

Ideologically ill-adapted and financially under-provided, the Irish Poor Law has had a mixed press from historians of famine.[27] That it failed is not in doubt, but could any system have coped? In part its failure arose, as Dr Kinealy explains, from the uneven regional impact of the Famine. Nevertheless, reading accounts of workhouses officials hounded for debts incurred in fighting off starvation, it is difficult to deny that the failure was more fundamental. Mokyr claims that 'in the frightful summer of 1847 the British simply abandoned the Irish and let them perish'.[28] If so, this was also an abandonment by the state of a responsibility for victims of famine that had been evolving for more than two centuries.

According to Ó Gráda the soup kitchens set up by the government in the Spring of 1847 'at least tackled the problem of starvation head-on'.[29] Indeed, but Dr Crawford's essay suggests that filling famine-bloated bodies with watery soup did more harm than good. Also meeting starvation, or rather its consequences head-on, were doctors and others who struggled with the harvest of typhus, relapsing fever, dysentery, marasmus, scurvy and cholera. On the eve of the Great Famine there were infirmaries attached to most of the workhouses and a plethora of medical charities staffed by a profession that was as well trained as any in Europe. These were reinforced by temporary fever acts in 1845 and 1847, a central board of health created to supervise medical aid, and a daily five shilling fee for physicians attending fever patients. It cannot be claimed that the efforts of medical men achieved much to stem the tide of fever; their resources were insufficient, their knowledge of the nature of epidemic disease inadequate, and their treatment largely confined to isolation and hope. But the mortality among doctors, including some prominent figures in the profession, justify Sir Peter Froggatt's conclusion that they 'emerge with credit'. Unlike Whitehall administrators medical men did not turn their back on famine.

III

To identify community responses to famines is also to identify their social and human consequences. The most immediate effect of harvest failure was on agricultural incomes. Tenants were unable to pay their rents, landlords lost revenues as rent arrears mounted, and consumers watched their real incomes wither as food prices soared. The decline in purchasing power throughout society caused a fall in demand for industrial goods, leading to widespread depression. The need to import food and the loss of food exports created problems with the balance of trade which aggravated economic depression still further.

Variations on these economic consequences can be seen at most times of crisis. They are at most evident in Dr Gillespie's account of the events of 1621-4. Indeed, in the absence of all but the most shadowy demographic indicators, economic repercussions of harvest failure provide his main source of evidence. They can also be seen at various times in the eighteenth century. The severe dearths of 1726-9 and 1740-41 occurred at a time of deep economic gloom. Similarly, harvest failures and difficulties in the linen industry coincided in Ulster in the 1750s. In the nineteenth century the subsistence crisis of 1816-18, the worst in the decades immediately preceding the Great Famine, was made no easier by economic depression following the end of the Napoleonic wars and was probably worsened by it.

The wider economic consequences of famine have generally been overlooked by Irish historians. Nowhere is this more evident than in treatments of the Great Famine. Neither of the standard modern texts discusses them — with the important exception of emigration — and they are not considered by Dr Daly in her new survey.[30] However Ó Gráda's most recent account of the Great Famine shows how bank deposits and note circulation, indicators of more general economic performance, both declined and also how Ireland switched from being a net grain exporter to a net grain importer during the famine years.[31]

Solar's essay points out that the change in Ireland's position from a net exporter of cereals to a net importer continued for the rest of the century; it was, he notes, 'one of the persistent effects of the potato blight'. So, too, were the lowered potato yields, which fell during the Great Famine and did not recover. The reasons are unclear but were possibly associated with a reduction in the amount of labour available to cultivate the soil following an increase in the cost of labour. In a direct fashion, therefore, the Great Famine caused a major long-term transformation in the structure of Irish agriculture.

Ultimately the burden of famine and starvation fell upon people. This human impact was of three kinds: migration, morbidity, and mortality. The mass emigration resulting from the Great Famine is well-known. Between 1846 and 1854 two and a half million people left the country. Emigration had long been an Irish experience but the Great Famine accelerated the flow and changed its character. Furthermore it persisted. 'Between the Great Famine and the great Depression [the 1930s] emigration accounted for more than half of each rising generation . . .'[32] This was an experience unique among modern western nations.

The scale of emigration in earlier centuries is not so well understood. There had been a small outward trickle during the seventeenth century, more than matched by immigration from England and Scotland, and a growing net outflow during the eighteenth century. Much of the emigration to North America in the 1720s, 1740s, and 1750s, particularly from Ulster, was of small farmers and artizans escaping from harvest failure. Many others went to England and Scotland, swelling the substantial Irish communities already settled there.[33] In the 65 years before the Great Famine possibly one and three-quarter million people left Ireland.[34]

There was also a movement of people within Ireland in search of succour during periods of food shortage. Dr Lyons's account of late medieval famines hints at beggars roaming the countryside seeking relief; and in the 1620s municipal and central governments were troubled by bands of wandering people looking for food. No doubt this happened in later crises too, but it is difficult to distinguish subsistence migration, of the kind widespread in sixteenth and early seventeenth century England, from other kinds of population movements such a booleying — common in pastoral societies — and internal colonisation as settlers moved from place to place in search of better opportunities. As Professor Cullen has pointed out, early modern Ireland was an exceptionally mobile society and hungry people were simply one more ripple on a sea of movement.[35] This sort of migration may have become less important during the eighteenth century, but starving wanderers scouring the land for food until they could walk no more were common figures in the Great Famine countryside.

Famished migrants were a sure means of spreading disease. Historians have long been aware of the close association between famine and disease and thirty years ago Sir William MacArthur provided the classic account of the medical history of the Great Famine.[36] Typhus, relapsing fever, dysentery and scurvy were rife throughout the famine, and cholera was present also in 1849. Medical diagnoses for earlier periods are more uncertain, but it is apparent from the work of contemporary medical writers that a similar crop of diseases, apart from cholera, was present from the mid-eighteenth century.[37]

The nature of the connections between hunger and illness, however, has been only very imperfectly understood by historians. As Dr Crawford shows, none of the infections commonly associated with famine are directly caused by lack of food, not even typhus, the classic 'famine fever'. The relationship is much more complex. Starvation depletes protein in the body which makes individuals more prone to infections. At the same time certain infections, measles for instance, impose severe nutritional stress thus heightening the chances of other ailments.

There are, nevertheless, direct consequences of malnutrition. These include the doleful physiological steps towards starvation traced by Dr Crawford and all evident in medical writings on Irish famines. They also include the vitamin deficiency diseases such as scurvy, xerophthalmia, and pellagra. The first was well known to physicians in Ireland long before the Great Famine, even though not very common, but the presence of others is revealed only by the nutritionist's eye. Even more elusive are the effects of prolonged hunger on physical and mental development. Was a long term legacy of the Great Famine a population cohort stunted and intellectually impaired because it starved during childhood in the hungry forties?

The final outcome of starvation is death. Few people die directly of starvation. Far more perish from related epidemic diseases, although the distinction is probably of little interest to the victims. To the total of deaths we should add the loss of births caused by a decline in the marriage rate during subsistence crises and perhaps also by a fall in fecundity resulting from severe deprivation.

Unfortunately it is precisely on this central issue that our evidence is at its weakest. When William Wilde's source tells him that 'above three thousand starved in Tyrone' in 1602 and one thousand men lay dead and unburied in a small district of County Antrim, we can be sure that his source was plucking phantoms from thin air; the implied mortality rates would have practically obliterated the entire population of the two counties. The burial registers analysed by Dickson are valuable for pinpointing years of crisis but less helpful in determining the scale of mortality. The best known of the eighteenth century crises is 1740-41. Drake, on the basis of contemporary guesses, puts the mortality at between 200,000 and 400,000. If we are prepared to accept a more recent estimate that almost 20 per cent of the population died in these years, the true mortality exceeded 400,000. Assuming that 'normal' mortality accounted for around 70,000 deaths annually, then a quarter of a million people were the victims of famine in 1740-1.[38] The only other crisis before the Great Famine for which we have a national estimate is 1816-18 when contemporaries guessed that 65,000 people died of famine related disease.[39]

Thanks to the work of Mokyr and Ó Gráda the excess mortality during the Great Famine is now firmly established.[40] Around a million died, over one-ninth of the population, with massive concentrations in parts of the West, among the poor, the very young and the elderly. Most died of fevers and dysentery. Some died of starvation and a few of vitamin deficiency diseases. All died because they were hungry and all were hungry because their potatoes were blighted.

IV

This brings us to the final theme of the volume, implicit throughout and explicit in the title of Dr Solar's contribution. Was the Great Famine a unique event or does its reputation depend on its being the last of the line and, like the Great Plague therefore, the one that is remembered? There is no simple answer to the question. Major famines were always unusual occurrences in Ireland and even lesser crises of subsistence did not happen more than five or six times in a normal life span. Coddled in modern twentieth-century comfort we would find such frequency intolerable, but in past time — at least before 1845 — Irish men and women were no worse off than most Europeans in this respect.

The Great Famine was a great human tragedy, but its mortality was perhaps not quite the worst that Ireland ever experienced. Famine and famine-related diseases killed one-ninth of the population in six years, but in 1740-41 they carried one-tenth of the population to their graves in only two. Furthermore, to widen the perspective, 'in a comprehensive world history of famines the Great Irish Famine . . . would hardly rank as major . . . In northern China in 1877-8 a famine accounted for 9 to 13 million deaths and in 1932-3 in the Ukraine another for probably at least 5 million; [and] . . . the dreadful Bengali famine of 1940-3 carried off ten millions'.[41]

But in three distinct ways at least, the Great Famine 'was no ordinary subsistence crisis'. In the first place, the extent of the crop failure was beyond normal experience; whether it had been exceeded in 1740 is impossible to say, but it was quite unprecedented in the nineteenth century. From this point of view the wonder is not that so many died but so few. The reason is that the burden of famine fell almost exclusively on the lower, potato-eating, strata of society, leaving perhaps sixty per cent of the population more or less unscathed. In this respect 1845-9 was different from 1740-1. Secondly, the Great Famine had long-term economic and demographic consequences that, if not unique, were highly unusual. Population continued to fall because of emigration and delayed marriage long after the crisis had passed. For those remaining in Ireland, incomes rose — a modern variant of the Black Death effect whereby a diminishing number of people share the remaining wealth.

Finally, as Ó Gráda reminds us,[42] the Great Famine, took place at the middle of the nineteenth century in the United Kingdom, the most industrialised and richest nation in the world. Because of this the Great Famine has left a political and ideological legacy unsurpassed by any other subsistence crisis in Ireland. The experience of famine may not be a recurring theme in Irish history but it is an ever-present issue in historical mythology.

References

1. George O'Brien, *The Economic History of Ireland in the Eighteenth Century*, Dublin and London, 1918, p. 102.
2. Cormac Ó Gráda, *Ireland Before and After the Famine: Explorations in Economic History, 1800-1925*, Manchester, 1988, Chapter 3.
3. See Amartya Sen, *Poverty and Famines: An Essay on Entitlements and Deprivation*, Oxford, 1981, pp. 39-44.
4. In addition to the essays by Gillespie and Dickson in this volume see Michael Drake, 'The Irish Demographic Crisis in 1740-41', in *Historical Studies VI*, (ed. T.W. Moody, 1968), pp. 101-24; J.D. Post, *Food Shortage, Climatic Variability, and Epidemic Disease in Preindustrial Europe: The Mortality Peak in the Early 1740s*, Ithaca and London, 1985.
5. Raymond Gillespie, 'Harvest Crises in Early Seventeenth-Century Ireland', *Irish Economic and Social History*, vol. XI (1984), pp. 5-18.
6. For the most recent discussions see Joel Mokyr, *Why Ireland Starved: A Quantative and Analytical History of the Irish Economy, 1800-1850*, London, 1983, Chapter 9; Ó Gráda, *Ireland Before and After the Famine*, Chapter 3.
7. See B.J. Graham, 'The Towns of Medieval Ireland', in R.A. Butlin (ed.), *The Development of the Irish Town*, London, 1977, p. 45; Gearoid MacNiocaill, 'Socio-Economic Problems of the Medieval Irish Town', in David Harkness and Mary O'Dowd (eds.), *The Town in Ireland*, Belfast 1981, pp. 18-9; S.G. Ellis, *Tudor Ireland: Crown, Community and the Conflict of Cultures, 1470-1603*, London 1985, p. 37; Nicholas Canny, *From Reformation to Restoration: Ireland 1534-1660*, Dublin, 1987, p. 7.
8. For references to these episodes, based on the Irish state papers, see Gillespie, 'Harvest Crises', p. 7.
9. *Cal S.P.D., Ireland, 1600*, p. 244.
10. A.B. Appleby, *Famine in Tudor and Stuart England*, Liverpool, 1978, pp. 121-7, 145-8.
11. Cullen, *The Emergence of Modern Ireland*, p. 96.
12. In addition to Wilde, see Cullen, *The Emergence of Modern Ireland*, p. 96; George O'Brien, *The Economic History of Ireland in the Seventeenth Century*, Dublin and London, 1919, pp. 107-7.
13. Cullen, *The Emergence of Modern Ireland*, p. 96.
14. L.M. Cullen, 'Economic Development, 1691-1750', in T.W. Moody and W.E. Vaughan (eds.), *A New History of Ireland, IV, Eighteenth Century Ireland, 1691-1800*, Oxford, 1986, pp. 132-5.
15. David Dickson, *New Foundations: Ireland 1660-1800*, Dublin, 1987, p. 96; L.A. Clarkson, 'Irish Population Revisited, 1687-1821', in J.M. Goldstrom and L.A. Clarkson (eds.), *Irish Population, Economy and Society: Essays in Honour of the late K.H. Connell*, Oxford, 1981, p. 26.
16. In addition to Dickson's essay see Cullen, 'Economic Development, 1691-1750', pp. 144-5.
17. William Macafee and Valerie Morgan, 'Mortality in Magherafelt, County Derry, in the early Eighteenth Century reappraised', *Irish Historical Studies*, vol. XXIII, no 89 (1982), pp. 50-60.
18. For general accounts of conditions in Ireland, that mostly reiterate Wilde, see

O'Brien, *The Economic History of Ireland in the Eighteenth Century*, pp. 103-4; J.L. McCracken, 'The Social Structure and Social Life, 1717-60' in Moody and Vaughan (eds.), *A New History of Ireland, IV, Eighteenth Century Ireland*, p. 33; Cullen, 'Economic Development, 1691-1750', p. 145. For England see T.S. Ashton, *Economic Fluctuations in England 1700-1800*, Oxford, 1959, p. 18; L.A. Clarkson, *Death, Disease and Famine in Pre-industrial England*, Dublin, 1975, p. 35; and for Scotland, Michael Flinn *et al, Scottish Population History from the 17th Century to the 1930s*, Cambridge, 1977, pp. 212-3.

19. Post, *Food Shortage*, p. 32.

20. The dating of these minor crises varies from source to source, indicating, perhaps, their localised nature and uncertain impact. Compare the dates given in Dickson, above; Ó Gráda, *Ireland Before and After the Famine*, pp. 2-5; K.H. Connell, *The Population of Ireland 1750-1845*, Oxford 1950, pp. 144-5; O'Brien, *The Economic History of Ireland in the Eighteenth Century*, pp. 103-6; M.E. Daly, *The Famine in Ireland*, Dundalk, 1986, pp. 38-43.

21. The chronology of mortality is taken from Ó Gráda, *Ireland Before and After the Famine*, pp. 84-6.

22. J.S. Donnely, jr, 'The Irish Agricultural Depression of 1859-64', *Irish Economic and Social History*, vol. III (1976), pp. 46-50.

23. See E.M. Crawford, 'Indian Meal and Pellagra in Nineteenth-Century Ireland', in Goldstrom and Clarkson (eds.), *Irish Population, Economy and Society*, pp. 118, 127-31.

24. Quoted in O'Brien, *The Economic History of Ireland in the Eighteenth Century*, p. 112.

25. David Dickson, 'In Search of the Old Irish Poor Law', in Rosalind Mitchison and Peter Roebuck (eds.), *Economy and Society in Scotland and Ireland 1500-1939*, Edinburgh, 1988, pp. 149-159.

26. S.A. Royle, 'Irish Famine Relief in the Early Nineteenth Century', *Irish Economic and Social History*, vol. XI (1984), pp. 44-58.

27. Contrast Ó Gráda, *Ireland Before and After the Famine*, pp. 110-8; Daly, *The Famine in Ireland*, pp. 113-16.

28. Mokyr, *Why Ireland Starved*, p. 291.

29. Ó Gráda, *Ireland Before and After the Famine*, p. 116.

30. R.D. Edwards and T.D. Williams (eds.), *The Great Famine: Studies in Irish History 1845-52*, Dublin, 1956; Cecil Woodham-Smith, *The Great Hunger: Ireland 1845-9*, London 1962; Daly, *The Famine in Ireland*.

31. Cormac Ó Gráda, *The Great Famine in Irish History*, London, 1989, forthcoming. See also Ó Gráda, *Ireland Before and After the Famine*, pp. 88-109; Philip Ollerenshaw, *Banking in Nineteenth-Century Ireland*, Manchester, 1987, pp. 65-72.

32. Ó Gráda, *Ireland Before and After the Famine*, p. 161. For surveys of the emigration literature see Daly, *The Famine in Ireland*, pp. 105-109; David Fitzpatrick, *Irish Emigration 1801-1921*, Dundalgan Press, 1984.

33. For a survey of early Irish emigration to the New World see K.A. Miller, *Emigrants and Exiles: Ireland and the Irish Exodus to the New World*, Oxford, 1985, pp. 131-279. There are many scattered reference to Irish migrants in England in Peter Clark and David Souden (eds.), *Migration and Society in Early Modern England*, London 1987.

34. Connell, *The Population of Ireland,* p. 27.
35. Cullen, *The Emergence of Moden Ireland,* pp. 89-92.
36. Sir William P. MacArthur, 'Medical History of the Famine', in Edwards and Williams (eds.), *The Great Famine,* pp. 263-315.
37. The literature is summarised in Post, *Food Shortage,* pp. 243-6.
38. Drake, 'The Irish Demographic Crisis of 1740-41', p. 121; David Dickson, Cormac Ó Gráda, Stuart Daultrey, 'Hearth Tax, Household Size and Irish population Change 1672-1821', *Proceedings of the Royal Irish Academy,* vol. 82, C, no. 6 (1982), p. 167.
39. Daly, *The Famine in Ireland,* p. 39.
40. Mokyr, *Why Ireland Starved,* pp. 262-8; Ó Gràda, *Ireland Before and After the Famine,* pp. 82-8.
41. Ó Gráda, *The Great Famine in Irish History,* forthcoming.
42. Ó Gráda, *The Great Famine in Irish History,* forthcoming.

INDEX